FOUR HATS IN THE RING

American Presidential Elections

MICHAEL NELSON

JOHN M. MCCARDELL, JR.

FOUR HATS IN THE RING

**THE 1912 ELECTION AND
THE BIRTH OF MODERN
AMERICAN POLITICS**

LEWIS L. GOULD

UNIVERSITY PRESS OF KANSAS

Published
by the
University
Press of Kansas
(Lawrence,
Kansas 66045),
which was
organized by the
Kansas Board of
Regents and is
operated and
funded by
Emporia State
University,
Fort Hays State
University,
Kansas State
University,
Pittsburg State
University,
the University
of Kansas, and
Wichita State
University

ISBN 978-0-7006-1564-3

Printed in the United States of America
Book Club Edition

CONTENTS

Twentieth and twenty-first century presidential elections typically have been two-party affairs, matching the Republican nominee against the candidate chosen by the Democrats. In the twenty-seven elections that took place from 1900 to 2004, the major-party nominees combined on all but four occasions to win more than 90 percent of the national popular vote. Significant third-party or independent candidates occasionally have arisen—for example, H. Ross Perot won 19 percent of the popular vote (but, because he failed to carry any states, no electoral votes) in 1992 and George C. Wallace won 13 percent of the popular vote and, with a regional base in the Deep South, 46 electoral votes in 1968. But the Democratic and Republican nominees finished first and second in both of these elections—indeed, in every presidential election except one.

The one exception was 1912, which, as Lewis Gould emphasizes in this volume, was contested not by two or even three significant candidates but by four. The Democrats nominated Woodrow Wilson, the governor of New Jersey. The Republicans anointed William Howard Taft, the incumbent president. The Socialist Party chose Eugene V. Debs, who had won about 400,000 votes in the 1904 and 1908 elections and was bidding to substantially increase the Socialist vote in 1912. (He did: Debs won 901,551 popular votes, 6 percent of the national total and the high-water mark for his party in American presidential elections.) Former president Theodore Roosevelt, running as the candidate of the newly formed Progressive Party, was the other candidate to, in his phrase, throw his "hat in the ring."

Roosevelt had not planned a third-party candidacy; instead he had challenged Taft for the GOP nomination, adopting the Progressive mantle only when, despite winning nine of twelve Republican state primaries, he lost the nomination to the incumbent at the convention. On Election Day, Roosevelt and Taft divided the Republican vote and Wilson coasted to victory. Wilson's 42 percent of the national popular vote was sufficient to carry 40 states and 435 electoral votes. Roosevelt was second with 27 percent and 88 electoral votes. Finishing third, Taft won a smaller share of the popular vote (23 percent) and fewer electoral votes (8) than any reelection-seeking president or major-party nominee in history.

As Gould points out, Wilson's victory was not a lonely landslide. The Democrats gained more than sixty seats in the House of Representatives, substantially increasing their majority in that chamber. They also netted enough additional senators to win control of the Senate away from the GOP. As president, Wilson mobilized his congressional party to pass a raft of new legislation and in 1916 became the first Democrat since Andrew Jackson to win a second consecutive term.

Many scholars judge Wilson to have been a significant presidential innovator. His New Freedom legislative agenda established a significant role for the federal government in the American economy, presaging the New Deal and Great Society. His speechmaking efforts to rouse public opinion in support of that agenda made him, in the political scientist Jeffrey Tulis's phrase, the first "rhetorical president." One of Lewis Gould's particular achievements in this book is to make these innovations less surprising than they usually have seemed. The election that brought Wilson to power, after all, marked the birth of modern American politics.

The judgment that the election of 1912 represented a presidential and congressional contest of unusual historical significance came into being just after the end of World War II. Two distinguished historians, George E. Mowry and Arthur S. Link, made the election seem of enduring relevance. Mowry offered the first contribution in 1946 with the publication of *Theodore Roosevelt and the Progressive Movement*. Based on his doctoral dissertation at the University of Wisconsin, Mowry's book traced the way in which Theodore Roosevelt moved toward a decision to bolt the Republican Party in 1912 and the consequences of that judgment for American reform. The lively prose and thorough research in the Theodore Roosevelt papers helped Mowry's work become an instant classic. His analysis of Roosevelt's New Nationalism and its links to the New Deal had a great impact on lectures and textbooks.[1]

A year later, Link began his multivolume biography of Woodrow Wilson. In *Wilson: The Road to the White House* (1947), Link emphasized the ideological duel between his subject and Roosevelt in the fall of 1912. The discussion of how the roots of Wilson's New Freedom campaign grew from the thoughts of Louis D. Brandeis provided a gripping account of progressive reform at a crucial moment in its evolution. Link echoed Mowry in seeing this confrontation as pivotal in the way in which the political history of the twentieth century unfolded.[2]

Other important historians during the 1950s and 1960s built on the Mowry-Link analysis. John Morton Blum's *The Republican Roosevelt* (1954) further revived Theodore Roosevelt's reputation as a serious politician and social thinker.[3] William H. Harbaugh's biography of Roosevelt, which appeared in 1961, added to the conviction that Roosevelt's career was central to the story of reform.[4] During the decade, Link's biographical volumes on Wilson as president confirmed the centrality of the 1912 contest.[5]

The first book devoted to the election itself came out in 1961. Frank K. Kelly wrote *The Fight for the White House: The Story of 1912* based on some research done for him from news articles in the *New York Times* and published accounts of the major participants in that race. Organized into chapters covering each month, Kelly's narrative synthesized Mowry and Link. He lamented that "the sense of a National Mission has been lost—and we are seeking to recover it."[6] To that end, he concluded, "The times call for a leader, as the times called in 1912." There is not much evidence that Kelly's work had great influence on how historians considered the 1912 election.[7]

Almost three decades passed before another book devoted to the 1912 election appeared. Francis L. Broderick, *Progressivism at Risk: Electing a President in 1912* (1989) considered the implications for reform of this electoral contest. Broderick relied for the most part on published sources and did not break much new ground in an analytic sense.[8] Fifteen years later, James Chace, *1912: Wilson, Roosevelt, Taft and Debs—The Election That Changed the Country* (2004), was an account derived from secondary sources, cluttered with factual errors, and not really all that focused on the events of the election itself.[9]

What then are the new contributions of this study? Unlike previous treatments of the election, this narrative rests on research in the numerous manuscript collections of the politicians who fought the election of 1912. President Taft's role is discussed in richer detail than in earlier books. The key part of Robert La Follette in opposing Roosevelt comes into sharper relief. Research into Roosevelt's speeches during the fall campaign, a source not used to the same extent by other writers on the election, makes possible a more nuanced analysis of the confrontation with Wilson during September and October.

A major substantive goal of this book is to restore the tariff issue to its central place in the 1912 contest. Historians do not like to engage the tariff. To them, it is only a word in a Gilded Age that comes with technical complexity, dry arguments, and the hint of selfishness among proponents of a protective policy. Yet for Americans between the mid-1880s and the start of the First World War, protection and free trade were major domestic issues in the minds of both Republicans and Democrats. Wilson, Taft, and even Roosevelt spent much more time on the tariff than historians have recognized. In many respects, 1912 was the last presidential election in which the tariff played a significant role in the outcome.

Because 1912 is an election that has excited historians, the assumption has grown that Americans at the time must have been captivated as well. Yet students of voting behavior have identified a decline in voter participation and turnout during the first two decades of the twentieth century (and beyond). In 1912, the voters confirmed that trend as turnout fell from four years earlier. From all indications, the passions of the Taft-Roosevelt rivalry, the heated race for the Democratic nomination, and the presence of four active presidential candidates in the fall contest did not activate the electorate to come out and take part. This book identifies some answers to that seeming paradox in the rise of distracting media events during the course of 1912. The sense after July that Woodrow Wilson was a likely winner also drained drama from the contest.

The importance of the election was thus threefold. The Taft-Roosevelt split and the emergence of the Progressive Party pushed the Republicans in the rightward direction that they adopted for the rest of the century. That same division insured Wilson's election and Democratic dominance of Congress in the new administration. The ideas debated in both the New Nationalism and the New Freedom set the agenda for reform and social change within the Democratic Party for decades to come.

As the title of the book suggests, there were, of course, four candidates for the White House in 1912. I have tried to examine Eugene V. Debs and the Socialists on the same terms as the other aspirants for the presidency. If Socialists missed an opportunity to become a real alternative to the major parties in 1912, some responsibility rests with Debs as a political leader. The question is usually posed as, why did the Socialists do so well in 1912? Another way to put it is, why did not Debs do better in a year that promised so much for the party?

In terms of American political history, the 1912 contest had everything. There were two bitter and protracted primary contests within the two major parties. These battles led to two of the most exciting and hotly disputed nominating conventions of all time. Out of the Republican donnybrook came the third-party candidacy of Theodore Roosevelt, or perhaps it was a fourth-party race since Eugene V. Debs and the Socialists were already in the field. There was the debate of ideas between Wilson and Roosevelt, an attempted assassination of Roosevelt, an enhanced role for women in politics, and continuous campaigning on a larger scale than ever before. A good case can be made that it was in 1912 that patterns were set, and thus the year of four hats in the ring was the first true twentieth-century presidential election. With this electoral contest, modern American politics began.

So much seemed to be at stake for Americans in that distant time before the First World War erupted. The men and women who battled at Armageddon with Roosevelt, who enlisted in the Wilson campaign, who stayed with Taft, or who waved red bandanas for Debs all sensed that something important was involved in how that election came out. While the electorate may not have shared the passion of the activists, politicians, social thinkers, and party workers who fought the election of 1912, all felt that this was a decisive moment in the nation's history. The ensuing narrative seeks to tell why the people inside those campaigns were even more right than they knew at the time.

The research for this book began four decades ago as part of a project on the history of the Republican Party from 1897 to 1913. As sometimes happens with historical subjects, that endeavor turned into books about the presidencies of William McKinley and Theodore Roosevelt and a study of American politics from 1900 to 1921. In the intervening years, I continued to accumulate materials about this crucial election. I welcomed the chance when the editors of this series, John McCardell and Michael Nelson, asked me to contribute a volume on this election.

Thanks to the teaching of such fine historians as John Morton Blum and Howard R. Lamar, as well as the friendship of H. Wayne Morgan and R. Hal Williams, my initial interest in the Gilded Age and Progressive Era deepened over time. That fascination has never dimmed for me. The world of Theodore Roosevelt, Woodrow Wilson, William Howard Taft, and Eugene V. Debs comes alive each time I dip into their correspondence, read a newspaper of that day, and consider the legacy of the men and women of these decades for the modern United States. I hope this book will convey some of that sense of possibility and loss that for me still surrounds that distant era.

Space permits only a brief acknowledgment of the people who have helped to make this book a reality. The staff of the Manuscript Room at the Library of Congress were helpful at every opportunity during my visits there between 1961 and 1990. The Perry-Castaneda Library at the University of Texas at Austin has rich holdings on the years 1880–1920, and those materials facilitated my research while I taught and since my retirement. The Center for American History, under the direction of Don E. Carleton, provided original source documents in abundance for the study of Texas and national politics. Wallace F. Dailey at the Theodore Roosevelt Collection, Houghton Library, Harvard University, helped locate copies of Roosevelt's 1912 speeches.

Friends who have assisted me with the research and writing on 1912 over many years include Norman D. Brown, Charles Calhoun, Bill Childs, Thomas Clarkin, Stacy Cordery, Judith Kaaz Doyle, Larry

Easterling, the late Sara Hunter Graham, Gene Gressley, Clarence G. Lasby, Jonathan Lee, John Leffler, the late Herbert F. Margulies, Kristie Miller, Bradley R. Rice, Craig Roell, Patricia Schaub, Bill Shade, and Steve Stagner. Ron Yam is a constant source of timely expertise on computer issues.

John Milton Cooper generously shared with me the excellent chapters on the 1912 election from his forthcoming biography of Woodrow Wilson. Cooper's book promises to be a masterful account of Wilson's life and times. Stacy Cordery was also generous in letting me consult the manuscript of her superb biography of Alice Roosevelt Longworth.

R. Hal Williams read the entire manuscript and offered incisive criticism. John Morton Blum improved the opening chapters with his wise insights and then read again the complete book to my great profit. The editors of the series supplied detailed and perceptive comments on the text that also clarified what I was trying to do. Fred Woodward was the soul of patience and understanding throughout the work on the book.

For assistance with recurring health issues, I owe thanks to Larry Breedlove, David M. Ferguson, Martin Stocker, and Garth Weaver. Elizabeth Sylvester and Kelly Inselmann helped me understand how post–traumatic stress disorder has shaped my life. Their rich experience and deep understanding as psychotherapists helped to restore my capacity to tackle a project such as the election of 1912. Their human sympathy and professional insights were crucial in dark personal moments.

Karen Gould surmounted her own personal challenges with a bravery and resolve that inspired me to write this book.

For any mistakes of fact or interpretation in this account of the election of 1912, I alone am responsible.

Lewis L. Gould

When Americans picked up their daily newspapers on Monday, 1 January 1912, they learned that the New Year had come in without the usual festivities and hoopla. Since New Year's Eve fell on Sunday, thousands of people stayed home from the ceremonies in New York, Chicago, and other cities where freezing cold also kept the crowds down. In Manhattan, the *New-York Daily Tribune* surveyed businessmen, scientists, and religious leaders about what the next twelve months would bring. The railroad magnate, James J. Hill, told the newspaper "there is nothing to fear, no menace of any kind, and everything to hope for." The New York State banking superintendent was equally positive. "The political disturbances usually attendant on a Presidential campaign appear to me to have been largely discounted in 1911."[1]

Some of the stories that greeted readers on that morning suggested the presence of more social problems than the *Tribune*'s commentators had identified. In Chicago, Volunteers of America provided meals for 9,000 of the city's poor. "We fed more people than we have done in any former year," said the official in charge of the project, because "lack of occupation and want were more general in Chicago this winter than for many years." Residents of Sallisaw, Oklahoma, lynched "a negro named Turner" who had stolen a railroad engine, fled the scene, and then murdered a farmer and assaulted the man's wife.[2]

Over the next twelve months, important events made 1912 a year that lingered in the national memory. In April the British ocean liner *Titanic* sank on its maiden voyage with heavy loss of life. The tragedy that surrounded the fate of this "unsinkable" vessel dominated news coverage for weeks as congressional committees probed the cause of the disaster. A generation's faith in technology came into question as stories of both heroism and cowardice among the passengers filled endless columns of both gossip and serious analysis.

While big-time sports had not yet arrived, as it would a decade later, the year provided evidence of the growing celebrity of major athletes. The Olympics in Stockholm, Sweden, saw Jim Thorpe win gold medals in the pentathlon and decathlon and be dubbed the greatest athlete in the world. Only later would he be stripped of his medals because he had played professional baseball. The African American boxing champion, Jack Johnson, had defeated all the "great white hopes" sent against him in the ring. In 1912, legal troubles over his relationships with white women came when the government prosecuted him under the Mann Act, which barred the transportation of women across state lines for "immoral" purposes. Eventually, Johnson fled the country to escape prosecution and racism.

Baseball was the major sport of the day, and newspapers supplied full reports of every good play and botched grounder. In the World Series, the heavily favored New York Giants, managed by the legendary John McGraw and with their star pitcher, Christy Mathewson, went down before the underdog Boston Red Sox by four games to three. Because of a tie game, it required eight contests to decide the series. In the crucial final tilt, Giants outfielder Fred Snodgrass dropped a routine fly ball and allowed a Bosox runner to advance to scoring position. Eventually, the runner crossed the plate with what proved to be a crucial tally. So intense was the coverage of the series that, for the rest of his life, this miscue haunted Snodgrass. Even though major league baseball was played only as far west as St. Louis in those years, it remained the national sporting obsession in 1912. The presidential candidates in the autumn would vie for attention with the diamond exploits of professional ballplayers.

Although the twentieth century was still young, sensational trials had already become a feature of public life that consumed ample newsprint. In 1912, Herman Rosenthal, a gambler with close ties to the emerging world of organized crime, died in a fusillade of bullets from a gangland hit in the Tenderloin District of New York City. Police Lieutenant Charles Becker went on trial as the alleged mastermind of the crime in the autumn of 1912. Newspapers across the nation followed the proceedings with close attention throughout the ensuing weeks until Becker was convicted. Political news had to compete with sensational accounts of sports, human tragedies, and big-city crime for attention. The prominence of partisan politics in national life was continuing a slow decline that lasted throughout the century.

For those who tracked politics, however, there were interesting signals of the special quality that 1912 would impart to national affairs even on that quiet New Year's Day. The *Chicago Tribune* reported that President William Howard Taft and Theodore Roosevelt were at odds over Taft's proposal for treaties to arbitrate disputes among nations. Roosevelt had assailed the idea, and the reporter following the story wrote, "That President Taft and former President Roosevelt can be brought together on any understanding with regard to politics is deemed an impossibility."[3]

Readers of the *Atlanta Constitution* were told that progressive Republicans were assembling for a conference in Columbus, Ohio, on New Year's Day to explore their options for the coming presidential election. Reflecting the growing bitterness between Roosevelt and Senator Robert M. La Follette of Wisconsin, insiders said that no presidential candidate who might run against Taft would be endorsed at the gathering. La Follette himself was starting a three-day campaign swing in Michigan to promote his own chances. For the Republicans, usually so cohesive and united, the transition from 1911 to 1912 left them in the divided state that had been their lot ever since William Howard Taft had assumed the presidency on 4 March 1909.[4]

Three years earlier in January 1909, the impending shift from the administration of Roosevelt to that of his hand-picked successor had seemed a renewal of the dominance that Republicans had enjoyed since the election of 1896. The friendship of Taft and Roosevelt was already a byword in American politics. How had these two men, once so close in their policies, sentiments, and expressions of mutual regard, become such intense enemies? To understand the way in which the presidential election of 1912 developed, it is necessary to commence when the friction between Taft and Roosevelt surfaced. That moment came just after Taft won his decisive victory over William Jennings Bryan in the 1908 presidential contest.

PROGRESSIVE POLITICS, 1909–1910

Teddy, come home and blow your horn,
The sheep's in the meadow,
The cow's in the corn.
The boy that you left to tend the sheep,
Is under the haystack, fast asleep.
—*Life*, 1910[1]

The key events that shaped the outcome of the 1912 race for the White House commenced almost as soon as the 1908 election was over. On 3 November 1908, the Republican candidate, William Howard Taft, defeated William Jennings Bryan. The Democratic nominee had now made his third unsuccessful race for the presidency. Despite the later perception that he was not a strong vote getter, Taft forged a decisive victory. He received more than 7,675,000 votes to some 6,400,000 ballots for Bryan. In the electoral count, Taft amassed 321 votes while Bryan garnered 162. The number of Americans casting their ballots rose some 1,367,000 over the 1904 result. Estimates were that on Election Day, 65.5 percent of the eligible electorate turned out.

It was the fourth consecutive presidential election victory for the Grand Old Party. In many respects, the 1908 contest resembled the struggles between William McKinley and Bryan in 1896 and 1900. Of the sixteen states that Bryan carried against Taft, he had won thirteen of them—eleven from the South plus Colorado and Nevada—twice before. Four years earlier the lopsided race of Roosevelt against Alton B. Parker had failed to bring Democrats to the polls. In 1908, Bryan increased Parker's total by more than 1,400,000 ballots. At the same time, Taft saw his own count rise by 50,000 votes over what Roosevelt had amassed in 1904.

Other than Bryan, the most disappointed candidate was Eugene V. Debs of the Socialist Party. He had garnered 400,000 popular votes in 1904 and hoped to double his total in 1908. The party had raised the money to provide him with a campaign train, the Red Special, from which he had taken his message of an impending revolution to large, friendly crowds. Yet on Election Day, his result stood at just under 421,000 votes. The party's message had not convinced the electorate as much as Debs hoped it would.

A signal feature to contemporary election observers was the ticket splitting that shaped the 1908 returns. In five of the states that Taft carried, including Indiana, Ohio, and Minnesota, Democratic governors won the statehouse. Since the polarizing election of 1896, partisan intensity had declined across many states. Even 65.5 percent was fourteen points down from the voter turnout in the first Bryan-McKinley contest in 1896. One hallmark of this period was the increasing suspicion about the value of political parties and their hold on the electorate. Roosevelt's close friend Elihu Root, an eminent conservative, put the cause as "a growing irritation and resentment caused by the failure of party machinery to register popular wishes correctly and that conventions and legislatures give their allegiances first to managers and second only to the voters."[2] The next four years would see many calls to reform the rules of politics to give greater expression to the will of the people.

On Election Night, President Theodore Roosevelt was outwardly jubilant. "We have beaten them to a frazzle," he said as the returns came in. His handpicked successor had trounced the Democrats. More important, as Roosevelt told an English friend, the voters had understood "that Taft stood for the policies that I stand for and that his victory meant the continuance of those policies." Taft had been secretary of war in Roosevelt's cabinet, and the president explained before his friend was nominated that "he and I view public questions exactly alike." Thus all seemed to be coming up electoral roses for the Grand Old Party and Roosevelt.[3]

But the friendship of Roosevelt and Taft did not have a solid basis in real political agreement. A small gesture from Taft kicked off the process that ended in the bitter rupture between the two men three years later. Four days after the voting, Taft wrote the president a thank-you letter. He called Roosevelt "the chief agent in working out the present status of affairs" and then added a phrase that first irritated and later outraged his predecessor. "You and my brother Charlie," Taft said, "made that possible which in all probability would not have occurred otherwise."[4]

Charles Phelps Taft was the millionaire half-brother of the president-elect. His newspaper empire provided the wealth that had underwritten much of his sibling's campaign. At the time, Roosevelt gave no sign that he had been offended. His correspondence with Taft continued in the usual friendly manner. But in Roosevelt's mind the comparison stung. As he said a year and a half later, giving Charlie Taft and Roosevelt the same credit was like saying that "Abraham Lincoln and the bond seller Jay Cooke saved the union." For Roosevelt, who liked to think of himself as an updated version of the Great Emancipator, no other words could have indicated how deeply he had been wounded.[5]

How could such a small incident initiate such large consequences? The problem was that, for all their surface rapport, Theodore Roosevelt and William Howard Taft were not all that close in personality, attitude toward the presidency, and political philosophy. They had worked well together when Roosevelt was the chief executive and Taft a cabinet officer from 1904 to 1908. When their roles changed with Taft's election as president, their underlying differences came to the surface. In a process that stretched over the next four years, their friendship turned to opposition and bitterness.

The president and his successor provided a vivid contrast in reputation and achievement in November 1908. The fifty-year-old Roosevelt was nearing the end of two terms in the White House that had made him an international figure. The people of the United States had watched his rise from New York politics through his exploits during the Spanish-American War to his accession as president after William McKinley's death in 1901. For more than seven years, Roosevelt's attacks on trusts, his wielding of a "big stick" in diplomacy, and his recurrent battles with Congress had dominated the headlines.

By the time he left office, Roosevelt had emerged as a political celebrity. He may have thought that he could be a private citizen again, but as his friend Elihu Root remarked, "He cannot possibly help being a public character for the rest of his life." As an ex-president, he would be in the limelight, whether it was serving as a contributing editor for the *Outlook* magazine, hunting big game in Africa, or acting as the conscience of the reform wing of the Republican Party. He did not intend to seek a quiet retirement but rather expected to remain active in pursuit of a more just society.[6]

Whether in office or as a former president, Roosevelt exuded passion and vitality. His facile mind darted from issue to issue. He energized his followers and captivated the public. A sense of excitement followed him. His magnetism "surrounded him as a kind of nimbus, imperceptible but irresistibly drawing to him everyone who came into his presence— even those who believed they were antagonistic or inimical to him." At the center of this personal electricity was a serious thinker who believed that the nation needed to adopt social justice reforms to avert violent revolution. Social justice, he believed, was a "movement against special privilege and in favor of an honest and efficient political and industrial democracy." By 1909 Roosevelt sought to broaden the reach of presidential power and the role of the national government to engage these pressing needs.[7]

William Howard Taft, on the other hand, brought public geniality rather than charisma to the practice of politics. He was one year older than Roosevelt, and the race for the presidency was his first for major elective office. A Yale graduate and a lawyer by training, Taft had been a judge in Ohio, solicitor general of the United States, and a federal Court of Appeals judge before William McKinley tapped him to head the commission to provide civil government for the Philippine Islands in 1900. Taft then became governor-general of the islands. His strong performance in that job led Roosevelt to make him secretary of war in 1904. From then on, he functioned as a troubleshooter for the White House. Roosevelt once quipped that he had left the portly Taft "sitting on the lid" of potential trouble while the president was away from the White House on one of his many trips.[8]

When he searched for a successor in the run-up to the 1908 election, Roosevelt found that Taft was the logical choice. The secretary of state, Elihu Root, considered himself too old. Governor Charles Evans Hughes of New York struck Roosevelt as overly independent, and Senator Robert La Follette of Wisconsin had assumed a more radical stance on railroad regulation than the president. Searching, as he was, for a continuance of his legacy, Roosevelt turned to his friend Taft. He had been a loyal lieutenant in the Cabinet, was a resident of the crucial state of Ohio, and he seemed an ideological soul mate. By late 1906 and early 1907, President Roosevelt was Taft's most enthusiastic booster.

Since they both needed each other, the two friends minimized their philosophical and political divergences. Roosevelt thought that the president should be able to push the boundaries of the Constitution to do good for the people. Taft believed that the chief executive should stay within the limits of the constitutional precedents. As a cabinet member, Taft chafed in private at his chief's tendency to meddle in the affairs of the government departments. He liked the president personally but had less regard for Roosevelt's more reformist associates in and out of government. Roosevelt thought Taft a good subordinate who would therefore become a strong leader. He never asked himself if he and the secretary of war really shared as many principles as he believed they did. Once their working relationship changed with Taft's rise to the presidency, the two strong-willed individuals would find that they had very little in common.[9]

An erosion of their friendship marked the period of transition before Taft took office in March. The president-elect's wife, Helen Herron Taft, and other family members advised him, "Be his own king." In choosing his cabinet, Taft dropped some members of Roosevelt's official family as he had every right to do. The problem was that Roosevelt remembered an earlier pledge from Taft to retain his cabinet. By the time that power passed to Taft, relations were very strained. An invitation from the Roosevelts to stay at the White House the night before the inauguration produced a very awkward evening that Taft later recalled as "that funeral." So while all was pleasant on the surface as Taft became the next president, in private, tensions mounted.[10]

Roosevelt left three weeks after the inauguration for a hunting trip in Africa. He and his successor did not correspond during the next year. Each expected the other to write first. As time passed and the new administration moved further away from Roosevelt's policies, the prospects for misunderstanding increased. On his safari, Roosevelt reached the conclusion that Taft had been a satisfactory cabinet officer but was not up to the task of governing the nation as president.

In office, Taft revealed a different governing style than the frenetic energy that had marked the Roosevelt years. The new president worked hard but had difficulty at first managing the flow of business. His personal secretary, Fred W. Carpenter, was in over his head and soon fell behind in his work. Lacking a good sense of public relations, Taft kept the press at arm's length and did little to encourage favorable news stories

Stepping Out of the White House

Uncle Sam congratulates Theodore Roosevelt at the end of his presidency as William Howard Taft prepares to assume the presidential duties. The actual transition was not as friendly as this image suggests. (Cartoon from the New York Evening Mail, *1909, in Albert Shaw,* A Cartoon History of Roosevelt's Career *[New York: Review of Reviews, 1910])*

out of the White House. He did not have Roosevelt's sense of what pleased the public. Pictures of the president playing golf with rich men at exclusive clubs conveyed a sense that he was out of touch. A tendency to procrastinate in writing speeches produced some public gaffes. An unkind senator quipped that Taft was "an amiable island, entirely surrounded by men who know exactly what they want."[11]

Believing that his presidential role was to be a party leader who maintained GOP unity and helped enact their legislative program, Taft stressed working with the Republican establishment in Congress. Once he became identified with Nelson Aldrich, the dominant Republican in the Senate, and Joseph G. Cannon, the autocratic Speaker of the House, Taft raised suspicions among party reformers and friends of Roosevelt. In turn, the president resented opposition to his policies. He moved rightward toward his natural allies among Republican conservatives.

The nation over which William Howard Taft presided in March 1909 was in the midst of the period that historians have dubbed the Progressive Era. Since the end of the depression of the 1890s, the United States had experienced an age of political and social reform. In a series of campaigns to improve the quality of life, activists had sought an enhanced role for government at all levels in regulating business, supervising morality, and purifying the political system. Within the general consensus that the United States was a nation that God favored to set an example for the world, progressives, as they called themselves, argued that people were basically good. The right application of government support could make them even better.

Since the accession of Theodore Roosevelt to the presidency in September 1901, the impulse for reform had grown stronger. Roosevelt had placed his intense personality behind the idea that a more just society would prevent a social revolution and class warfare. Many middle-class Americans responded to this call. The reform elements within the Democratic Party, too, applauded parts of Roosevelt's program and contended that even more regulation of business was necessary. The election of 1912 would be waged largely on domestic issues growing out of these concerns.

Unlike the 1890s, when hard times determined political responses, the political struggles leading up to 1912 occurred during an era of general economic prosperity. Since the presidency of William McKinley, economic indicators had much improved. The gross national product, which stood at an annual average of $17.3 billion between 1897 and 1901, would rise to $40.3 billion from 1912 to 1916. The average wage earner among the 95 million Americans brought in $592 per year in 1912, up from $454 in 1901. For that sum, the same individual worked fifty-six hours each week for a little more than 27 cents an hour. Ten years before, a comparable worker would have labored 58.7 hours weekly for 22 cents per hour. In that respect, the economy during the first decade of the twentieth century had produced real gains for most Americans.

For those Americans who toiled in the factories, mines, and fields of the United States during Taft's administration, their working conditions were often harsh, brutal, and dangerous. A sensational tragedy symbolized these problems in March 1911. A fire broke out at the Triangle Shirtwaist Company on the Lower East Side in New York City. As workers, most of them women, fled to the exits they found locked doors and no escape. The blaze left 146 women dead, either burned to death or killed when they jumped to the street below. The New York legislature probed the disaster and in time enacted some reforms. But the episode illustrated how fragile was the social fabric for those on the lower end of the economic ladder.[12]

The prosperity under Roosevelt and later Taft did not disturb the disparities of income that had grown with the triumph of capitalism. The top 1 percent of the population controlled almost 15 percent of the national income by the time Taft left office in 1913. The chance for working Americans to rise out of the economic status to which they had been born was very slight. Meanwhile, inflation pressed hard on the resources of the lower-middle- and lower-class families. Gold discoveries in the Yukon and South Africa at the end of the 1890s increased the amount of money in circulation. A growing population intensified demands for goods and services, especially in the cost of agricultural products. The result was a worldwide upward pressure on consumer prices that in the United States became a hot political issue between 1909 and 1912. Because the Republicans were identified with the protective tariff that added to the cost of imported goods, they suffered the most political damage from this trend. The festering question of what to do about the tariff now confronted Taft during the early weeks of his administration.

The battle over what became the Payne-Aldrich Tariff of 1909 now seems an arcane dispute over an outmoded public policy. In modern times, when the goal of freer global trade is an economic orthodoxy and the stated policy of the U.S. government, it is hard to recapture a time when the nation and a major political party clung to protectionism with an almost religious fervor. Because the tariff was the major source of government revenue, it represented as important a political issue as the income tax does today. While there had been advocates of high tariffs and protectionist ideas since the founding of the country, the Republican Party after the Civil War took up the high tariff philosophy as its basic ideological creed. It was, said one writer, "the sacred temple of the Republican party."[13]

Protection appealed to Republicans because it fit their vision of promoting business enterprise, using the power of the national government to expand capitalism, and pursuing social harmony. Since society consisted of a network of interdependent producers, the benefits of the tariff would provide employment and markets for rich and poor alike. Labor would also obtain higher wages in a protected home market. For businesses and industries that confronted imports from Canada and Mexico on such trades as cattle raising, coal mining, and lumbering, the tariff was a necessary line of defense. Companies that faced competition from less expensive British, French, and German goods added their voices to the protariff coalition. But the tariff was to Republicans more than just the sum of the economic interests that endorsed its operation. To many in the party, the tariff embodied patriotism, social cohesion, and an alluring vision of a bright economic future.[14]

The protectionist policy, which had been translated into legislation in the Dingley Tariff of 1897, had been a hallmark of Republican success during the first decade of the century. By 1909, however, the appeal of the doctrine and the intensity of feeling about the issue were showing indications of political obsolescence. As American industries matured, they felt less need for the sheltering arm of the government. Mechanization, cost cutting, and intensified marketing were better ways to secure business in the competitive pre–World War I environment. Even though they were the principal source of revenue for the expanding federal government, customs duties had limitations in the amounts they could bring in annually. For a growing federal government, the tariff did not provide the needed funding for regulatory programs and social spending.

Republicans had divided over the tariff during Roosevelt's second term. The protectionist wing remained in firm control, but there was growing dissent from orthodoxy among middle western senators and representatives. These lawmakers heard from their constituents that the agricultural crops they grew received no protection while duties were too high on the industrial goods they purchased. The outcome of these intraparty battles was a pledge in the 1908 Republican platform to call a special session in the spring of 1909 to consider "a revision of the tariff." While the direction of such revision was not specified, everyone understood that the promise meant a reduction in some tariff rates. Taft echoed the platform in his campaign speeches during the fall of 1908.[15]

The new president summoned lawmakers into session in March 1909. He had already signaled his willingness to work with Speaker Cannon. A potential revolt against the Speaker's leadership fizzled when it became clear that Taft would not endorse the move. The president wanted prompt action on the tariff, and Cannon seemed to be the means to that end.

At first things went Taft's way. The House Ways and Means Committee reported out a bill in early April that the full House then passed. The measure, named after Sereno Payne of New York, chair of the House Ways and Means Committee, lowered the rates on sugar, iron, and lumber while placing coal and cattle hides on the free list, meaning such imports paid no duties.

The problem for Taft and the Republicans lay in the Senate, where the lawmakers produced their own version of a tariff law. The key phase would then occur in the House-Senate conference committee, where the actual bill would be written. With the Republicans enjoying a sixty-one to thirty-one edge in the upper house, the leader, Nelson Aldrich of Rhode Island, should have been able to tailor the bill as he wished. There were, however, about ten progressive Republicans who disagreed with Aldrich's views on the tariff. If they voted with the Democrats, the large Republican majority was reduced to about a dozen votes. Protectionist senators from the west saw their chance. They made it clear to the leadership that the price of their votes would be increased rates on the products of their states, such as wool, lumber, and cattle hides. As a result, Aldrich had to make concessions to these politicians to get a bill out of the Finance Committee. Some 800 amendments took rates not downward but back toward the levels of the Dingley Tariff.[16]

The progressives (or, as they were known, "insurgents") rebelled and attacked Aldrich. Robert La Follette of Wisconsin, Albert J. Beveridge of Indiana, and Jonathan P. Dolliver of Iowa led the assault. A version of the bill passed on 8 July by a vote of forty-five to thirty-four, with ten Republicans recorded against Aldrich. Both sides now looked to President Taft for support. He went with Aldrich, much to the disgust of the insurgents, who complained that they "received no support whatever in this tremendous fight we have made from the White House."[17]

In mid-July, the House-Senate conference committee set to work. Taft sought reductions on key products, including coal, wood pulp, lumber, and cattle hides. The president secured these concessions as he stood firm against Aldrich and Cannon. However, he did not pursue lower rates on more controversial items such as wool, cotton, and industrial products. Had he done so, he would have lost to the protectionists. Taft believed he had obtained the most possible. The progressives countered that he had failed to deliver the kind of leadership Roosevelt had provided. The Payne-Aldrich Tariff passed in early August, and Taft put his signature on the bill. Seven of the insurgents opposed the bill on final passage, and a key House procedural vote produced an administration victory by a scant five votes.[18]

The first major legislative confrontation of Taft's presidency left much bitterness among Republicans. The insurgents believed that Taft had failed them and betrayed his principles. The conservatives within the party resolved to take revenge on their dissenting colleagues. When Taft made a nationwide tour during the fall of 1909, protectionists pressed him to defend the Payne-Aldrich law "with a strong forceful statement." The president did so at Winona, Minnesota, on 17 September 1909. He called the measure "the best tariff bill that the Republican party ever passed" and praised the lawmakers who had supported it.[19]

There was immediate and bitter resentment from the insurgents about what the president had said. The president explained that he had written the speech hastily and had not been as clear as he should have been. Factionalism marked the last months of 1909. From the perspective of Taft's chances for renomination in 1912, the most ominous development was the increased public talk that Roosevelt, upon his return from Africa, should come out against the president. There were "back from Elba" clubs formed to have Roosevelt emulate Napoleon and reclaim his title to the Republican Party. The last thing Taft needed at this point in his first year was any controversy that put him in direct opposition to any of Roosevelt's policies.[20]

Yet that is precisely what happened. One of Roosevelt's proudest initiatives was his campaign for the conservation of natural resources. His closest adviser in that endeavor had been the chief forester, Gifford Pinchot. Roosevelt and Pinchot had wielded executive power to create national parks, preserve bird sanctuaries, and manage rangelands, coal reserves, and forests. When Taft came into office, he and his secretary of the interior, Richard Achilles Ballinger, sought to rein in Pinchot and pursue policies on natural resources that, in the president's mind, conformed more to the letter and spirit of the law.[21]

The result was a bureaucratic struggle over conservation policy that threatened to burst into view during the first half of 1909. Pinchot and his supporters used publicity to make their case to Congress and the nation. By the fall the news regarding the dispute spread. The charge was that Secretary Ballinger had favored special interests when he made decisions regarding coal lands in Alaska. Taft worried that he might have to fire Pinchot with all the ensuing consequences for his relationship with Theodore Roosevelt. Pinchot brought about his own dismissal in January 1910. He leveled criticism at both Ballinger and Taft in an open letter to Senator Dolliver. Faced with insubordination, Taft fired Pinchot. The resulting furor led to a congressional investigation. From the probe came an impression that Taft had something to hide and that Ballinger was at fault. The interior secretary resigned his post in the spring of 1911.[22]

Since Pinchot and Roosevelt were so close, Republicans feared that this development would mean trouble for the president and his reelection chances. A California politician wrote that "I should hesitate to set a limit to the extent to which the fires started by it may spread." A midwestern Republican said of Taft in the wake of the incident that he was "a hopeless blunderer; his blundering is about in proportion to his avoirdupois." Much depended on how Roosevelt would react to the news. "I am getting more and more puzzled at what attitude Father will take when he gets home," wrote Roosevelt's oldest son.[23]

When the former president heard of Pinchot's dismissal, he wrote that "I cannot believe it," adding that "it seems to me absolutely impossible that there can be any truth in this statement." When his mail caught up with him, he learned that his onetime aide had been fired. Roosevelt began to reappraise his relationship with Taft and to consider whether he had judged well in supporting him for the presidency. He admitted to himself that Taft "had gone wrong on certain points; and then I also had to admit to myself that deep down underneath I had known all along he was wrong, on points as to which I had tried to deceive myself, by loudly proclaiming to myself, that he was right." As he began his journey home, Roosevelt thought about what he would do when he reached the United States and reentered the world of national politics.[24]

In that realm, the second year of the Taft administration had not produced much joy for the beleaguered Republicans. The regular session of Congress that opened in December 1909 intensified the discord among the president's party and gave unexpected hope to the Democrats that they might win back the House of Representatives. Outside of Congress, economic conditions worked against the party in power. Higher prices for consumer goods sparked public protests in major cities. The cost of living index, which stood at 100 in 1898, had risen to nearly 130 by 1910. In that context, the protective tariff no longer seemed a major asset for the GOP. A reform journal said that public suspicion about the connection between tariffs and inflation "may well cause uneasiness in the mind of any Republican member of the House who voted for the present tariff and whose majority in his district at the last election was small."[25]

The White House at first took a harsh position toward its Republican opposition. Taft informed the progressives in Congress that he would not allocate patronage to them if they continued to block administration measures. In some states the president encouraged those who disliked the insurgents. Meanwhile, in the House itself, a revolt against Speaker Cannon resulted in a reduction of his power. That change did not assist Taft, who was by now identified with the conservative leadership of Cannon and Senator Nelson Aldrich. "In the world of men," said the editors of Collier's Magazine, Taft was "the toy of the politicians, lawyers, and money-makers with whom he plays golf, walks, and eats—the most gullible President, in regard to his associates since Grant left the battlefield for the White House."[26]

At the end of the congressional session in the spring of 1910, the White House dropped the confrontational stance and worked better with lawmakers. This temporary entente led to some victories for the president, such as the Mann-Elkins Act, which broadened the power of the Interstate Commerce Commission and created one of Taft's pet projects, a Commerce Court. The legislators passed a postal savings measure, legislation on conservation, and regulations about campaign contributions. Republicans told themselves that they might win in the fall elections after all. They could always count on Democratic mistakes that made them act, said one Republican, as "the fool in our favor at the right time."[27]

But in 1910 the Democrats did not cooperate with Republican expectations. In fact, they were well positioned to take advantage of the erosion of Republican unity. It had been a long road back to political competitiveness for the Democrats after the disastrous intraparty split over free silver in 1896 and the two losing presidential campaigns of William Jennings Bryan in that year and again in 1900. The joke was that "there is no Democratic party and William Jennings Bryan is its leader."[28] The party hit bottom with the candidacy of Alton Brooks Parker in 1904. A colorless New York judge, Parker went down before the charismatic presence of Theodore Roosevelt. Parker carried only the solid Democratic South and trailed the popular president badly in the popular vote. The electoral landscape tilted against the Democrats. They had their solid southern base, and some support in the Far West in the states where free silver once resonated. The Northeast and Middle Atlantic states were Republican bastions, as were many parts of the industrial Middle West.

Four years later, William Jennings Bryan improved on Parker's performance in his losing race against Taft. Yet once again the Democrats had come up short with the voters. Bryan was no longer a credible candidate for the party, but he remained a force that any potential presidential hopeful had to win over to become a likely nominee. Amid the gloom, there were small signs of hope. In five states that Taft carried in 1908, Democrats elected governors. Other Republicans trailed Taft's total at the top of the ticket. Should Republican unity fray, the Democrats had a chance for a comeback.

Democratic resurgence did not come at once in 1909. There were divisions over the proper strategy to pursue toward the Payne-Aldrich Tariff. But the rising prices moved consumers against high tariffs and made charges that protection promoted inflation seem plausible. In fact, the upward pressure on prices came from worldwide causes, but in the context of American politics, the trend helped the Democrats. "The high cost of living," said one typical Democratic leader, "is directly chargeable to the unnecessarily high duties on the commodities of life, such as building material, food and clothing."[29]

With unexpected unity, the Democrats went into the 1910 contest on an optimistic note. Strong candidates appeared in state after state where the Republicans were in disarray. Judson Harmon made an effective campaign for reelection as governor of Ohio. John Worth Kern battled the Republican insurgent Albert J. Beveridge for the Senate seat in Indiana. Attracting great national attention was the gubernatorial race in New Jersey. The former president of Princeton University, Woodrow Wilson, had captured the Democratic nomination. With the

Republicans badly split in the state, Wilson began the fall race with a good chance to emerge victorious. If he did so, there was talk that he could be a powerful candidate for the 1912 nomination. "He condemns backward looking," wrote a friendly journalist of Wilson that summer, "he is for a constructive and definite program, though he is by no means a nationalist."[30]

Meanwhile, the implicit tensions between Roosevelt and the president mounted. During Taft's first year, the new president had found more and more reason to be suspicious of his predecessor. Writing his wife about the onset of the Ballinger-Pinchot controversy, he said, "the whole administration under Roosevelt was demoralized by his system of dealing directly with subordinates." He expected to have Roosevelt's support for his renomination and wanted it at an early date.[31]

Roosevelt felt alienated by what his former lieutenant had done in office. The firing of Pinchot was a major grievance coming as it did after Taft had not retained Roosevelt's cabinet. Other friends of the former president had been moved out of their government posts. Within Taft's own family, his wife, Helen Herron Taft, made clear her disdain for the Roosevelts because of her suspicion that the former president would challenge her husband in 1912. One close observer of Washington society noted that "the war on the Roosevelt section has gone to a point of scandal." The failure of the two men to correspond while Roosevelt was away prevented any opportunity to work through their mutual grievances.[32]

Roosevelt returned to the United States in mid-June to a welcome in New York that brought cheering crowds to acclaim his arrival. He had emerged as a celebrity who made news just by being himself. He could not walk on the street without attracting a crowd. Mail deluged his office and he had more potential speaking engagements than any one person could handle. Yet this notoriety depended on the chance that he might run for president in 1912.

Since he was unwilling to acknowledge Taft as the leader of the party, Roosevelt decided that he had to bring unity back to the GOP. That judgment increased the problems that confronted the former president. His capacity to exercise influence rested on the possibility that he might challenge Taft in 1912. Once he endorsed Taft's candidacy, Roosevelt would become just another Republican voice. So he withheld that kind of statement. In turn, the anti-Taft forces looked to Roosevelt to lead the opposition to the president. By keeping his options open in 1910, Roosevelt increased the likelihood that he would have to come out against Taft. In his search for a leadership role, Roosevelt promoted disunity as the only means of keeping himself in the public eye.

As a result, relations with Taft did not improve. The two men met at the Tafts' summer White House in Beverly, Massachusetts, on 30 June 1910, where they exchanged pleasant compliments but did not address what divided them. To the dismay of the White House, Roosevelt entertained a number of Republican progressives at his home at Oyster Bay, New York. By now he was also complaining about what Taft had said regarding Charles P. Taft's contributions to the president's victory in 1908. When newsmen asked for comments on Roosevelt's guests, the president's secretary snapped, "Our position is that we don't know what Oyster Bay is going to do and we don't give a damn."[33]

In fact, President Taft was highly concerned about what a member of his cabinet called "the pilgrimage of insurgents to the shrine on Sagamore Hill" at Oyster Bay.[34] To forestall Roosevelt, the president and his allies took a more active part in the developing battle among Republicans. Unhappily for the president, these tactics of withholding patronage from Taft's enemies produced defeat for the administration in several key states such as Iowa, Kansas, and Wisconsin, where progressives prevailed. A newspaper editor in Minnesota defined the predicament in which Taft and Roosevelt now found themselves: "Oyster Bay is not the summer capital of the United States, but it is the home of the leader of the Republican party, and, unless we are mistaken, it will remain such for years to come."[35]

Seeing himself in precisely that role, Roosevelt decided to assert his intellectual leadership of the Grand Old Party during a three-week speaking tour of western states starting in late August. His goal was "to announce myself on the vital questions of the day, to set a standard so that it can be seen, and take a position that cannot be misunderstood." The political doctrine that Roosevelt proclaimed on his trip he called the "New Nationalism." It proved to be a key opening move in the presidential campaign of 1912, and it set priorities that dominated the national debate for the next two years.[36]

Roosevelt began his campaign with a speech in Denver on 29 August 1910. He had long resented the way that courts had imposed limits on the ability of the federal government to conduct regulation of business through executive agencies. He now charged that federal and state courts had "tended by a series of negative decisions to create a sphere in which neither nation nor state has effective control; and where the great business interests that can call to their aid the ability of the greatest corporation lawyers escape all control whatsoever." Since such rulings were "fundamentally hostile to every species of real popular government," he argued that the people, through their elected officials, should "have complete power of control in all matters that affect the public interest." For conservative Republicans, with Taft among them, Roosevelt's attack on the judiciary seemed radical and dangerous.[37]

At Osawatomie, Kansas, two days later, Roosevelt confirmed the fears of traditional Republicans and delighted the party's progressive wing. Speaking in commemoration of John Brown and his role in Kansas before the Civil War, Roosevelt showed how far his political ideology had evolved. He called the address "The New Nationalism," a phrase he borrowed from author Herbert Croly, whose book, *The Promise of American Life* (1909) echoed Roosevelt's thinking on social problems.[38] Some 30,000 people heard Roosevelt enumerate a program of government activism more sweeping than what any major Republican or Democrat had proposed before him. His remarks addressed the influence of corporations on politics, asked for revision of the tariff by experts, and called for legislation to provide workmen's compensation and regulation of child labor. His summary statement moved well beyond his previous positions on the role of government embodied in the "Square Deal" of his first presidential term. "I stand for the square deal," he said, "But when I say that I am for the square deal, I mean not merely that I stand for fair play under the present rules of the game, but that I stand for having those rules changed so as to work for a more substantial equality of opportunity and of reward for equally good service."[39]

A key element in his proposal was the role of the president. "This New Nationalism," he went on, "regards the executive power as the steward of the public welfare." A president must be even more of a champion of reform than Roosevelt had been before 1909. He had words for the judiciary, too. Judges must be "interested primarily in human welfare rather than in property," while legislatures at every level should "represent all the people rather than any one class or section of people."[40]

After Roosevelt gave the New Nationalism speech and another on conservation in Minnesota, a British diplomat concluded that "the power of Mr. Roosevelt in the West seems indeed to be very great, and it is undoubted that he has greatly strengthened his position by his recent triumphal tour, although there are not wanting persons in the east to assure one that he has killed himself politically." Among progressives Roosevelt's words evoked praise. In contrast, eastern Republicans were unhappy with "his queer gyrations and don't take any stock in his 'New Nationalism.' "[41]

There was enough negative reaction that Roosevelt took a few steps back toward party orthodoxy. He told an audience in Syracuse, New York, that his new philosophy was "nothing but an application to new conditions of certain old and fundamental moralities." He also compared his position to Abraham Lincoln's criticism of the Dred Scott decision during the 1850s. Henry Cabot Lodge wrote that the outcry against Roosevelt came "wholly from the people who control vast masses of wealth and wish to control the government of the country at the same time." Nonetheless, the hammering at Roosevelt had an effect.[42]

In New York, Roosevelt bested the conservatives at the party convention in 1910. He secured the nomination of his friend, Henry L. Stimson, for governor. Yet Roosevelt also had to accept a platform that endorsed the Payne-Aldrich Tariff and spoke well of Taft's administration. Roosevelt did not come out for Taft in 1912, as the president had hoped he would. Nonetheless, progressives in the West believed that the former president had caved in on the important question of the tariff. "T.R. fell down badly in his platform making in N.Y. *He doesn't see*," wrote Ray Stannard Baker, a muckraking journalist. The Republican ticket in New York seemed headed for defeat as a Democratic tide rose in the nation.[43]

Among the happy Democrats in the fall of 1910, one state race attracted particular attention. New Jersey had been a reliable Republican bastion since the mid-1890s. Now in the wake of GOP factionalism and unhappiness with the high cost of living, the Democrats saw their opportunity to make inroads in an industrial state. The Democratic Party boss, James Smith Jr., knew that he needed an attractive candidate without previous ties to the state organization to have a chance to win. He decided that Woodrow Wilson, the president of Princeton University until a few months earlier, would be an ideal choice. Fifty-three years old in 1910, Wilson had headed Princeton since 1902. After eight years, academic controversies and the erosion of his support among alumni and students had left Wilson embattled. He had opposed the university's social clubs and quarreled with influential faculty and alumni over Princeton's future plans. By the spring of 1910, he was on his way out of office.

Wilson appealed to conservative Democrats in New Jersey because he seemed to be one of them. For years he had made public statements that placed him on the right among his party where state rights and limited government still held sway. In 1907 he said that it would be fatal "to our political vitality really to strip the States of their powers and transfer them to the federal government." He had also made comments critical of William Jennings Bryan. In 1906 and again in 1908 there had been talk in conservative circles in the east about how Wilson might make an excellent candidate for president.[44]

When opportunity came again because of Republican divisions in 1910, Wilson pronounced himself ready for "the rough and tumble of the political arena." The first step in getting Wilson to the White House was to win the New Jersey governorship. George Harvey, the conservative editor of *Harper's Weekly*, proposed to Smith that Wilson be designated as the Democratic nominee. Since the alternative was a Democratic re-former, Smith agreed to Harvey's notion. The bosses had to fight to convince the delegates at the state convention to anoint Wilson. Once they did so, Wilson told the gathering that if elected there would be "absolutely no pledge of any kind to prevent me from serving the people of the State with singleness of purpose."[45]

Wilson proved to be a better candidate than anyone could have anticipated. He leveled his attacks at the leaders of the GOP in a manner that left Republican voters sympathetic to him. He assailed boss rule and overt partisanship and thus identified himself with the progressive spirit. His candidacy captured the attention of Democrats nationally. In Texas, the *Dallas Morning News*, the state's leading newspaper, reprinted Wilson's speeches and wrote on the eve of the balloting that his victory "would be, to our way of thinking, about the most inspiring event that it is possible for the ballot boxes to give forth next Tuesday."[46]

Throughout the nation, optimism soared among Democrats as the election neared. Champ Clark of Missouri, the party leader in the House of Representatives, said that his party was now "a courageous, vigilant, hopeful, militant band, not only ready but eager for the fray." Democrats in New York assailed the New Nationalism as "this exaltation of Federal centralization power" and warned that "whatever advance its adoption would bring is advance toward socialism." Everywhere the Democrats pounded their adversaries about the high cost of living and the impact on consumers of the Payne-Aldrich Tariff.[47]

Election Day on 8 November 1910 brought gloom to the Republicans. The Democrats regained control of the House for the first time since 1894 with a majority of sixty-seven seats. In the East, twenty-six seats moved into the Democratic column from New Jersey, New York, Pennsylvania, and West Virginia. The GOP dropped ten seats in the Senate. Notable casualties included the insurgent Republican, Albert J. Beveridge, who lost to Democrat John Worth Kern in Indiana. While the Republicans retained nominal control of the upper house by a margin of fifty-one to forty-one, their position was weaker than it seemed. When the insurgent Republicans voted with the Democrats, that coalition controlled the upper house. Democrat Champ Clark would be the new Speaker of the House, and he promised vigorous action on measures to lower tariff rates.

The Democrats had additional reason to celebrate results on the state level. In New York, their candidate, John A. Dix, trounced Henry Stimson in a strong rebuke to Roosevelt. The party also reelected Judson Harmon in Ohio and added state executives in Massachusetts, Maine, and Connecticut. The success that drew the most notice came in New Jersey, where Woodrow Wilson swept into office and helped the Democrats win the lower house of the legislature. At once there was mention of Wilson as a White House hopeful. "I am for you for President of the United States in 1912," wrote one enthusiastic Texan to the governor-elect. Since the Democratic nomination for president was now worth something for the first time in twenty years, Wilson would have to compete with a large field in his own party should he decide to run.[48]

The biggest personal loser in 1910 was Theodore Roosevelt. The defeat of Stimson in New York and Beveridge in Indiana sparked charges that the Republican setbacks were the former president's fault. "Just at the present time," wrote a New York Republican, "he has lost many friends." Roosevelt's wavering between reform and conservatism during the campaign even strained his friendship with Gifford Pinchot for some weeks. Pinchot himself concluded that "T.R. will bob up again later, but not in 1912." To those who talked of him as a candidate in 1912, Roosevelt discouraged such speculation. "As things are now it would be a serious mistake from a public standpoint, and a cruel wrong to me, to nominate me," he wrote in January 1911.[49]

The result in 1910 also cast grave doubts on Taft's reelection chances. In search of hopeful signs, he predicted that his links with Roosevelt would improve. "The coolness will wear away," he wrote before the voting, "and our old relations will be restored." Meanwhile the party debated what to do next. Taft told an Iowa Republican of his aim to forge "a working agreement with all elements of the party." That would not be easy to accomplish in view of the disillusion with Taft's leadership among GOP stalwarts. "While he is a well-meaning President and aims to do what is right," observed Senator Knute Nelson of Minnesota, "some how or other he has not been able to catch the sympathy or heart of the public."[50]

By the end of two years in office, Taft was pessimistic about his own prospects in 1912. He was not, however, ready to step aside for a third Roosevelt term or in favor of a Republican progressive such as Robert M. La Follette. The president believed that his policies were sound, prudent, and, in his mind, progressive. In the crucial area of the tariff, the administration was moving toward a new initiative that the president hoped would improve his political fortunes as well. Behind the scenes, a trade agreement with Canada was in the works that Taft believed would reduce prices for American consumers. Instead, the tariff reciprocity plan that Taft negotiated would further intensify Republican factionalism in 1911 and contribute to the prospects for Democratic victory in the 1912 presidential contest.

As 1911 began, the impending presidential election shaped up as a contest between the Republicans and the Democrats like the ones that had occurred since the mid-1890s. The Democrats were optimistic, as they had been before the presidential race in 1908. This time Democratic hopes had a more solid basis. The Republicans saw problems ahead but counted on the mistakes of their opponents to bring an expected victory. Reporters and political observers assumed that President Taft would be renominated and that his major challenger would come from the crowded Democratic field. Few anticipated the four-cornered contest that would be launched eighteen months later.

All the potential contenders for the presidency in 1912 also had to deal with significant changes in the way Americans conducted their politics and elections at the end of the first decade of the twentieth century. During 1911, the implications of this shift in the way presidential contests were waged combined to shape the strategies of each of the Republicans and Democrats with ambitions to win the White House. The run-up to the events of 1912 proved crucial in determining how this pivotal presidential race would be decided.

PRELUDE TO THE PRESIDENTIAL RACE, 1911

Has anybody here seen Teddy?
TE Double DY.
Has anybody here seen Teddy,
Did you meet him passing by?
Oh, his head is clear, and his heart is true,
He is an Insurgent through and through,
Has anybody here seen Teddy,
Teddy from Oyster Bay?
—A newspaper parody, 1910[1]

The congressional elections of 1910 reshaped the political landscape as leaders of both parties reappraised the situation for the presidential race in 1912. While the optimistic Democrats and the wary Republicans digested the returns and examined which potential candidates might succeed, they did so within an electoral system that had certain well-defined characteristics. The election of 1912 looked forward to the contemporary ways in which presidential contenders seek the White House, but there were important historical differences, too, that still separated this election from its modern counterparts. These older customs would come under pressure as 1912 unfolded.

The Progressive Era at the outset of the twentieth century had some key procedural priorities about the role of political parties in public life. Reformers who had grown up in the mobilized mass politics of the late nineteenth century now believed that the dominance of parties and partisanship during that period had not served the nation well. The emphasis on caucuses, loyalty to the party, and voting on a strict partisan basis had, so critics contended, made the Republicans and Democrats the tools of special economic interests. One of the main means for society to improve itself, these reformers asserted, was to reduce the role of parties in national affairs. "The people are inclined to be suspicious of any partisan organization," wrote one exponent of this point of view. "It suggests exclusiveness, possibly some sinister purpose and at least the chaining of big men to little or corrupt men. There is a loss of force in party action. We are living in a new age which none of us understand."[2]

Yet, Americans still had to work through the existing party system to nominate major presidential candidates. While retaining the old forms, the champions of progressive change sought to reshape the rules to their advantage. In 1904, for example, few delegates to the national conventions of the Democrats or Republicans came out of primaries where voters made the key decision about who would attend these gatherings. Four years later, William Jennings Bryan and William Howard Taft both became the nominees of their party through the traditional route of caucuses and conventions. Party regulars by and large determined who the delegates to the national convention would be. At the precinct and county level, the process was relatively open to interested voters with the time to show up and participate. For the most part, however, public opinion did not bear in a direct way in the selection of those who chose the nominee for the White House.

During the four years that followed the 1908 contest, a few states in the West adopted primaries as a means of choosing their delegates to the national convention of each party. Nebraska led the way with a system that linked slates of delegates to prospective presidential candidates. The parties could in theory disregard the will of the voters, but doing so would be a liability for anyone who attempted that course. Six states (Wisconsin, New Jersey, North Dakota, South Dakota, Nebraska, and California) adopted primaries in 1911. Three other states (Maryland, Massachusetts, and Illinois) followed suit in early 1912. In Ohio and Pennsylvania, voters would choose the delegates from individual congressional districts. State conventions in those two states would then allocate at-large delegates.

Among Republicans, the election of delegates was tied to the various congressional districts within an individual state. Thus, to create a statewide primary that would choose delegates at large conflicted with long-standing party rules. In California, for example, the progressive Republican governor, Hiram W. Johnson, sought to persuade the legislature in late 1911 to adopt a statewide primary law for delegates even though the president had enough voting strength in the state to make him the favorite against La Follette. Johnson believed that the principle behind a primary justified the political risk. After all these states had acted, it still remained the case that most of the delegates in both parties would be chosen through the old style of conventions and caucuses.

For the Democrats, the primary proved easier to adopt because their rules were looser than for Republicans. In addition, most southern states had turned to primaries in the early twentieth century as a way of keeping African Americans out of the process of candidate selection for state offices. Voters had to demonstrate that they were both white men and Democrats before they could participate in a primary contest. Moreover, William Jennings Bryan had campaigned in 1908 under the slogan "Shall the People Rule?" which positioned the Democrats more in favor of primaries as they popped up in selected states. As the front-runner for 1912, for example, Woodrow Wilson anticipated the need to win primaries in the thirteen states that offered them.[3]

An unintended consequence of the adoption of primaries for both parties would be greater demands on the candidates to travel around the country seeking votes for potential delegates in a number of states. In the past, prenomination campaigns had been the province of surrogates for the candidate. These individuals did the hard work for their favorite in the party. The candidate stayed off the hustings except perhaps for a few carefully staged appearances.

Now in 1912 the aspiring candidate would have to take to the road to see voters and make a case in public. Such a campaign also meant that the presidential hopeful had to have speeches ready to sustain interest over the many days of a campaign. Aspiring candidates could no longer adopt a silent posture, as Alton B. Parker had done in 1904 as a candidate for the Democratic nomination. The positions of the candidates on the issues would also come under more intense and continued scrutiny than in the past.

Sharing the arena with the direct presidential primary were other procedural changes designed to restrict the power of the parties in the conduct of government. The initiative allowed voters to propose legislation on their own; the referendum placed disputed questions before the electorate to decide what had once been the sole province of the legislature.

Conservatives regarded these measures as providing an unhealthy dose of direct democracy into the process. "The initiative and referendum as a substitute for representative government found its birth in the ranks of the Socialist party," said a Senate candidate in Texas in 1912. When Woodrow Wilson became a staunch advocate of such innovations in 1911, he raised fears about his safeness and conservatism among the more cautious members of his party.[4]

The most controversial of these procedural reforms in 1911–1912 had to do with the judiciary. Judicial recall, as it was known, came in two varieties. When a jurist rendered a decision with which the people of a city or state disagreed, there should exist the right to hold the judge to account through an election to determine whether continuance in office was justified. This proposed procedure disturbed conservatives who feared that judges might be intimidated from making unpopular decisions because of a potential outcry from the voters. "It drags him from his high position of an independent judicial expounder of the law to the position of a mere puppet who must, perhaps, make his decrees and judgement false to his reason, to his conscience, and to the law in order to avoid the degradation brought about by the recall petition," said one opponent of the reform.[5]

Recognizing the faith in the judiciary that many Americans felt, reformers turned instead to what was known as "the recall of judicial decisions." In this procedure, the judge would not be the target. The goal would be to overturn a particular decision through an election. Faced with rulings that invalidated social or economic legislation, the populace could express an opinion on the merits of such decisions. Theodore Roosevelt became the leading champion of this approach as a way of curbing the power of courts to overrule regulators and administrative commissions. He said that when a judge "decides what the people as a whole can or cannot do, the people should have the right to recall that decision if they think it wrong." Conservatives did not like this version any better than they did the outright recall of judges. Any intrusion of actual voters into the judicial process threatened to break down the legal system, as they saw it. For a candidate to take up judicial recall in any of its forms would risk a backlash from conservative and moderate voters.[6]

The recall became a national issue when the territory of Arizona presented a constitution to Congress as a prelude to statehood. The fundamental document of the state contained a provision for the recall of judges. When it reached Washington, Taft announced that he would not accept the language and insisted upon its removal. After Congress failed to do so, Taft submitted a veto message that prompted lawmakers to remove the offending clause. Taft called it "something of a victory." Once Arizona was admitted to the Union, the new state amended its constitution to put back in the language that Taft disliked. After that, judicial recall slipped out of the popular consciousness for the last several months of 1911, but it was still on the active and involved mind of Theodore Roosevelt.[7]

A less controversial political reform in the context of 1911 was the direct election of U.S. senators by the people of their states. Since the beginning of the new century, the perception had grown that the upper house of Congress was an exclusive club for rich politicians selected through a corrupt process. Popular sentiment had mounted to remove the power to choose senators from state legislatures and give it to the voters. Scandals over the tainted elections of senators in Wisconsin and especially the alleged vote buying associated with the 1909 election of William Lorimer in Illinois fueled this campaign for change. In 1911 the Senate adopted a constitutional amendment for direct elections. The measure then stalled in the House until the opponents relented in mid-May 1912. The proposal went to the states where ratification seemed assured. Senate elections in 1912, however, would occur under the old system.[8]

Among the striking new aspects of the 1912 presidential election was the enhanced role that women played in the contest from the outset. Part of that greater participation grew out of the success of the woman suffrage movement since the previous presidential race. In 1908, women could cast votes for president in four states—Wyoming, Colorado, Utah, and Idaho. Washington State followed in 1910. The big prize came in October 1911 when California voters added woman suffrage to the state's constitution. Anna Howard Shaw, a leader among reform advocates, said that "the politicians are also sure to realize that the women are winning their long fight and will climb on the band wagon with the rest of us."[9]

With some 1,300,000 women of voting age in these six states, women now had enough electoral clout to make direct appeals for their ballots a worthwhile strategy. Women born in the years between 1885 and 1891 were more interested in politics than their predecessors. Many of them had gone to college, worked in settlement houses in the cities, and participated in conservation and public health campaigns. Seeing a potentially exciting, hotly contested election before them, women of all shades of opinion prepared to take part in the process in a much more organized fashion. These developments happened with such speed that male politicians were in the midst of change before they quite knew what had happened. As one woman involved in the Progressive Party put it, "The crusaders' spirit is abroad in women for womankind, and the parties and their leaders are but instruments in the cause."[10]

Signs abounded in late 1911 of the intensifying involvement of women with policy questions and electoral strategy. Several of the major participants in the coming battles of 1912 had already taken their places. Mrs. J. Borden "Daisy" Harriman, president of New York's Colony Club, declared herself for Woodrow Wilson. Meanwhile, Jane Addams of Hull House and Lillian D. Wald joined other social workers in handing a petition to Taft about labor unrest. The document asked for a federal commission "to gauge the breakdown of our machinery of industrial Government." Out of their action would come the federal Commission on Industrial Relations. Among the Republicans, Helen Varick Boswell had taken over the leadership of the Women's National Republican Association after the death of its longtime head, Mrs. J. Ellen Foster. During 1912 itself, the opportunities would expand for these and other women to involve themselves in politics in ways unheard of a few years earlier.[11]

While white women were finding a greater role in national politics in the prelude to 1912, African Americans of both genders remained marginalized. The politics of reform in this crucial presidential election did not include the interests of black Americans in a substantial way. In the South, decades of disenfranchisement had left most blacks outside the decisions of the dominant and racist Democratic Party. In such states, like Texas, Republicans had sought without success to purge their party of African Americans to make the organization "lily white." Once that was accomplished, members of the Grand Old Party believed that they could appeal to Democrats on economic issues without the distraction of race. This tactic had not brought a noticeable increase of white voters to the Republican side, and African Americans constituted a large number of what existed of southern Republicans in 1911.[12]

The Great Migration of southern blacks to northern cities had just begun in the years before World War I. These new arrivals had not yet reached sufficient numbers to change voting patterns. They brought

Daisy Borden Harriman, as the most visible Democratic woman for Wilson in 1912, helped implement the party's strategy of criticizing the Republicans on the tariff issue. (Prints and Photographs Collection, Library of Congress)

with them their sympathy for the Republicans to new homes in New York, Philadelphia, Chicago, Detroit, and other cities. At the same time, Roosevelt and Taft had not given blacks much reason to maintain this loyalty. Both presidents had used African Americans to win presidential nominations. Once that process had been completed, the Republican presidents had resorted to wooing Democratic converts from the white South.

Roosevelt had dismissed black soldiers from the army in the Brownsville, Texas, episode of 1906, in a miscarriage of justice. He had also begun to doubt whether there was any future for a Republican Party in the South based on the votes of African Americans. President Taft in turn offered blacks little cause to admire his record in the White House. He named a racist southerner as his secretary of war and made it clear that the fewer African Americans involved in government and Republican affairs the better. There was a strong undercurrent of disillusionment with the GOP among some activist blacks on the eve of the 1912 campaign. Some of them even looked at the Democrats with a small amount of hope.[13]

The Democrats on the surface displayed little appeal in their ideology to move potential black defectors from the Republicans. The opposition party believed in white supremacy and segregation. Southerners dominated the higher councils of the Democrats with defenses of lynching, attacks on the Fourteenth and Fifteenth Amendments, and rationales for violence against blacks. A few prominent African Americans in the North, holding their noses, had contended that unswerving loyalty to the GOP had not worked. Accordingly, they voted for Bryan in 1908. If the Democrats selected a palatable candidate in 1912, there might be some opportunity for limited gains among black intellectuals such as W. E. B. Du Bois and William Monroe Trotter.

The surge of immigration into the United States during the first decade of the century raised the political consciousness of ethnic groups looking to better themselves through the electoral process. At the same time, there was a backlash against these newcomers. On the West Coast, restrictions on Asians were popular in California, Washington, and Oregon. The Democratic platform in 1908 was "opposed to the admission of Asiatic immigrants who cannot be amalgamated with our population, or whose presence among us would raise a race issue and involve us in diplomatic controversies with Oriental powers." For their part,

Republican officials warned of the perils, in their minds, of unregulated immigration.[14]

The newcomers organized themselves into associations to advance their own political agenda and to influence national candidates. The Irish Americans had long supported Democrats while German Americans leaned toward the Republicans in the Middle West. The emerging issue of prohibition of alcohol affected the Democrats as their southern base clamored to restrict liquor, while in the North the urban, immigrant constituents of the party resisted any limits on their cultural tolerance for beer and wine. Under Roosevelt, Republicans had made inroads into ethnic blocs of eastern European and Jewish voters. The Democrats expected to counter these shifts with appeals to immigrants in 1912.[15]

The issues of foreign policy played a peripheral role in the run-up to the 1912 contest,. Although the outbreak of World War I was just three years away, the possibility of such an international cataclysm seemed remote as the nation prepared to choose the next president. Newspapers kept the public well informed of events overseas, but to Americans a general European war seemed improbable. Industrial nations, people believed, were too advanced and mature to descend into a pointless conflict that would threaten civilization. There was a revolution in neighboring Mexico in 1911, but even that volatile incident did not intrude on the presidential race. The outside world seemed very distant as Americans looked at the possible contenders for the presidency during the year before the actual campaign commenced.

In the aftermath of the 1910 elections, politicians in both parties recognized that the presidential contest in 1912 would be competitive in a way that had not occurred for two decades. For the first time since Grover Cleveland's third race for the White House in 1892, the united Democrats had a serious opportunity to challenge Republicans outside of the states that went for William Jennings Bryan in 1896, 1900, and 1908. No one foresaw a split among Republicans into two rival tickets, as happened eighteen months later, but Democrats believed that they could, with the right candidate, beat their faction-ridden opponents in a two-way race.

During 1911, many of the key decisions were made that determined the outcome in November 1912. William Howard Taft did not regain his national popularity, but he did seize an advantage in the quest for renomination. Theodore Roosevelt could not make up his mind about challenging the president. As a result, when he did become a candidate in early 1912, he had to play catch-up and never gained the initiative. The third Republican in the race, Robert La Follette of Wisconsin, used 1911 to make himself a credible progressive alternative to Roosevelt. The failure of this effort relegated La Follette to subordinate status. He did not recognize how slim his chances were by the end of the year, and his persistence in the contest hurt the chances for a progressive alternative to Taft other than Roosevelt to emerge.

Among the Democrats, their newly won control of the House of Representatives focused press attention on the two lawmakers who seemed probable rivals for the prize in 1912. Both Champ Clark as Speaker and Oscar W. Underwood as majority leader believed that their legislative successes would translate into delegate votes at the next national convention. For Clark, that strategy brought him quite close to the nomination in late June 1912. What he did not take fully into account was the presence of a non-Washington alternative in the governor of New Jersey, Woodrow Wilson.

Throughout 1911 and, indeed, in 1912 as well, events broke Wilson's way at propitious times. Of course, he was also a good-enough politician to seize the opportunities that positive developments presented to him. He demonstrated this quality within a few days of his election in 1910. The boss of the Democrats in New Jersey, James Smith Jr., saw his chance to return to the U.S. Senate now that his party had enough seats in the assembly to put him into office. The U.S. Congress had not yet adopted a constitutional amendment to have the people choose senators. That task remained with state legislatures. So Smith anticipated that he would now collect on the political chits that he had amassed over the years.

Yet, for many in New Jersey, Smith exemplified corruption and boss rule in political life. He had spent one undistinguished term in the Senate from 1893 to 1899 and now wanted the personal vindication another six years would provide. Few observers anticipated his candidacy before the voting because a Democratic majority in the legislature seemed improbable. Another candidate had been selected in a senatorial primary, but that process seemed irrelevant until the Democrats won control of enough legislators to choose a senator. Wilson regarded the Democrat who had won the primary, James E. Martine, as a laughingstock hopeful. He also assumed that Smith would not enter the contest. Five days after the election, however, Smith told the press: "If I find that my friends think I should make the fight, I will enter the race and I will win it."[16]

Faced with immediate outrage among New Jersey progressives about Smith, Wilson decided that he had to block the former senator from returning to Washington. If Wilson was going to have any chance at the presidency, he had to demonstrate his reform credentials in a dramatic way. Allowing Smith to win would probably have ended the governor's national prospects. So, after a final, futile conference with Smith to persuade him to withdraw, Wilson came out against his former patron on 8 December. The governor's statement urged legislators to vote for Martine despite the candidate's modest qualifications. During the month that followed, Wilson cajoled Democratic lawmakers, delivered public speeches against Smith, and threw his prestige into the campaign. Martine was elected in the end, and the first great confrontation of Wilson's young public career came to a victorious conclusion. "Here, obviously," said a Texas newspaper, "is the exponent of new political ideas."[17]

Wilson then proceeded to have the New Jersey legislature adopt laws providing for workmen's compensation, the direct primary, regulation of utilities, and the outlawing of corrupt practices. The party had found a Democratic state executive who could govern. These accomplishments appealed to Democrats across the country eager for a newer direction and a fresh face for the party. A Texas editor said that "the scholar turned statesman, is the toast of every decent citizen of his adopted State and the man toward whom millions of his countrymen are turning for national leadership." Woodrow Wilson clubs sprang up and invitations to address audiences around the country poured in to Wilson's office. His friends put together the beginnings of a presidential campaign structure.[18]

By the summer of 1911, the New Jersey governor had taken an apparent lead in the race for the Democratic nomination. His original conservative backers had cooled after the Smith episode. Wilson's endorsement of the initiative and referendum as needed reforms did not please party members on the right. Yet, with his move to the left, Wilson became more appealing to Democratic reformers who saw him as an improvement over either Clark or Underwood. "We must make our fight clean cut—progressive policies and progressive men against reactionary policies and reactionary men," said one reporter friendly to Wilson. "You cannot nominate Woodrow Wilson for President upon a straddle."[19]

For Wilson, a man of great self-confidence and little humility, the prospect of becoming president seemed to be the fulfillment of his own sense of historic destiny that he had thought about since college. As he began to speak around the country during 1911, it was evident that he had the talent to connect with friendly audiences. He attacked Republican tariff policy and asked for greater openness in politics. While he had now grabbed the spotlight as the front-runner, it remained to be seen what would happen when his rivals in the party began criticizing his public record. In his writings as an academic and in several of his private letters, the governor had provided ammunition for his opponents with derogatory statements about immigrants. They would use these comments in early 1912. For most of 1911, Wilson set the Democratic pace.

The other Democratic hopefuls for 1912 seemed off stride while Wilson surged. Judson Harmon, the governor of Ohio, appealed to conservatives because of his service in Grover Cleveland's cabinet as attorney general from 1895 to 1897. A dull, colorless campaigner, "Uncle Judson" rested his hopes on his base in the Middle West and the prospect of a deadlocked convention. More serious as the candidate of the South was Oscar W. Underwood of Alabama, chair of the House Ways and Means Committee. A cautious advocate of lower tariffs, Underwood clashed with William Jennings Bryan over the pace at which rates should be lowered. On procedural reforms such as the initiative and referendum, Underwood's opposition pleased party conservatives. Pinned down with congressional duties and perceived as a regional candidate, the fifty-year-old Underwood would be a late entrant into the 1912 contest.[20]

The major Democratic contender was Champ Clark, the Speaker of the House. During 1911, the performance of the party in Congress belied the predictions that they would be disunited and ineffective. Since taking formal control of the House in March, the party had demonstrated unexpected cohesion and purpose. They had pushed their low-tariff agenda in the face of Taft's vetoes and had battled the White House on issues from conservation to probes of the president's record. By the time the special session, called to address Canadian reciprocity, adjourned in August, surprised commentators said that the Democrats in Congress were "making good." The verdict was that "their legislative work is constructive in aim, not destructive, and their leaders are showing a conservatism and poise wholly lacking since the free silver hysteria rent the party in twain fifteen years ago."[21]

The solid performance of the House Democrats improved Clark's chances. He rested many of his claims to consideration for the White House on his record in Congress. When he announced for president, he

Woodrow Wilson campaigns in Texas. A key to Woodrow Wilson's eventual nomination was his support from such states as Pennsylvania and Texas. In October 1911, he spoke at the Texas State Fair, where he met with Governor Oscar B. Colquitt (middle) and Senator Charles A. Culberson (right). (Center for American History, University of Texas at Austin)

said that he would not "allow my candidacy for the Presidential nomination to interfere with the duty I owe my party in the House." As a presidential hopeful, Clark had the benefit of an impressive record within the mainstream of the party, especially on the need for lower tariffs. Working against him was a feud with William Jennings Bryan and a reputation as a leader with a penchant for awkward statements and gaffes. During the debate over Canadian reciprocity, he proclaimed a desire to annex "every foot of the British North American possessions no matter how far north they extend." That comment naturally unsettled the Canadians and hurt the chances for approval of the reciprocity agreement north of the border. Clark's loose tongue and Missouri border manner explained why many Democrats hoped for a more respectable and credible nominee. Nonetheless, the prospect of victory ran through the ranks of happy Democrats throughout 1911.[22]

The Democrats were not the only opposition party preparing to challenge the Republicans during 1911. While press coverage focused on the struggle between the major parties, another presidential contender was engaged in what he believed was the process of transforming the United States from capitalism. Eugene Victor Debs was fifty-six in 1911. Running as a Socialist for the White House, he had secured 98,000 votes in 1900, 400,000 votes in 1904, and 420,000 votes in 1908. With reform in the air and greater receptivity to socialism after 1909, hopes flared that the party could do even better in 1912. For Debs, the key was not just the amassing of votes or even the electoral count in any individual state. He wanted to promote "the stern and uncompromising spirit of a revolutionary party."[23]

Within the Socialist ranks there were bitter divisions over how best to attain the revolution. In cities like Milwaukee, Wisconsin, and Syracuse, New York, Socialist mayors had been elected in protest against the corruption and lack of responsiveness of the major parties. These achievements, said one journal, meant that "the American Socialist is no longer a creature of hoofs and horns" in the minds of middle-class citizens. Yet to the extent that Socialists made the inevitable compromises that governing entailed, they risked losing some of their ideological edge.[24]

When, however the Socialists spoke of violence and dramatic attacks on the social order, as did William "Big Bill" Haywood of the Industrial Workers of the World, they frightened middle-class voters. Debs struggled with the dilemma in 1912 as he had done in previous years. But the emphasis on the Socialist side in 1911 was more on their hopes than their problems. Should the Democrats choose a moderate candidate and the Republicans opt for the conservative Taft, Socialists might have a good chance to win over some sympathetic progressives from both of the major parties. One enthusiastic writer on the left predicted that the Socialists could poll as many as 2 million votes. Debs himself caught the spirit: "Let us make this our year! Let us make the numerals 1912 appear in flaming red in the calendar of the century."[25]

The Republicans, of course, had no intention of letting the Democrats, much less the Socialists, displace them from the power they had enjoyed since 1896. President Taft, as the party leader, sought to mend fences with Roosevelt following the election of 1910. This effort seemed to succeed during the early months of 1911. The two men corresponded again and exchanged views on pressing issues. Roosevelt praised Taft's campaign for tariff reciprocity with Canada and told friends that he did not expect to oppose the president's renomination in 1912. While the old intimacy had vanished, the bitterness abated, at least for the moment.

On the national scene, Taft showed that he could still lead the Republicans. He negotiated the reciprocity agreement with the Canadian government of Sir Wilfred Laurier that lowered tariff rates for both countries. Taft believed that such a trade pact would offset his reputation as protectionist. The arrangement, however, was not popular in the states along the Canadian border where Republicans, competing with their northern economic rivals, saw their interests threatened. The high-tariff wing of the GOP also saw this initiative as proof that Taft was not really one of them as well. Theodore Roosevelt initially endorsed the Canadian reciprocity proposal, though he would soon change his mind as the opposition to the agreement from progressives and farm-state Republicans mounted.

The president summoned Congress into special session in April 1911 to enact the legislation necessary to put the trade understanding into effect. Using the power of his office to win GOP lawmakers to his cause, Taft persuaded enough Republicans and some willing Democrats to enact the program into law. Since many progressives opposed the measure, Taft also exposed the apparent hypocrisy of several of his most visible congressional critics. The British ambassador, James Bryce, told the governor-general of Canada: "Taft is doing admirably, if not for his party, which is cleft in twain, yet for his own character and reputation as a man of integrity and courage."[26]

With the momentum he had gained from this victory, Taft decided to launch his bid for another nomination. He now had a skilled operative as his personal secretary. After two men had flopped in the post, Charles Dewey Hilles came to the White House early in 1911. A conservative from New York, the forty-four-year-old Hilles brought organizing energy and a sense of urgency to his new job. It was time, he and the president concluded, to get Republicans on the record for Taft. Early in June 1911, Hilles sent out a letter to party leaders around the country asking their opinion of Taft's prospects. The document laid out Taft's claims for re-nomination as an effective president and thus put Republicans on notice that Taft would want their public endorsement for 1912. By August 1911, confident Taft backers were telling friendly reporters "that as far as the result of the convention is concerned it is all over but the shouting."[27]

Hilles and the president also laid plans for a presidential tour of the country in the fall. Taft enjoyed traveling, and this trip gave him a chance to seem nonpartisan in his formal remarks. On another level, the junket was designed to secure delegate commitments in advance of the nomination process that opened early in 1912. By getting the unoffi-cial phase of the race for delegates started so early, Taft and Hilles seized an initiative that they never relinquished through the national conven-tion in June 1912. For the president, his primary goal was to insure that Roosevelt did not win the nomination. His reelection chances became secondary to that overriding objective.

Opposition to Taft among Republicans lacked a clear alternative to the president. With Roosevelt on the sidelines, party members who sought lower tariffs, procedural reforms, and fresh leadership had to look else-where for a viable candidate. They had one potential challenger in Sena-tor Robert M. La Follette of Wisconsin. La Follette very much wanted to be president and believed that he deserved the backing of progres-sives over Roosevelt. In La Follette's mind, Roosevelt was an opportunist who had too often compromised with big business and GOP conserva-tives. The Wisconsinite believed that he represented the true essence of progressivism and therefore should receive the backing of all genuine friends of meaningful reform. During the summer of 1911, while he was willing to run for the nomination, La Follette had yet to commit himself fully to the race. He lacked the drive to pursue a prize he thought should be his by right.

Because he advocated so many reform causes, "Battle Bob" La Follette has often been depicted as the selfless crusader he thought he was. On the wall of his study on his Wisconsin farm, he hung words from Robert Browning that summed up his approach to politics: "Never dreamed, though right were worsted, wrong would triumph / Held we fall to rise, are baffled to fight better / Sleep to wake." He had served in the House during the 1880s and then became a foe of the conservative Wisconsin Republican political organization that frustrated his efforts to win the governorship several times during the 1890s.[28]

He finally won the governorship in 1900 and embarked on a program of railroad regulation through a commission, the direct primary to choose candidates, and heavier taxes on business. After two terms as governor of Wisconsin, he came to the U.S. Senate in 1906 intent on using that body as his ticket to the White House. He read out the roll-call votes of his reactionary colleagues to audiences around the country. In 1908 he filibustered a banking bill in dramatic style that included his exaggerated charge he had been poisoned on the Senate floor. Most of all, he let everyone know that he alone was the true symbol of Republican reform. In his mind, Roosevelt represented expediency and could not be trusted. Based on his public record, La Follette asserted that he was the best progressive candidate to beat Taft.

That premise of electability rested on very thin evidence. In fact, La Follette had no chance to seize the GOP nomination in 1912. His perceived radicalism limited his support in the East. "What the people in the Middle West do not understand is the fact that La Follette has never made the faintest impression, practically, East of Ohio," wrote Mark Sullivan, a progressive journalist. For other Republicans, his "French" name evoked images of that revolutionary country. His confrontational speaking style alienated many regulars. More important, La Follette wanted the nomination only if the quest did not interfere with his Senate duties and his own convenience. He shrank from launching the all-out speaking campaign that might have given him a slim chance for victory. One Republican House member called him "a grandstand politician, taking up certain issues and handling them effectively. But so far as the day in and day out work is concerned, he is little of a factor."[29]

Following the election of 1910, La Follette encouraged the organization of the National Progressive Republican League. Beginning in January 1911, the league included such reformers as Gifford and his brother Amos Pinchot, James R. Garfield, who had served in Roosevelt's cabinet, and the urban reformer Frederic C. Howe among its members. Its goal was to build on the successes of 1910 and create an organization to

Senator Robert La Follette, progressive candidate for the Republican nomination, believed that he was the true reformer in the race to defeat Taft. (Robert M. La Follette, La Follette's Autobiography: A Personal Narrative of Political Experiences *[Madison: Robert M. La Follette Co., 1913]).*

push for progressive causes. News releases said that the group favored the direct election of senators, the initiative, referendum, and recall, and laws to curb corrupt practices. But the league never found a clear focus and lacked enough funds to succeed. It did not prove to be an effective monitor of what Congress was doing or how state legislatures operated. Instead, most politicians regarded it as a cover for La Follette's White House ambitions and a gimmick.

La Follette eased into the presidential race with an announcement of candidacy in June 1911 that was too guarded in its wording and too general to stir excitement. Supporters raised some money and sent out literature, but a flourishing national organization never emerged. Among the backers of La Follette was the Boston lawyer, Louis D. Brandeis. He shared La Follette's suspicion of bigness in industry and was looking for a candidate who did not share Roosevelt's sympathy for large corporations. La Follette had no doubts about Brandeis's loyalty. The senator, however, knew that many of his backers preferred Roosevelt. A tension between the La Follette loyalists and the admirers of the former president pervaded the campaign from the outset. La Follette hammered the Taft administration over the tariff all during the summer. He cooperated with Democrats to block the president on several initiatives. It seemed a strange way to win the votes of Republican convention delegates. Much to the frustration of his allies, the candidate stuck to his Senate work and wrote his autobiography for the *American Magazine*. None of these moves did much good outside of loyal Wisconsin. Yet for progressives such as the Pinchots and Garfield, La Follette was "the only man in sight" so long as Roosevelt refused to make the race against Taft.[30]

La Follette's candidacy was a nuisance for Taft, but the threat of Theodore Roosevelt menaced the president's chances. As he had done since his return from Europe, Roosevelt declined to endorse Taft throughout the early months of 1911. The friendlier attitude of the two men that grew up after the 1910 election defeat persisted until early June. At a public event for a prominent Roman Catholic clergyman, the former friends met in Baltimore. The press announced that Roosevelt would soon endorse Taft; the ex-president repudiated the stories. He blamed the White House for what seemed to him a blatant leak. In fact, a Taft cabinet member and former ally of Roosevelt, George von Lengerke Meyer, was responsible for the story.[31]

During the rest of the summer, Roosevelt criticized Taft's plan for arbitration treaties to settle international disputes. In the pages of the *Outlook*, he hit out again on issues regarding conservation policy in Alaska. Mutual suspicion now dominated the mood of the former friends. "The truth is," wrote Taft, "he believes in war and wishes to be a Napoleon and die on the battlefield. He has the spirit of the old Berserkers."[32]

Roosevelt's political judgment had not been good since his African safari. He lost touch with the American political scene, and without the authority of the presidency he seemed less skilled about internal Republican affairs. Out of power, he listened to advisers such as the Pinchots whose sense of the Republican base was at best limited. Moreover, he took his continuing celebrity as confirming evidence of his genuine popularity within the Grand Old Party.

His situation during the summer of 1911 reflected his muddled thinking. If he did not plan an all-out race in 1912, coming out for Taft would have cleared the air. Assuming a Taft loss in 1912, Roosevelt would then be the presumptive nominee for 1916. If he intended to challenge Taft, waiting to enter the contest only increased the president's advantage as leader of his party. Unsure of what to do, Roosevelt dithered. His fame and popularity rested on the possibility that he might come out against Taft. He soothed his conscience during the rest of the summer with his critiques of White House positions on arbitration and conservation.

If Roosevelt decided to run, one of the centerpieces of his campaign would be his evolving stance on government regulation of big business. The rise of industrialism and the consolidation of the movement had pushed the question of controlling corporations to the front among political issues. While only the Socialists talked of government ownership and control of large firms, the extent to which big business should either be broken up or regulated divided the parties and policy makers.

Among Republicans, President Taft was a committed advocate of the Sherman Antitrust Act (1890) as a weapon to control corporations. Indeed, his Justice Department filed more such prosecutions than were started under Theodore Roosevelt. Under Roosevelt, suits against the tobacco trust and Standard Oil had begun, and these prosecutions went forward after 1909. Taft's attorney general, George Wickersham, believed that if the Supreme Court endorsed breaking up the tobacco trust and Standard Oil, "the business community will voluntarily conform its organization to the law." Taft's commitment to this policy produced some erosion in his support from corporate America during 1911.[33]

For all of his reputation as a trustbuster and enemy of big business, Theodore Roosevelt seemed a more sympathetic figure to corporate

President William Howard Taft in a contemplative moment of his difficult presidency. Despite his problems, he believed that he deserved renomination in 1912. (Prints and Photographs Collection, Library of Congress)

executives during this period. He believed, as he had done in the White House, that the government should distinguish between businesses that served the public good and firms that violated the law and its spirit. Through executive agencies within the federal government, Washington could encourage good behavior and punish wrongdoers. Speaking of the tobacco trust, Standard Oil, and United States Steel, Roosevelt argued that "we should be able to put our hands on these two big corporation as well as on Judge [E. H.] Gary [of United States Steel], and tell them just what they are to do in any matter where we think they are conserving to the public ill."[34] The means would be a regulatory agency, modeled on the Interstate Commerce Commission, which would have some capacity to set the maximum prices that firms could charge. The predictability inherent in this kind of supervision seemed to some in the business community a better deal than Taft's antitrust approach. Despite his perceived radicalism, Roosevelt enjoyed unexpected support from some of the more conservative elements within the Republican coalition.

Another latent issue for Roosevelt had to do with the third-term tradition in national politics. In 1904, on the night of his election in his own right, Roosevelt had announced that he would not be a candidate for another nomination in deference to the custom that presidents served only two terms. "The wise custom which limits the President to two terms regards the substance and not the form. Under no circumstances will I be a candidate for or accept another nomination." His three years after the death of William McKinley, he said, meant that he had in effect held the presidency for two terms. In the next several years he renewed his pledge and, of course, in 1908 stepped aside to enable the Republicans to pick Taft as his successor. There is some evidence that he came to regret while president having made such a categorical pledge, but there was no way to undo the strong words he had uttered in November 1904.[35]

As the possibility of another race loomed for the former president, however, he began to back away from what he had said on that election night. He developed a distinction between his situation in 1908 when he was in office and four years later when he lacked the power of the presidency. Roosevelt told friends that should he become a candidate he would not be seeking a third consecutive term. Without the clout of incumbency to dole out patronage and sway party conventions, he should not be evaluated in the same light as a sitting president trying for a third nomination. While his argument made sense to him, it did not seem likely to quiet the fears of his enemies about the prospect of a third try for the White House. Roosevelt did not appreciate with sufficient insight how the third-term issue, coupled with the recall of judges, could serve as a drag on his possible candidacy to oppose Taft.

As the summer of 1911 drew to a close, the political scene in the United States was more fluid than it had been in any presidential election since 1896. A member of the British Embassy staff in Washington told the ambassador in early September that "it seems in the last few weeks to have become something of a commonplace that Taft's chances of reelection are absolutely nil. A Democrat seems a certainty."[36] That assumption gave hope to the opposition and drove Republicans to consider their alternatives to the president's renomination. During the last months of 1911, events shaped themselves in a manner that guaranteed a bitter fight for the Republican prize. The Democrats, with increasing confidence of victory, opened the process of choosing someone who might return them to the national power they had not seen for almost sixteen years. Few could have foreseen the political tumult that lay ahead for all concerned as 1912 began.

ROOSEVELT VERSUS TAFT IN 1912

I'm twice as great as Washington,
I'm twice as great as Grant;
Because third terms they didn't get
They needn't think I can't.
I'm twice as great as Jefferson
And Madison combined
I'm twice as great of all the lot
Of Presidents, I find!
—Anti-Roosevelt poem, 1912[1]

The contest between Theodore Roosevelt and William
Howard Taft for the Republican presidential nomination in 1912 has been treated as one of the great melo-
dramas in the nation's political history. According to the
main story line, the popular, progressive Roosevelt, eager to enact the New Nationalism, yielded to the public
clamor for his selection and became a declared candidate during the winter of 1912. An inept, befuddled Taft,
a pawn of party conservatives, faced down the Roosevelt
challenge. Although the president failed to connect with
the GOP's rank and file, he won in the end through par-
liamentary muscle and control of the party machinery.
By all rights, this interpretation continues, Roosevelt
should have been the Republican nominee. Outraged
at having the prize snatched from his grasp, Roosevelt
bolted, formed his third party, and insured Republican
defeat and only one term for the hapless Taft.

The story is compelling because much of it fits the
evidence. In its simplicity, however, it misses the dilem-
mas of 1912 for the Republicans. By giving Roosevelt

the sole starring role in the saga, it depicts the political loser as the winner and thus understates Taft's capacity as a party politician. That Roosevelt made a series of mistakes and unwise decisions gets overlooked. It also leaves out the crucial contributions of Robert La Follette to the triumph of the Republican conservatives. In a battle that foreshadowed the campaigning style of modern politics, Roosevelt and his progressive allies missed chance after chance to seize control of the Grand Old Party. The consequences of their missteps would shape American politics for decades.

In the case of Taft, he had likely given up any realistic hope for reelection in 1912 but was determined to gain a renomination and frustrate Roosevelt. That goal shaped his strategy throughout the intraparty conflict that followed. While not ignoring electoral considerations altogether, Taft and Charles D. Hilles, his campaign manager, assigned them less weight than otherwise would been the case. They used delegates from the South, where the GOP did not exist as a real force, to build a majority for the president. They focused on exploiting the rules that favored an incumbent president to maximum effect. Roosevelt and his allies never grasped the essence of Taft's strategy until it was too late for the opposition to succeed.

Compared with Taft, Roosevelt displayed a much weaker sense of how his party operated in choosing presidential candidates. He waited too long in making a decision to run in January 1912, and he failed to shape an approach aimed at creating a majority coalition in the national convention. The former president seemed to think that a wave of favorable opinion would sweep him to the nomination when he so desired. He thus allowed valuable time to be wasted before he began to campaign in earnest. Sure that he ought to win, he gave little thought to what would happen if he lost and then had to endorse Taft. From the outset of his race, Roosevelt had placed himself in a position where bolting to a third party might become his only option. His unwillingness to step aside for a compromise nominee attested to Roosevelt's willfulness.

Robert La Follette is usually portrayed as a supporting player in the larger Taft-Roosevelt drama. That judgment understates the importance of the Wisconsin senator. The existence of his progressive campaign complicated Roosevelt's thinking throughout the fall of 1911. La Follette's disastrous speech in February 1912 is the point where he usually drops out of the main narrative. In fact, his continued presence in the race divided the progressive assault on Taft during the spring of 1912.

The unwillingness of "Battle Bob" to cooperate with Roosevelt at the national convention prevented the selection of the only announced candidate who could possibly command a majority of the delegates. At the same time, La Follette's intransigence also blocked the emergence of a compromise choice. Largely out of personal pique, La Follette stood against a victory for the Republican progressives.

Within the party that all three men sought to control, the president had the better grip on the levers of power. The Republican National Committee was a bastion of Taft strength. Its members had been chosen in 1908 at a time when Roosevelt and Taft were allies engaged in fending off conservative opposition to Taft's nomination. No one anticipated that a subsequent falling out would make the committee pivotal in deciding contested delegates. During the week before the national convention, the Republican National Committee would make up a temporary roll of delegates and hear contests over disputed delegate slates. Taft thus held the institutional high ground from which in time Roosevelt would seek to dislodge him.[2]

Another powerful Taft advantage lay with the southern Republicans. In that day, Democrats dominated Dixie politics as the party of state rights and white supremacy. Republicans represented a shadow party of only a few whites eager for patronage or heretics from the Democratic fold. Black party members, the majority of southern Republicans, associated the GOP with Abraham Lincoln and the end of slavery. During a time of racial oppression, those African Americans within the ranks of Republicans in the South aligned their delegate votes with the presidents who could provide federal offices and campaign cash. "Referees," as they were called, decided who got offices; Taft decided who the referees were. In Texas, for example, Cecil Lyon, a friend of Roosevelt's, had doled out the spoils for a decade. Taft moved to replace him in late 1911.[3]

By the end of the summer of 1911, Taft was well ahead of both potential challengers to his renomination. Though the selection of delegates could not commence until after the Republican National Committee issued its call for the convention in January 1912, Hilles encouraged the president's allies to create organizations loyal to Taft. These groups would be ready to act in the new year, especially in the South. As for Taft himself, his extensive and well-publicized cross-country trip during the fall had as its real goal, in the words of Hilles, to "put a crimp in the inflated boom of the opposition in a few states."[4]

Nonetheless, Taft's problems persisted. After expending large amounts of political capital to get the Canadian reciprocity agreement through Congress, his dream collapsed in September 1911 when voters in Canada turned out the Liberal government of Wilfred Laurier that had negotiated the trade accord. All Taft had to show for his effort was the deep unhappiness of Republicans in the states that bordered Canada. The president also encountered opposition from both Roosevelt and Senate Republicans to his arbitration treaties designed to preserve peace through international agreements. Meanwhile, business leaders complained about the campaign of the Justice Department to enforce the antitrust laws.[5]

Taft came out fighting for his renomination in late August 1911. He spoke at Hamilton, Massachusetts, on the 26th, where he excoriated both the Democrats and the insurgent Republicans for their efforts to lower tariff rates. The president singled out La Follette for specific criticism. He said nothing about Roosevelt, though inwardly he resented his predecessor's attacks on his conservation policies toward Alaska. Strong within the Republican Party because of his control of the party apparatus and his status as the best candidate to block Roosevelt, Taft had less attractive prospects for reelection as he began his six-week tour of the country.[6]

With Roosevelt silent in public about a White House run and assuring friends privately that there were "no great issues at stake" in the upcoming elections, progressive Republicans believed that they must look elsewhere for an anti-Taft candidate. The logical choice was Robert La Follette, who wanted the nomination and saw himself as the one true reformer within the Grand Old Party. His opposition to Canadian reciprocity because it threatened the interests of Wisconsin farmers undercut his claims, and those of his insurgent colleagues, to low-tariff virtue. "Reciprocity pinches their feet and they squeal in exactly the same tones as the stand-patters," wrote the cynical *New York Times* reporter Oscar King Davis.[7]

At bottom, La Follette seemed too radical to most Republicans. He had assailed railroads, criticized the voting records of his conservative senatorial colleagues, and made little secret of his disdain for eastern business and its methods. To nominate La Follette, regular party members would have to abandon the core beliefs that made them Republicans in the first place.[8]

These difficulties plagued La Follette's campaign during the fall of 1911. Supporters wanted him to become a more active presence among Republicans through speeches and tours, steps he declined to take. Encouraging reports came in to La Follette headquarters about Taft's unpopularity. These correspondents promised that if Roosevelt chose not to run there was latent sentiment for the Wisconsin senator. Money remained tight, and La Follette's campaign manager, Walter L. Houser, sent pleading letters to well-heeled progressive donors asking for more cash. They replied that as soon as La Follette showed strength money would be forthcoming. In the meantime, the campaign sputtered.[9]

A mid-October meeting of progressives in Chicago was designed to relaunch La Follette's candidacy. The gathering on 16 October endorsed him over the objections of James R. Garfield, a Roosevelt ally. But the La Follette movement did not attain much energy during the fall of 1911. The senator's reluctance to leave Washington and abandon the writing of his autobiography frustrated his supporters. "For God's sake, Houser, do not delay in getting him out if you have to blow up the American Magazine to accomplish it," wrote the La Follette leader in Ohio. Despite these pleas, La Follette did not make important public speeches until the end of December. By that time, Roosevelt's boom had started.[10]

What would have happened had La Follette been the only anti-Taft Republican in the race? Given the president's troubles, the challenger would have garnered some delegates. Yet it would have been an uphill struggle. Taft, on the one hand, would have received most if not all the southern votes plus New York and the rest of the Northeast. Such a result would have left the president with more than half the 540 votes needed for the nomination. La Follette, on the other hand, would have had Wisconsin, the Dakotas, a sprinkling of western delegates, and not much else. So, if Roosevelt had not come into the contest, a first-ballot Taft selection was all but a certainty.

But of course Roosevelt did enter the race to deny Taft a renomination. In mid-1911, the former president seemed to have found an uneasy but viable political balance. He would not endorse Taft, but he also told friends that he did not expect to be a candidate in 1912. Then in June 1911 came the mix-up about an endorsement of Taft. Feeling betrayed at the hands of the White House, Roosevelt changed his tune. He wrote friends and family in August 1911 that the president was "a flubdub with a streak of the second-rate and the common in him, and he has not the slightest idea of what is necessary if this country is to make social and industrial progress." Having expressed such thoughts aloud, it would be hard for Roosevelt to find a way to endorse Taft as a potential Republican nominee.[11]

The political situation among Republicans remained complex during September and October. Taft made his national tour to court potential delegates, but his junket did not convince party stalwarts that he could be reelected. La Follette stayed in Washington waiting for political lightning to make his long-shot bid viable. Roosevelt hovered on the sidelines, neither in nor out of the 1912 contest.

While the three principal potential candidates weighed their options, the Supreme Court ruled during the spring that both the American Tobacco Company and Standard Oil had violated the Sherman Antitrust Act. The Justice Department under Attorney General George Wickersham decided that United States Steel would be the next target of such a prosecution. As the summer ended, the attorney in charge of the case began to prepare an indictment of the giant steel company. That took the government lawyer into a political controversy that still raged for members of both major parties.[12]

A key aspect of a potential case against U.S. Steel was the episode in 1907 when President Theodore Roosevelt approved the company's acquisition of the Tennessee Coal and Iron Company. At the time and later there were allegations that the executives of U.S. Steel, in the midst of the Panic of 1907, had deceived Roosevelt about the true value of the transaction. That was in fact the case as the steel magnates got the better of both the deal and the president. Ever reluctant to admit that he had been wrong, Roosevelt reacted with anger whenever the charge surfaced. He had done so in his testimony to a committee of the House of Representatives in early August. So if the government took the position that Roosevelt had been duped, the reaction from the former president would be predictably loud and impassioned.

Acting as lawyers to make the best case possible, Jacob M. Dickinson, Taft's former secretary of war serving as a special assistant to the department, and Wickersham put together a set of charges against U.S. Steel that included a discussion of the Tennessee Coal and Iron matter. Roosevelt, they wrote, "was not made fully acquainted with the state of affairs" about the merger and thus had been misled into an unwise action that served the financial interests of the steel company and not the well-being of the nation.[13]

Dickinson and Wickersham went ahead and filed the indictment on 26 October 1911. Taft had not seen the document before it was submitted in court and only learned about it after the fact. The president did not review such pleadings before they were made. Wickersham, in briefing Taft about the case, left out the Roosevelt link. Not one of the three men involved stepped outside their training as attorneys to ask what the political ramifications of naming Roosevelt might be. They did not have to wait long to find out.

As soon as he read about the suit in the newspapers, Roosevelt exploded. He told James R. Garfield that Taft "and Wickersham are playing small, mean and foolish politics in this matter." More important, he wrote an article that outlined his objections to Taft's antitrust policy. The government should attack "not the mere fact of combination but the evils and wrongdoing which so frequently accompany combination." Roosevelt's position appealed to the business interests that had once denounced him as a dangerous radical. The president of the pro-business National Civic Federation wrote to a friend about "that bully article of Colonel Roosevelt's." A railroad president said: "It would not surprise me a bit to see the Republican Convention stampeded for him, but of course a lot of things can happen in this country in seven months."[14]

During the remainder of 1911, sentiment for Roosevelt mounted in the wake of his article. As that emotion gained support in the political world, the issue of a third term assumed greater relevance, especially among those opposed to Roosevelt's candidacy for other reasons. His standard answer became that since he was out of office and lacked power, there was no danger of dictatorship. As he wrote in early 1912 in an effort to address the issues, "Frequently when asked to take another cup of coffee at breakfast, I say "No thank you, I won't take another cup." This does not mean that I intend never to take another cup of coffee during my life; it means that I am not accepting the offer as applying to that breakfast, and that my remark is limited to that breakfast."[15]

That consoling formulation did not quiet his critics. At the same time, he kept the door open for a run against Taft. "If the matter of my candidacy should appear in the guise of a public duty, then however I might feel about it personally, I could not feel that I ought to shirk it." His friends read such statements as a tacit command to shape public opinion to conform to "a public duty," which they did throughout December 1911.[16]

Taft for his part secured his hold on the inner workings of the Grand Old Party. The Republican National Committee had its regular annual meeting in Washington on 11 December and decided that the national convention would meet in Chicago in mid-June. There would be 1,078 delegates with 540 needed to select a presidential candidate. Senator William E. Borah of Idaho proposed that states be allowed to select their delegates through a primary system that would be done in a state at large. The Taft forces wanted to retain the older procedure of basing representation and delegate selection on congressional district. Since the better-organized conservatives could maximize their strength on a district-by-district basis, the usual approach also favored the president's chances. The committee rejected the Borah proposal by a count of seven in favor and forty-four against. Despite the procedural victories for Taft, the talk at the meeting was all about Roosevelt. "If Roosevelt keeps still he will be nominated," said one Taft supporter. "The thing for him to do is to keep still, and I am going over to New York to tell him so."[17]

During the closing weeks of 1911, each of the three potential Republican candidates moved toward a confrontation. Senator La Follette toured Ohio in the last ten days of December but then failed to win an outright endorsement from Ohio progressives in Columbus on New Year's Day. The Wisconsin lawmaker's suspicions of Roosevelt's friends and their motives increased. For his part, President Taft and his campaign for renomination were forging ahead with their efforts to secure delegates. He told his military aide on December 27 that "I am going to be renominated and reelected." Only Roosevelt stood in his way, but Taft wagered that his predecessor would not make the race. There was, however, little disposition on the part of the president and his men at this stage to reach out to Roosevelt and defuse his candidacy.[18]

The key to the Republican political situation lay with Theodore Roosevelt and his White House ambitions. By early January, his long-time position shifted. Where he had once downplayed the idea that there might be a genuine groundswell for his nomination, he had by 9 January 1912 decided that if a nomination "comes to me as a genuine popular movement of course I will accept, and that is all there is to it."[19]

Roosevelt is often portrayed as a master politician, but his thinking on this score lacked clarity. Since he could not endorse Taft, any expression of interest in the nomination was bound to trigger a fight with the president. Yet if he could not swallow Taft before a contest for the nomination, how would he reconcile himself to a victory for the president at the convention? Thus, the prospect of a bolt and a third party were implicit once Roosevelt decided to yield to the clamor he had encouraged.

Why did Roosevelt decide to run in 1912? Having been out of the presidency and bored with private life, he could feel fulfilled only in the White House once again. To be sure, he had laudable social justice goals to pursue, but only if he could be the person to carry them into action. He felt betrayed at Taft's performance in office. Yet their policy positions were not so far apart that cooperation was impossible. La Follette he dismissed as an impractical dreamer and minor irritant. In the end, Roosevelt believed that what he wanted and needed for himself was what the country also needed and wanted. That some of his enemies found in such thinking the basis for a rationale for one-man rule was not that surprising.

During the transition from a noncandidacy to an open race, Roosevelt made several decisions that shaped the ensuing struggle against Taft. Once he became an active campaigner, he would face the president's early start in collecting delegates, especially among southern Republicans. To avoid newspaper stories showing a big lead for Taft in pledged delegates, Roosevelt agreed to have a Republican operative, Ormsby McHarg, go south and stir up sentiment for the ex-president. That strategy involved fomenting flimsy challenges to Taft that placed several southern states in the "contested" column. In the short run, this move helped Roosevelt seem competitive with his rival. By June 1912, it meant that the Taft-dominated Republican National Committee would have a large role in resolving these disputes. Roosevelt believed, however, that these contests were not bogus but, rather, reflected the real sentiment for him in the South. He came to think that the nomination should be his, no matter how spurious some of these contests were in reality.[20]

Having agreed to heed a call from the people, Roosevelt needed to find a way to orchestrate that sentiment into a tangible public expression. He and his advisers decided that seven progressive Republican governors would write him a letter. He would then respond with a statement of his readiness to run. In mid-January, the candidate began writing to the state executives about how such a document might be framed. Naturally enough, word leaked out about Roosevelt's intentions, especially since some of the letters in which he discussed his future moves were given to the press. More and more, Roosevelt was being drawn into active combat with Taft. He professed that he did not want such a bitter confrontation, but that was the most likely result of his course. Elihu Root warned him that "no thirsty sinner ever took a pledge which was harder for him to keep than it will be for you to maintain this position."[21]

As he neared an entry into the race. Roosevelt devoted less attention to La Follette, perhaps on the theory that the senator would either cooperate in an anti-Taft effort or simply drop out in favor of the former president. In any case, Roosevelt and his allies sought to reach an accommodation with La Follette, but with the proviso that the way would be cleared for Roosevelt. This tacit admission of being overshadowed La Follette could not swallow.

At that moment, fate seemed to resolve the matter. On 2 February 1912, the Wisconsin lawmaker was one of the featured speakers at a banquet of the Newspaper Publishers Association in Philadelphia. Distracted by the illness of his daughter and fretting about the problems of the campaign, La Follette found that his most reliable weapon, his gift for oratory, deserted him. His speech, which ran two hours by some accounts, proved a rambling, disconnected attack on his audience and the sinister influence of the press. Some listeners walked out as La Follette repeated himself and harangued his audience. In the wake of this personal and political disaster, support for La Follette outside of his immediate circle collapsed. Friends of Roosevelt, such as Gifford and Amos Pinchot, now had a ready excuse to switch their allegiance. One reporter said, "La Follette has gone to pieces physically and is now finished as a presidential candidate."[22]

That verdict was premature. La Follette rested for a time but did not leave the contest. He told a friend: "I have a hundred good fights left in me." His candidacy would prove a continuing distraction for Roosevelt and his campaign. They had to deal with attacks from La Follette about which anti-Taft candidate had the true progressive credentials. The senator stressed Roosevelt's alleged sympathy for big business as well as the former president's failure to attack the Canadian reciprocity agreement from the moment it was announced. Roosevelt did not try for rapprochement with La Follette. The venom that the two sides exchanged soon made any deal at the convention most improbable. Such a gesture on Roosevelt's part would not likely have worked, but it would perhaps have laid the basis for future cooperation when the convention voting took place.[23]

La Follette certainly had a right to stay in the presidential race as long as he wanted, but he also failed to think about the larger needs of the Republican progressivism he claimed to embody. If the hold of the conservatives on the party was to be broken, it was clear by the winter of 1912 that only Roosevelt could do it. La Follette had muffed his chance, and his campaign had gone nowhere. Now he had to recognize that his dream of becoming president would not happen in 1912. But his egotism and self-righteousness dominated his personality at this key moment. Anger at Roosevelt overrode his political judgment and led "Battle Bob" to engage the wrong enemy, a fellow progressive, at the wrong time for the wrong reasons.

For President Taft, the early months of 1912 were a painful period as he watched the remnants of his friendship with Roosevelt dissolve. He told Mabel Boardman, "I can never forget what Roosevelt has done for me, but his conduct has seared my soul." The president who was, according to Roosevelt, "one of the best haters he had ever known," had seen his regard for his one-time comrade wane during his years in the White House. His wife, conservative political allies, and those currying favor with him, had fed Taft evidence of Roosevelt's ostensible misdeeds. The president believed that he deserved another term and could not understand why Roosevelt had not endorsed him. Anything short of such a definitive gesture could not satisfy Taft's sense of partisan propriety.[24]

Yet Taft also stirred the political pot during these weeks. He displayed his dislike for the policy proposals that Roosevelt was considering. On 20 January, he spoke to the New York State Bar Association. That same week, Roosevelt had published an article in the reform periodical the *Outlook* on the wisdom of judicial recall. "Judicial recall! Judicial recall!" said Taft, "The words themselves are so inconsistent that I hate to utter them." Three weeks later he took what many commentators believed was a direct slap at Roosevelt. The president spoke of "extremists" who "would hurry us into a condition which could find no parallel except in the French revolution or in that bubbling anarchy that once characterized the South American Republics. Such extremists are not progressives—they are political emotionalists or neurotics" who had lost a sense of proportion about the American political system. Since there had often been charges among conservatives that Roosevelt lacked all his mental faculties, Taft's comment hit his potential opponent hard. "I have no doubt he honestly thinks that he is loyal to Lincoln Republicanism," Roosevelt told a friend, "but in reality he is the spiritual heir of the cotton whigs of Lincoln's time." The more red meat Taft provided to his supporters, the more the breach with Roosevelt widened.[25]

The White House sent emissaries to Roosevelt to glean his intentions. Henry L. Stimson, the secretary of war and a Roosevelt friend, went to Oyster Bay to sound out "the Colonel" on his plans. To Stimson and others, Roosevelt repeated his statement that he did not wish to be a candidate but would, if the people called, signal a willingness to accept. Roosevelt yearned for a confrontation. He told intimates that Taft would likely be nominated, but part of his personality expected that the Republicans would abandon Taft for him. Like other politicians who challenged incumbents during the twentieth century, Roosevelt was never so strong as in the days leading up to the formal announcement.[26]

To introduce himself as a formal candidate, Roosevelt intended to issue a response to the seven governors in a public letter. He also sought an appropriate forum to lay out his policy views. Meanwhile, a National Roosevelt Committee, organized by some of the more eager supporters, began operating in Chicago. A suitable place for Roosevelt to speak out appeared. The state of Ohio was in the process of writing a new constitution. Roosevelt decided to address the delegates on 21 February and thus launch his candidacy with a statement of his progressive policy views. With the assistance of Amos and Gifford Pinchot, both of whom wanted him to be as progressive as possible, Roosevelt drafted a speech that would take "a sufficiently well-defined radical position."[27]

This major address, intended to persuade Republicans why he should be their nominee, proved a political disaster that changed the direction of the ensuing campaign. Part of the problem was that Roosevelt was out of touch with changes in how campaigns were being run. It had been fourteen years, in his race for governor in New York in 1898, since he had appealed to voters directly on his own behalf as an announced candidate on the stump. As the incumbent president in 1904, he had not campaigned, in keeping with the custom that sitting chief executives did not do so. In 1908 he had written letters for Taft and again in 1910 he spoke for his gubernatorial choice in the New York race. Of the intense, immediate scrutiny that would meet his utterances as presidential aspirant, he seemed either unaware or heedless.

Roosevelt arrived in Columbus on 21 February amid snow and rain "welcomed by crowds wherever he went." To a reporter, he tipped his hand about his intentions when he proclaimed "my hat is in the ring and I am stripped to the buff." Cartoons appeared showing his hat in a boxing ring or the political arena. In his remarks to the members of the Ohio convention, he provided a reprise of his program for regulation of big business. On purpose he said nothing about the tariff issue, a subject on which he had usually equivocated. To a large extent, the policy positions he outlined were those of the New Nationalism he had

A notable feature of the 1912 election was the intense campaigning that Roosevelt did throughout the year. For the most part, he attracted sizable audiences. (Theodore Roosevelt Collection, Houghton Library, Harvard University, Cambridge, Massachusetts)

advanced in 1910. What made the speech explosive was his extended treatment of the recall, both for judges and their decisions.[28]

As for the plan to subject judges to elections when their decisions displeased the community, he called it "one of expediency merely. Each community has a right to try the experiment for itself in whatever shape it pleases." If that phrasing was meant to placate potential critics, it did not do so. On the matter of applying the recall to specific decisions, that approach required "immediate adoption." In Roosevelt's mind, "when a judge decides a constitutional question, when he decides what the people as a whole can or cannot do, the people should have the right to recall the decision if they think it wrong."[29]

Roosevelt had been moving toward this idea since the latter years of his presidency. His commitment to the idea of reining in the conservative judiciary had grown in 1910–1911 as he chafed at state and federal rulings that such blocked progressive goals as workmen's compensation. By early 1912, in an article in the *Outlook* magazine he proclaimed his belief in recalling decisions in constitutional cases. So, in that sense, his stance in Ohio tracked what he had said for years about how judges had acted "almost to bar the path to industrial, economic, and social reform."[30]

While Roosevelt had consistency on his side, he had misjudged the impact of his position on judicial recall among moderate and conservative Republicans. The attacks on his speech came in from all across the party. One progressive senator told reporters, "After reading stuff like that a man must go off by himself for a long time to regain control of his nerves." The American Bar Association established a committee "to take such steps as it may deem best to expose the fallacy of judicial recall." Harry Daugherty, a conservative Republican in Ohio, commented that Roosevelt's attacks "upon the Supreme Court of the United States, and upon the Supreme Court of his own state, will do more harm than any speech ever made along that line." An ally of Roosevelt, Governor Herbert S. Hadley of Missouri, told him that sentiment in his state was that "the recall of judges would break down the independence of the judiciary and substitute a judgment of unpopularity for a judgment of unfitness or of wrongdoing, upon which alone a public officer should be removed." The governor urged Roosevelt to make his position "more clear" on the recall of decisions.[31]

The political effect of the Columbus speech was to interrupt the momentum that Roosevelt had built up since the start of 1912 and administer a jolt of energy to the Taft campaign. What Roosevelt had done at Columbus, said Henry Cabot Lodge, had "turned Taft from a man into a principle." Conservatives who flirted with Roosevelt or professed neutrality now flocked to the president. Roosevelt had allowed his opponents to define him, and so his formal statement of candidacy on 26 February came as a sort of anticlimax after the Columbus bombshell.[32]

In that announcement, Roosevelt released his letter to the seven governors. He would accept the Republican nomination "if it is tendered to me." Almost at once, the Roosevelt campaign, directed by Senator Joseph M. Dixon of Montana, called for presidential preference primaries to allow average Republicans to stand against "both political and financial privilege." Several states such as Massachusetts, Illinois, and Maryland quickly enacted such laws. If Roosevelt could stay in contention until these states voted in April and May, he might have a chance to win. He also faced races against Taft in Massachusetts and Ohio, where he and the president would be more evenly matched.[33]

The month of March did not go well for Roosevelt. The issue of a third term plagued him, and he had to deny dictatorial ambitions over and over. Backbiting over La Follette persisted as a drain on the energies of the Roosevelt camp. The Wisconsin senator defeated both Taft and Roosevelt when North Dakota held its primary on 19 March. Emboldened with this show of electoral support, La Follette would be in the race to the end. Roosevelt suffered another expected but still stinging reverse when his home state of New York chose in local conventions an uncommitted delegation loaded with Taft supporters at the end of March. Roosevelt had a mere fourteen delegates out of the ninety selected.[34]

Taft's campaign, with Representative William B. McKinley (no relation to the president) of Illinois as its official head, gathered in delegates from the South and the Middle West throughout March. Some of the battles in these state conventions were quite heated, complete with fistfights and charges of bad faith on both sides. Taft was still intent on minimizing his differences with Roosevelt during this stage of the race. He instructed his managers to avoid personal attacks and an exchange of recriminations with Roosevelt. "I want to be consulted about every paragraph that goes out of a critical or hostile nature, and especially of a personal nature with respect to Colonel Roosevelt or the canvass." The Taft headquarters, the president added, should avoid attacks on Roosevelt about his financial reliance on wealthy publishers for campaign funds.

Nor should the president's men make much of Roosevelt's friendly antitrust policies as president toward a large corporation such as International Harvester. This detached pose would collapse as the exchange of political invective intensified during April 1912.[35]

Since the hunt for delegates had gone Taft's way in March, there was increasing confidence in the president's camp as April began. The British ambassador wrote on 1 April that at the Republican Convention there would be "a considerable majority of delegates pledged to Mr. Taft." Hilles said on 6 April that "by the end of this month he will have secured such a number of delegates as to convince everyone of the outcome in June. Think our score on April 30th will be in excess of 500."[36]

During the latter part of March there began to be talk about a possible Roosevelt bolt from the Republicans to a third party of his own if he lost the nomination. Such an initiative represented a novel tactic in national politics. Roosevelt insisted that such rumors were false. "Any statement like that is a fake. Any time I have something to say on such a subject I will say it myself, and anything purporting to come from me, unless I say it myself is a fake." In the statement, Roosevelt did not disavow a bolt, and behind the scenes the possibility persisted in quiet talks among Roosevelt's supporters.[37]

Throughout March and into April the bitterness in the campaign intensified as both sides fought harder and harder to prevail. In a speech to the New York Republican convention on 9 April the president of Columbia University (and once a close friend of Roosevelt), Nicholas Murray Butler, said: "This contest within the party and this presidential election may decide whether our government is to be republican or Cossack." The third-term issue continued to trouble many conservatives. For his part, Roosevelt said of Taft that "a well-meaning man may vaguely think of himself as a Progressive without having the faintest conception of what a Progressive is." He added accusations of election fraud and the misuse of patronage at the hands of the president in the days that followed. Taft concluded that Roosevelt was "beside himself with rage" as the political tide ran against him.[38]

Then on 9 April, Illinois Republicans gave the challenger a resounding victory. In a landslide result, Roosevelt rolled up 139,000 more votes than Taft with La Follette a poor third. "We knocked them over the ropes in Illinois," Roosevelt said, "and I want to see them take the count in Pennsylvania" on 13 April.[39] The Illinois success gave Roosevelt fifty-six of the fifty-eight delegates under the state's primary law. That outcome

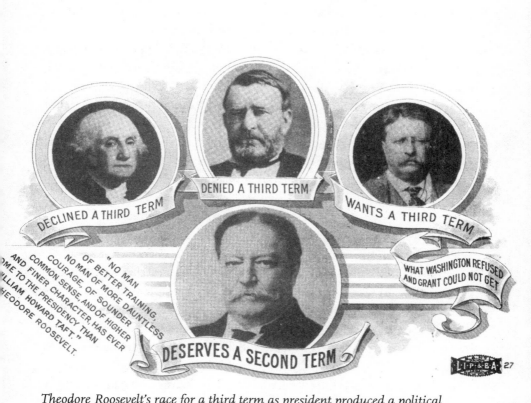

DECLINED A THIRD TERM

DENIED A THIRD TERM

WANTS A THIRD TERM

"NO MAN
OF BETTER TRAINING,
NO MAN OF MORE DAUNTLESS
COURAGE, OF SOUNDER
COMMON SENSE, AND OF HIGHER
AND FINER CHARACTER, HAS EVER
OME TO THE PRESIDENCY THAN
ILLIAM HOWARD TAFT."
HEODORE ROOSEVELT.

WHAT WASHINGTON REFUSED
AND GRANT COULD NOT GET

DESERVES A SECOND TERM

L·I·P·&·B·A 27

Theodore Roosevelt's race for a third term as president produced a political reaction that this critical postcard represented. (Lewis L. Gould Personal Collection) raised his total to 113, compared with Taft's 337, as Pennsylvania Republicans prepared to go to the polls. Roosevelt would have to win almost all of the contested delegates still to be decided to gain the nomination. If he could create a sense of momentum, however, he might be able to dislodge wavering Taft delegates from their allegiance.

The Pennsylvania primary also went Roosevelt's way. He was popular and enjoyed the backing of major GOP figures in the state, including William Flinn, the boss of Pittsburgh. As a result, Roosevelt in a sweeping victory added 65 delegates to his total, compared with 12 for Taft. McKinley told reporters: "President Taft is in the fight to stay." The twin results in Illinois and Pennsylvania rattled conservatives. The anti-Roosevelt newspaper, the *New York Sun,* said that the outcomes in Illinois and Pennsylvania "mean that the gravest danger which has confronted the nation since the civil war for disruption is not yet finally averted." On the Roosevelt side, the victories produced jubilation. If the primary outcome in Massachusetts, wrote Senator Dixon, "will repeat Pennsylvania, the fight will be ended."[40]

As the Taft-Roosevelt campaign hurtled toward a climactic encounter, public attention shifted to a disaster on the high seas. Late on the evening of 14 April, the R.M.S. *Titanic* hit an iceberg in the North Atlantic. Within three hours the "unsinkable" ocean liner disappeared. Of its 2,200 passengers and crew, 1,500 died. The 705 survivors reached New York on the *Carpathia* three days later. In the wake of the disaster newspaper readers across the country followed the listing of the dead, the stories of those who were plucked from the sea, and the probes into what had happened. Politics seemed less urgent before such an incredible tragedy as citizens struggled to understand how a technological marvel such as the *Titanic* had been lost.[41]

For Taft and Roosevelt, the loss was a personal one. Among the dead was the president's military aide, Archibald Willingham "Archie" Butt, who had served Roosevelt in the same capacity. Early reports had Butt dying a hero's death. Roosevelt called him "the highest type of officer and gentleman." Taft told the press, "I feel his loss as if he had been a younger brother." Throughout the rest of the spring the *Titanic* story gripped the headlines in what became one of the enduring narratives of the twentieth century.[42]

In the continuing race for the GOP nomination, Taft and Hilles recognized that their campaign faced a crisis in the Massachusetts primary. "It is necessary to go to Massachusetts," Hilles said of the vote in that state on 30 April. "If we lose in the primaries there, there will be a danger of a stampede." Southern delegates with easy consciences, wooed by money from Roosevelt backers, might defect and doom Taft's candidacy. Faced with these imperatives, Taft decided to abandon his above-the-battle position and make a personal reply to Roosevelt's assaults. His aides and cabinet had been telling him "that severe language is the only thing that can answer severe language." The president concluded: "I am afraid it will be necessary to reply to Roosevelt's attacks, but I am very sorry it is so. We will win." Taft would soon overcome these qualms.[43]

The offensive against Roosevelt began in Boston on 25 April. "I do not want to fight Theodore Roosevelt, but then sometimes a man in a corner fights. I am going to fight." Roosevelt should be defeated, the president argued, because "in such a nomination the Republican party will violate our most useful and necessary governmental tradition—that no one shall be permitted to hold a third presidential term." He accused his opponent of a flip-flop on Canadian reciprocity based on a letter that Roosevelt had written him early in 1911 supporting the agreement he now opposed. "I submit that Mr. Roosevelt's course on reciprocity is not in accord with the square deal." The president then denounced "the adroit appeals to discontent and class hatred Mr. Roosevelt is now making to the public." After a day of such speeches, all of them attacks on his challenger, Taft cried in private as he told a reporter, "Roosevelt was my closest friend."[44]

Roosevelt responded with bitter personal assaults of his own. Taft, he told reporters, "has been disloyal to every canon of ordinary decency and fair dealing such as should obtain even in dealing with a man's bitterest opponents." Taft had not behaved as a gentleman should when he released the private reciprocity letter. Moreover, Taft had shown a lack of gratitude for Roosevelt's support of him in 1908. "It is bad trait to bite the hand that feeds you," he proclaimed. Summing up, Roosevelt said, "I do not think Mr. Taft means ill. I think he means well. But he means well feebly, and during his Administration he has been under the influence of men who are neither well meaning nor feeble."[45]

The remainder of the Massachusetts campaign produced charge and countercharge from the two men. They jousted about whether the Roosevelt administration had delayed an antitrust suit against International Harvester in 1907 and what role each had played in the decision not to initiate legal action. These recriminations about their onetime collaboration underscored how far apart the former friends had grown. "I was a man of straw," Taft asserted in Lowell, Massachusetts, "but I have been a man of straw long enough: every man who has blood in his body and who has been misrepresented as I have been is forced to fight."[46]

The resulting public rancor probably aided Roosevelt since controversy provided the indispensable publicity that sustained his campaign. Roosevelt's friends were delighted with the spectacle of an open conflict with the president. "Taft certainly made a great mistake when he began to 'fight back.' He has too big a paunch to have much of a punch, while a free-for-all, slap-bang, kick-him-in-the-belly is just nuts for the chief." The bitterness of the two candidates, however, made it less likely that the party would unite behind the eventual winner.[47]

There was more to the Republican split in 1912 than just wounded egos and a broken friendship. While both Taft and Roosevelt claimed to be progressives, they differed in their view of what government should do and how presidents should act. Roosevelt believed that Republicans needed to stand for a greater degree of social justice through federal action. "In the long run this country will not be a good place for any of us to live in unless it is a reasonably good place for all of us to live in," he said in Philadelphia on April 10. Therefore the country needed "social and industrial justice" with an activist president in the lead pushing that agenda. The Constitution and the judiciary should serve such ends rather than frustrating them.[48]

Taft saw this approach as dangerous to the political health of the nation. Roosevelt, he charged, "is in favor of innovations and changes that would make the Constitution worth little more than the paper it is written on." The role of the president, in Taft's mind, was to stay within the framework of the law and not push the boundaries of his office just to serve immediate social needs. Judicial recall, aggressive regulation of business, and one-man rule of the kind that Roosevelt might establish caused Taft to regard himself as a defender of liberty in a time of political crisis for the nation.[49]

The Massachusetts primary on 30 April produced a narrow but clear victory for the president that stopped the erosion of his political strength and stemmed the Roosevelt tide at the end of April. Taft's plurality was only about 4,000 votes, but that was enough to ensure a split in the delegate votes with eighteen for each contender. "If we win in Maryland Monday it seems to us as if every ghost of a show Roosevelt ever had was gone," observed McKinley about the situation. Taft pulled out the rhetorical stops in Maryland. A newspaper story carried the quotation from a speech in that state: "I am a man of peace and I don't want to fight. But when I do fight I want to hit hard. Even a rat in a corner will fight." In private, Taft wrote friends that "it is agony of spirit to have to go out and drag the Presidential office down into the mire, but I believe I represent a great cause and that I am the only one who can fight it, and I must fight it and do the best I can." As for Roosevelt, he wrote an English friend that "Taft is not merely a fool, but he is a good bit of a blackguard."[50]

Roosevelt won the Maryland primary by fewer than 4,000 votes on 6 May. He also gained a victory in California where Governor Hiram Johnson's organization defeated both Taft and La Follette for Roosevelt. The climactic event in May would be Ohio's vote on the 20st. Roosevelt needed a sweeping triumph. For Taft, a loss in his home state would be a personal embarrassment as well as further evidence of his vulnerability a month before the national convention. Both sides poured speakers and resources into the contest.

Taft had by now dropped all pretense of political restraint. "I like a man to tell the truth straight out, and I hate to see a man try to honeyfugle the people by telling them something he doesn't believe," the president said. He defended his course on reciprocity, a hot issue in Ohio, and again accused Roosevelt of changing his position on the tariff agreement because it was "not popular with the farmers." At one point, the trains of both candidates stood near each other at Steubenville, but that was as close as the bitter rivals came to contact. Roosevelt announced, "I stand for the protective tariff. But I want to see part of it go into the pay envelope," a bow to the state's traditional support of higher duties. As for his opponent, Roosevelt pounded away on the theme that reciprocity had wounded the farmer. Since voters would choose delegates from congressional districts, the Roosevelt headquarters predicted "a practically complete sweep of the districts" on Election Day.[51]

Roosevelt gained a decisive victory in Ohio. He garnered thirty-four of the forty-two district delegates at stake on 20 May and statewide had a plurality of 25,000 votes. The Taft forces ultimately controlled six delegates selected at the state convention and had fourteen votes from the state. During the remainder of May, Roosevelt added victories in New Jersey and South Dakota. The primary season had now ended.

When Republican voters had a chance in 1912 to express their opinions at the polls, Roosevelt was the evident winner. He had amassed 1,164,765 votes to 768,202 for Taft and 327,357 for La Follette. Taft supporters countered that in some of the primaries open to non-Republicans the ballots from independents and Democrats had inflated Roosevelt's totals. On both sides, there was an unwillingness to grant any legitimacy to the other campaign. Reconciliation would not be easy. If the Democrats made "a good choice at their nomination convention in the end of June," wrote the British ambassador on 30 April, "they ought to win for the Republican party is being completely disrupted."[52]

The actual decision rested with the delegates to the national convention. As that event neared, delegate counts in the press gave Roosevelt 411 committed votes, Taft 201, La Follette 36 from Wisconsin and North Dakota, and Albert B. Cummins of Iowa 10 from his own state. There were 166 uninstructed delegates, but the great majority of them, from New York in particular, were in the Taft camp. Finally, there were 254 contested delegates whose fate the Republican National Committee would decide in Chicago the week before the convention opened. In June, despite Roosevelt's challenge, Taft's long-standing control of the machinery of the Republican Party proved the key to his ultimate renomination.

To assert dominance of the convention itself, the president selected Elihu Root as his choice for temporary chair of the proceedings. As an old, close friend of Roosevelt, Root was unassailable on personal grounds. On the issues, however, the conservative Root stood with the president. He could oversee the adoption of the delegate rolls in a manner favorable to Taft. The New York senator had begged off from actual campaigning for the president, but this request was not one he believed he could decline. Root's prestige as a former secretary of state under Roosevelt put the onus of opposition on to the challenger. From this point on, Roosevelt played from behind since Taft set the agenda for the convention and controlled its procedures. A search began within the Roosevelt high command for a plausible counter to Root's candidacy.[53]

On the membership of the Republican National Committee, there was little Roosevelt could do at such a late date to affect the political lineup of that body. Many of the Taft supporters on the committee had been named by the state parties with Roosevelt's tacit approval in 1908. Vice President James S. Sherman wrote on 24 May that "at the worst from the Taft standpoint there are 24 committeemen for the Taft end of it; 17 for Roosevelt and two for La Follette." That alignment underestimated Taft's strength. He had around thirty-five votes of the panel's fifty-three members. As the president recognized, "All that is necessary is for the National Committee to keep a firm hold on things in Chicago. I intend to 'follow through' and I expect to win out."[54]

Roosevelt could count, too. He knew that his chances before the Republican National Committee were not good. The committee began its work on 8 June and went through the states in alphabetical order. In the process, the weaknesses of many of the bogus contests that Ormsby McHarg and others had launched in states such as Alabama, Florida, and Georgia were exposed. The dubious nature of these Roosevelt contests undercut his chances in states where he had a more plausible case. The Taft forces maintained a running tally of how many votes the president had as each state's contest was considered and how many he needed for nomination. The process by which the national committee operated was a partisan one, designed to produce a Taft nomination. If their positions had been reversed, the Roosevelt forces would have behaved in the same manner. In 1912, however, believing they were entitled to win the contests, the Roosevelt camp began to cry fraud as the work of the national committee went on.[55]

In the end, the panel awarded 235 of the disputed delegates to Taft and 19 to Roosevelt. "The Nat Committee continues its course of theft of seats," James R. Garfield noted in his diary on 13 June. Four states struck the Roosevelt people as egregious examples of Taft thievery—Arizona, California, Texas, and Washington. In the case of Texas, the only state where a detailed analysis of the merits has occurred, Taft received thirty-one delegates and Roosevelt nine from the national committee. A modern tally concluded that Taft deserved nineteen and Roosevelt twenty-one. So instead of the 466 votes that he controlled, Roosevelt probably deserved at least another twelve to fourteen from Texas. That would have raised his total to 478 or 480, still well short of the needed majority.[56]

Analysis of the other contests, done in 1912, indicated that Roosevelt probably should have received another twenty or so delegates. That would have brought his total to around 500. That outcome would have meant for Taft that his delegate count also would have stood at or near 500 as well. Since La Follette had thirty-six votes and Cummins ten, this alignment would have meant that on an honest count neither Taft nor Roosevelt would have had a clear majority of the delegates in the 1912 Republican National Convention.[57]

President Taft's secretary, Charles D. Hilles (left), and Representative William B. McKinley of Illinois directed the president's race for renomination. (Great Leaders and National Issues of 1912 [Philadelphia: J. C. Winston Co., 1912])

Roosevelt's decision to focus on the alleged injustice done to him and his campaign had mixed results. It dramatized the perfidy of the Taft campaign in the eyes of the challenger and his supporters. Stealing delegates was easy to understand. Yet in the long run of the presidential election contest, it was not the plus that it seemed in June 1912. Taft's allies could make a case that many of Roosevelt's challenges were bogus, and there were reasonable issues on both sides about which delegates were honestly chosen and which were not. Was the theft of delegates a sufficient rationale for a bolt and a third party? As time passed and the presidential campaign heated up, the issue of the delegates lost much of its saliency for Roosevelt.

Equity and fairness aide, the decisions that the national committee reached during the week before the convention meant that Taft was likely to be nominated, despite his probable defeat in the fall. Could Roosevelt pull out the nomination despite the odds? His first task was to wrest control of the convention from his enemies. Though there was talk of a compromise third candidate even before the delegates assembled, Roosevelt made clear that he was going to go down fighting rather than give way to a dark-horse alternative.[58]

Before the convention opened, Roosevelt decided that he would go to Chicago to direct his campaign in person. That move broke with the tradition that announced candidates did not attend the convention themselves. Only after they were nominated would they be "notified" officially and accept as their party's choice. Such a ritual made sense in the nineteenth century, but modern communications were rendering that tradition obsolete. As he had from the beginning of the contest, Roosevelt hoped that his personal charisma would sway wavering delegates away from Taft. It was a high-risk move, but Roosevelt knew that customary behavior would not disrupt the likely outcome in Taft's favor.[59]

Since he knew he might lose the nomination even with his greatest exertions in Chicago, Roosevelt was already thinking about a bolt to form a third party. "I have absolutely no affiliations with any party," he wrote on 11 June a few days before he departed for the Middle West. Roosevelt had been hearing that even if "you should be counted out" progressives "still want a leader for the cause of the people which they regard as quite paramount to the welfare of a party now so largely run by bosses and machines." A bolt thus became alluring because "anything more scoundrelly than the attitude of the Taft supporters during the past six weeks we have not seen in American politics." By June 1912, Roosevelt could not envision himself agreeing to support Taft and the Republicans if the president was renominated at Chicago.[60]

The drama of Roosevelt's presence added to the tumultuous atmosphere that surrounded one of the most important conventions in American history. One participant recalled that "the streets were packed with people shouting 'we want Teddy.'" Daisy Harriman, a Democratic stalwart, described "a flat, flat lake, sizzling asphalt pavements, bands circling and booming 'Everybody's saying it, Roosevelt, Roosevelt.'" The bands turned out to be an expensive gimmick for the Roosevelt camp. They thought they were hiring one for a limited stint. Instead they had wall-to-wall bands at an eventual cost of $10,000. A Roosevelt partisan wrote of the scene that "the Taft headquarters were respectable; the Roosevelt headquarters were human."[61]

The leader of the Roosevelt campaign arrived in Chicago two days before the convention opened. A huge crowd greeted his train and cheered Roosevelt as he went toward his suite at the Congress Hotel. On 17 June he addressed a throng at the Chicago Auditorium where he proclaimed that the nomination he had won because of the support of the people was being taken from him by Taft and his allies. "We are fighting for honesty against naked robbery; and where robbery is concerned the all-important question is not the identity of the man robbed, but the crime itself." Some "sixty to eighty lawfully elected delegates" chosen at primaries or state conventions rightfully belonged in his column. If they were not fairly counted, then the result did not bind any Republican to support the ticket. He ended with the peroration that became a watchword for the third-party battle to come: "Fearless of the future, unheeding of our individual fates; with unflinching hearts and undimmed eyes; we stand at Armageddon, and we battle for the Lord."[62]

Roosevelt had the best rhetoric in Chicago during that exciting week, but he was not the skilled leader of his forces that the situation demanded. By pitching the issue as a moral one and accusing his opponents of thievery, he strengthened the resolve of the Taft men. As Hilles wrote to his daughter, "We are confronted with the most gigantic struggle in the history of this republic," and he regarded "Roosevelt's movement as the most horrible attack on constitutional government with which we have yet been confronted." Roosevelt would have been wiser to have based more of his appeal on the plausible grounds that Taft could not win in the fall election.[63]

On two occasions, Taft's hold on the convention might have been rattled. The selection of the temporary chairman on 18 June offered the first and best opportunity to shake up the situation. The Roosevelt forces knew that they did not have enough votes to put their own candidate in place. So they looked for someone who might draw votes from the La Follette delegates and those pledged to Senator Cummins of Iowa.

The Wisconsin delegation planned to put forward Governor Francis E. McGovern as the choice of the La Follette camp for temporary chair. Seeing an opportunity to maximize the strength of the progressives and win over delegates who were not in favor of Roosevelt, the challenger's men proclaimed that McGovern would be their choice, too.[64]

Victor Rosewater, the chair of the Republican National Committee, called the national convention to order on 18 June 1912. A small man, Rosewater could barely be heard, "but trumpet-voiced clerks, with megaphones, made the necessary announcements." The proceedings were conducted in a well-organized and well-seated hall in an atmosphere of raucous bitterness and intense partisanship. In the evenly divided Coliseum, 15,000 people sought to outdo their opponents with demonstrations and stunts. Fistfights punctuated the day's activities. Years later participants recalled the key moments. When the Taft forces exercised their control, Roosevelt delegates called it a steamroller. Their whistles and toots rocked the hall. One Mississippi delegate even raised a point of order "that the steam roller is exceeding the speed limit." William Jennings Bryan, covering the event for a newspaper chain, observed that "a national convention is not the best place in the world to decide questions of abstract justice."[65]

Once Rosewater's gavel fell, the Roosevelt camp, through Governor Herbert S. Hadley of Missouri, proposed that the seventy-two delegates in contention be banned from voting on their own cases. If adopted, such a move would have left the president's enemies in control. Rosewater ruled that the first order of business was the selection of a temporary chair. Nominations for the post put Elihu Root and Francis E. McGovern into the contest. For a moment, it seemed that the progressives might unite to gain control of the convention at the start. Then, Walter L. Houser, La Follette's campaign manager, gained recognition and said of McGovern: "This nomination is not with Senator La Follette's consent. We make no deals with Roosevelt. We make no trades with Taft."[66]

The voting then proceeded. During the count, the California delegation was polled and the name of Mrs. Florence C. Porter was called.

"And for the first time in the history of the United States, a woman, in a firm, clear sweet voice cast her vote in a national convention." The crowd cheered and the count went on. When it was done, the Taft forces had prevailed, with 558 votes to 501 for the other side, with a scattering for other names.[67]

La Follette's decision to oppose McGovern has not received much historical attention, but it proved to be a key moment in the history of progressivism and the Republican Party. Had McGovern been selected, Taft's men would have lost their shaky control, and the disputed Roosevelt delegates could have been seated. That in turn probably would have led to Roosevelt's nomination. At the least, it would have opened the chance for a multiballot convention and a candidate other than Roosevelt or Taft. By doing what he did, La Follette all but assured Taft's nomination. Out of personal pique at Roosevelt, some of it no doubt justified by the events of February 1912, La Follette made sure that the Republicans would remain a conservative party. Despite his talk about reform, La Follette's career was often more about himself than the ideas he sought to advance.

After Root's selection, the Roosevelt campaign had one more move that might stop Taft's selection. Hadley offered on the first day his motion to block the seventy-two disputed delegates from casting their votes. Of course, the problem was that such a tactic would enable any minority in any convention to disqualify enough votes to achieve a majority. After extended debate on 19 June, the second day of the convention, the Hadley proposal was referred to the credentials committee in a victory for the Taft side. Elihu Root then ruled that the contested delegates could continue to take part in the proceedings. Roosevelt and his supporters confronted the hard fact that Taft's renomination was almost certain. The question became whether to accept their defeat within the Republican Party or to bolt in favor of a third-party candidacy for Roosevelt.[68]

In the meantime, frightened Republicans outside the Taft and Roosevelt inner circles looked for a compromise candidate who could win in the fall. Because he did well in presenting Roosevelt's case about the delegates, Hadley began to be talked about as a possible dark horse. Retiring as governor at the end of the year, Hadley struggled with tuberculosis and could not have made the race. In any event, Roosevelt insisted that the disputed delegates be dropped from the convention roll before any compromise took place. For Roosevelt it was a "question of fundamental morality." Yet at the same time he knew that if the contested delegates were dropped, he would be nominated. In the end, Roosevelt would accept the Republican nomination or bolt.[69]

The possibility of a bolt had been under consideration for some time as the primary campaign unfolded. As the rancor surrounding the battles in state conventions and primaries bubbled up, the Roosevelt forces became persuaded that they were being cheated of a nomination that was rightfully theirs. Their leader agreed, and what he saw happening in Chicago only confirmed his conviction that he had won fair and square. To a great extent, Roosevelt simply looked past the rough methods his own side had used to secure delegates and discounted what Taft partisans claimed about their victories. He had warned friends that "if the stealing is flagrant no one can tell what the result may be." Now, in his mind, Taft and his allies had embarked on a clear course of larceny. Roosevelt could not tolerate a Taft nomination on that basis as a legitimate expression of the will of the Republicans.[70]

Discussions about a third-party race went on during most of 20–21 June in Roosevelt's suite of rooms. The big questions turned on organizing a separate party, getting Roosevelt's name on the ballot in all the states, and, most important, paying the expenses of a national canvass. The wealthy newspaper publisher Frank A. Munsey and the former corporate executive George W. Perkins told Roosevelt "we will see you through." All that remained was to exit the Republican Party in as advantageous a manner as possible. That would prove easier to contemplate than to accomplish.[71]

The problems that plagued the third-party effort for the rest of the year soon appeared. Was Roosevelt a Republican candidate taking the party name and organization in those states where he was strongest? Should he run as a third-party independent with his own partisan structure? He began with a statement that was read to the GOP Convention on 22 June. In it he said that "fraudulent delegates" were behind Taft's impending nomination. Therefore "the convention as now composed has no claim to represent the voters of the Republican party." He asked his delegates not to vote in the convention. That evening, in a speech at Orchestra Hall in Chicago, Roosevelt received the presidential nomination of his delegates. He asked those supporters to determine whether the sentiment in their state would sustain a new third party to advance progressive Republican ideals. For the moment, Roosevelt was not quite a member of the Grand Old Party, but neither had he fully committed himself to the course of a third party. The scene was one of wild enthusiasm for the hero of the moment, Theodore Roosevelt. One reporter noted that moving from the Republican Convention to Orchestra Hall was "like stepping from a board meeting of railroad directors, from a post-mortem in a coroner's office on a corpse, into a Zuni snake-dance."[72]

At the Republican Convention, the delegates nominated Taft while the Roosevelt contingent sat on their hands. The gathering renominated Vice President James S. Sherman as well, the first time an incumbent vice president had been so honored since 1832. The selection showed how little Taft was thinking about his electoral prospects. A colorless addition to the ticket in 1908, Sherman could not help him in New York, and, with the heart disease from which he suffered, he could not even campaign. Taft would have done better to have picked a younger Republican senator or governor to run with him.[73]

The Republican platform did not offer much excitement to the voters, either. It sought "the intelligent judgment of the American people upon the administration of William H. Taft. The country has prospered and been at peace during his presidency." The party restated "our belief in a protective tariff" that had been "of the greatest benefit to the country." As for the future, Republicans had been "genuinely and always a party of progress; it has never been stationary or reactionary." The only mention of Roosevelt was a reference to his Republican presidency.[74]

The Taft men had less concern with the fall election than with the defeat of Roosevelt, which they regarded, in the words of Hilles, "as the performance of a patriotic duty." Yet realism indicated that the road to victory in the autumn would be a difficult one. "It looks to me," wrote former senator John Coit Spooner, a Wisconsin conservative, "as if the party is making *progress* on its journey to destruction."[75]

The rift in the Republican ranks had been growing for almost a decade as the party divided over the issues of government regulation and political reform. All the major contenders for the nomination in 1912 bore some responsibility for the split becoming irreparable. La Follette had unrealistic expectations for his candidacy from the outset. He permitted his anger at Roosevelt to overrule good judgment. His tactics at the convention defeated the best chance party reformers had to achieve mastery within the GOP. For his part, President Taft pursued a renomination knowing he would lose in the general election. He was so determined to beat Roosevelt that he cooperated with the most reactionary and unsavory elements within his party. Though he showed skill as an infighter among Republicans, his energy and stubbornness could have been expended in a better cause.

The main architect of the divided Republican Party, however, was Theodore Roosevelt. His reasons for opposing Taft were ideological in public, but the dominant impulse for his race was personal. Tired of private life, Roosevelt sought the excitement and power of the presidency once again. In so doing, he refused to admit the possibility he might lose the nomination and would then have to endorse Taft if he remained a Republican. He convinced himself, against the evidence, that he deserved the disputed delegates and was being cheated out of the prize. Knowing that he could not win the presidency with a third party, he still insisted on a bolt from the Republicans and a race of his own. In the process, he eroded the power of reform among Republicans and defeated the goals he professed to seek.

One key element in Roosevelt's calculations about a third-party hinged on the action of the Democratic National Convention meeting in Baltimore three days after the Republicans left Chicago. In the past, Democratic mistakes had often helped the Republicans out of political difficulty. If the Democracy would oblige Roosevelt and select a conservative, or an uninspiring reformer, prospects for the third party would brighten. The nation's attention, riveted on the GOP throughout the first three weeks of June, now shifted to Baltimore. Republican discord had offered the opposition a chance to win. It was up to the Democrats to select a candidate to return them to the national power that had eluded them for sixteen years.

4 WOODROW WILSON AGAINST THE DEMOCRATIC FIELD

"I doan 'keer if he is a houn'
You gotta quit kickin' my dawg aroun'"
—Champ Clark campaign song[1]

Almost ten years after her husband lost the Democratic presidential nomination to Woodrow Wilson, Mrs. Champ Clark could still not figure out what had happened. With Wilson out of the White House and the former Speaker dead in 1921, she wrote to a Republican friend in January 1922 to ask "why Champ Clark was not nominated for President at Baltimore in 1912."[2] The simple answer, of course, was that Woodrow Wilson had prevailed in that dramatic convention. But Mrs. Clark had a point. After all, Clark had achieved a majority of the convention delegates and had only lost because of the Democratic rule that required a two-thirds majority for victory. How had Wilson, an improbable aspirant for the presidency in July 1910, risen with such speed to achieve the Democratic nomination and defeat the better-known Clark in the space of two years?

Woodrow Wilson's capture of the Democratic nomination and the presidency in 1912 is one of the great dramas in American political history. It was as if the fates had aligned themselves to speed Wilson's path. A Republican split in New Jersey eased the way of the former president of Princeton to win the governorship in 1910. Despite a lackluster campaign for the nomination in the primaries, he remained viable enough to block Clark and secure the prize in Baltimore. The Taft-

Roosevelt divide almost insured that Wilson would win in November. Well might Wilson tell an aide after his victory: "God ordained that I should be the next president of the United States." A more secular interpretation came a few years later when a Washington wit quipped that if the president "was to fall out of a sixteen story building ... he would hit on a feather bed."[3]

Luck followed Wilson in the early years of his national political career, but good fortune was not the only reason for his success. For the divided and fractured Democrats, Wilson, with southern roots and a base in the Northeast, offered the hope of national power with a fresh face and new ideas in 1911–1912. His skill as a campaigner and his capacity to arouse the faithful in his own party proved just what the Democrats needed. In the most rewarding of his runs for elective office, Wilson infused national politics with a blend of attractive moralism and partisan toughness that the Democrats had not enjoyed under William Jennings Bryan.

In his two presidential terms, Wilson would have notable accomplishments and decisive failures. The problems in his second term made him a rejected figure when he left office in 1921. The campaign of 1912 is thus instructive for what it reveals about the mixed record of Wilson in the White House. His style of campaigning, the obstacles he encountered and overcame, and the enemies he made cast shadows that affected his performance in the Oval Office. A full appraisal of Wilson in the 1912 election must do justice to his victory but must also measure the costs of his triumph in the years that followed.

In 1912, there were aspects of Wilson's character that did not reach the public gaze that would have made his campaign more difficult had they become common knowledge. Six years earlier he had suffered a stroke that for a time affected his vision and ability to read. He made an apparent recovery, but the underlying causes of his ailment had not been addressed. As events proved, he was able to discharge his presidential duties for most of his administration, but he had to avoid stress, work a limited schedule, and watch his health with care to make that record possible. Had his medical situation come to light, it would have cast serious doubt on his fitness to serve.[4]

Wilson was a man of intense romantic passion. His marriage to Ellen Axson Wilson was one of deep mutual affection. During his last years at Princeton, however, he had become infatuated with a divorced woman he met during his vacations in Bermuda, Mary Allen Hulbert Peck. As he did with other female friends, Wilson wrote her intense letters in which he poured out his feelings about people and events. There are suggestions that the relationship with Mrs. Peck may have gone further than that. Through adroit lies to his wife, Wilson found occasions to be alone with Mrs. Peck in her New York apartment. He would later tell his second wife of episodes about which he had repented. While it is not clear that he slept with Mrs. Peck, neither is it certain that he remained faithful to Ellen during their whole marriage. If Wilson's dalliance had become public, his political career would have been imperiled. There were whispers about his links to Mrs. Peck, but nothing definite came to light during the preconvention campaign. Had any of his letters become available for public discussion, he would have found himself in an awkward position.[5]

From the start of his presidential run in 1911, Wilson enjoyed inherent advantages over his major rivals. He was close to New York City, where the important newspapers and journals of opinion operated. As a former college president, he had a ready-made network of Princeton alumni in the news business and acquaintances among commentators who gave him favorable media coverage. For a president whose relations with the press would deteriorate over the course of eight years, Wilson as a candidate was unusually responsive and thoughtful to the scribes who followed him.[6]

As a platform orator, Wilson used the experience of making speeches as an academic to great advantage. He was a pleasing performer in a day when audiences would still listen with attention to a lengthy address. His repertoire included a reliance on limericks that he recited to loosen up the crowds and also to add a note of humorous self-deprecation. His favorite verse went:

For beauty I am not a star.
There are others more handsome by far,
But my face, I don't mind it,
For I am behind it,
It's the people in front that I jar.

Wilson combined religious overtones and traditional Democratic ideology into an appeal that seemed winning and fresh at the time. Among progressive Democrats, Wilson came across as respectable and high-toned in contrast to the Missouri border crudeness of Champ Clark and the provincial southern style of Oscar Underwood.[7]

Yet Wilson could be tough and pointed on the stump. He disclaimed any attempt to be personal in his attacks, but when assailed he gave as good as he got. When the publisher William Randolph Hearst came out against him and pledged to block his nomination with all the newspapers under his control, Wilson responded: "What a commentary it is upon our affairs when one man should suppose he can frame the affairs of the nation. What an exhibition of audacity. What an exhibition of contempt he must feel for the judgment and independence of the American people."[8]

In 1911, with his early start in the field, Wilson established a secure base in his home state, neighboring Pennsylvania, and the delegate-rich southern bastion of Texas. The solidarity of Pennsylvania and Texas would prove crucial in the high-pressure setting of the Baltimore Convention. While his support was more spotty elsewhere, Wilson had latent second- and third-choice backing that none of his rivals could duplicate. In a one-on-one contest against Taft or Roosevelt, Wilson had a better chance to carry northern industrial states than either Clark or Underwood. Logically, Wilson was the best Democratic choice, but as the Republicans divided and the prospects of success brightened, the other contestants—the most important of whom was Champ Clark—rose to forestall Wilson.[9]

One personal alliance that Wilson created in late 1911 had scant impact on the outcome of the 1912 election. Nonetheless, it proved significant for the candidate's future. In November he met for the first time Edward Mandell House of Texas. With an independent income and a taste for politics, the wily House wanted to exercise national power but knew he could not achieve that goal on his own. A reputed (if overrated) power broker in Lone Star State politics, House had been looking for a Democratic candidate for the White House he could support and influence behind the scenes. He let the Wilson campaign know that he was interested in meeting the candidate, and the encounter was arranged. In private, House said Wilson "is not the biggest man I have ever met but he is one of the pleasantest and I would rather play with him than any prospective candidate I have seen."[10]

House kept that tone of condescension out of his letters to Wilson. The two men had hit it off, and the deft Colonel (it was an honorary rank from the governor of Texas) struck just the right notes to persuade Wilson that they had so much in common. As a consummate bootlicker who exaggerated his importance in Texas and with the candidate, House wooed Wilson with practiced skill. The captivated presidential candidate had no way of knowing (and did not trouble to ask) whether House was as powerful a force in Texas politics as he claimed. The resulting friendship would prove a key element in Wilson's life while he was in the White House.

In 1912, however, House brought negligible assets to the Wilson effort. The New Jersey governor had rabid partisans in Texas who were already lining up the state's delegation for him. House played little part in the Wilson movement there. Leaders such as Thomas B. Love and Thomas Watt Gregory capitalized on the Wilson sentiment among the prohibitionist reform wing of the party in that state. One Wilson leader announced in March 1912, "There is every indication of an overwhelming majority for Wilson—it is simply a matter of organization and this, we are rapidly accomplishing." What House did was at most "entirely advisory."[11]

Wilson was the Democratic hopeful with the closest claim to a national organization, funded by his wealthy friends, and actual appeal across the country. William F. McCombs directed his campaign. An irascible New Yorker whose physical disability (he had fractured a hip as a child) and nasty temper made him hard to work with for many Wilson loyalists, McCombs had to share authority with William G. McAdoo. As a successful rapid transit executive in New York City with a good organizing mind, the southern-born McAdoo soon emerged as one of the strong figures in the Wilson camp. Thanks to Wilson's well-heeled backers, his presidential campaign could count on some timely financial support as the prenomination battle proceeded. By the end of 1911, Wilson appeared to be well ahead of his potential rivals.

Wilson had staked out a position on the left of the Democrats with a commitment to procedural reforms such as the initiative and referendum (but not the recall) along with attacks on the "money trust." His assaults on the Republican tariffs and their effect on the consumer, however, were the most effective means to build a wide base of support in all sections of the party. In that sense, Wilson appealed to a consensus among Democrats against Republican protectionism. He would remain true to that theme throughout the remainder of the presidential race. "It is in the tariff schedules," he noted in July 1911, "that half the monopolies of the country have found cover and protection and opportunity." He promised that, if elected, the Democrats would move slowly in revising customs duties downward so that business interests would not be disturbed. In October 1911, McCombs wrote to an aide that "everything [was] going forward satisfactorily" and that "the general tone of letters and newspaper comment is growing stronger and more confident."[12]

As 1912 began, however, the anti-Wilson forces coalesced to forestall any runaway for the nomination. Neither Oscar W. Underwood nor Champ Clark intended to abandon the race without a fight. As Wilson came under scrutiny, moreover, his earlier writings and public statements supplied ample ammunition for his detractors. Though the Democratic battle took place within the shadow of the Roosevelt-Taft donnybrook, the preconvention contest became a matter of Wilson against the field during these months.

Underwood told a family member in late December that "if conditions remain as good as they are today it looks like I could be nominated." The Alabama congressman, round-faced and genial, relied for his appeal on his southern base, where he expected to secure a cohesive bloc of delegates. Since the Democrats required that a nominee receive a two-thirds majority, Underwood wanted to have at least a third of the convention votes to remain viable. Everyone expected the convention to consume multiple ballots before a nominee was decided. The problem that Underwood faced was that Wilson could easily match his claims in the South. Many of the delegates pledged to the Alabamian looked to Wilson as their natural second choice. Most Democrats also knew that nominating a southerner would be unwise in an era when the Civil War still shaped popular attitudes toward Dixie and the politicians who originated there.[13]

Champ Clark presented a more serious challenge to Wilson's chances for the nomination. He had been a Democratic stalwart for more than two decades and had reached the legislative pinnacle when he became Speaker of the House in 1911. Born in Kentucky in 1850 as James Beauchamp Clark, he believed "that a man had as much right to cut off part of his Christian name as to trim off part of his hair." Known thereafter as "Champ" Clark, he taught in West Virginia, moved to Missouri in the mid-1870s, practiced law, and then went into politics. He was elected to Congress in 1892 and was defeated in the Republican landslide of 1894. He then returned to Washington in 1896. From that point on, he had a safe seat and rose to be Speaker in 1911.[14]

In his ascent to national prominence, Clark built up a network of friends and acquired contacts that Wilson as a political newcomer could not equal. Clark also gained from the success of his party in Congress. The ability of the Democrats in the House to remain united on Canadian reciprocity and on lowering the tariff validated Clark's leadership. In many respects, Champ Clark represented the middle ground of the Democrats. "I sprang from the loins of the common people, God bless them!" said Clark, "and I am one of them."[15]

That closeness to the common people, however, was what bothered Democrats about Clark and eventually cost him the nomination. His campaign song that urged supporters to "quit kickin' my dawg around" seemed seedy and provincial to eastern Democrats. Wilson labeled him "a sort of elephantine 'smart aleck.'" The Speaker seemed bland and tacky at the same time. He did not have Wilson's ability on the stump, and he displayed a tendency to utter indiscreet statements at bad moments. His comment about annexing Canada in 1911 was the one most often cited. So Clark offered an inviting target for pro-Wilson commentators who wrote about him in their journals during the first half of 1912. They dubbed him "a fine example of the old-fashioned partisan politician." Even with those strikes against him, Clark proved to be popular with Democratic primary voters and a formidable rival to Wilson as 1912 went forward.[16]

One drag on Clark's candidacy was the opposition he faced from William Jennings Bryan. After his third failed race for the White House in 1908, the ambitious Bryan had to come to terms with the end of his dreams of being president. It was not a transition that came easily to the "Great Commoner," whose appetite for adoring audiences and political adulation never waned. While it was easy to caricature Bryan, the Nebraskan was a formidable opponent when aroused. As the British ambassador later said of him, Bryan was "like a horrid mass of jellified sentimentality from which a sharp beak occasionally pokes out and snaps."[17]

Though he disclaimed any intention to run another time in 1912, Bryan insisted on having a large voice in who the party's nominee would be. He rejected Judson Harmon as a reactionary and was cool toward Underwood. Champ Clark became his primary target during the 1911 special session of Congress. While the Democrats there sought to lower tariff rates, they encountered problems over the wool schedule. Bryan wanted to place wool on the free list. Clark did not have the votes to accomplish that feat within his own caucus or to override an anticipated

Champ Clark, Speaker of the House. Woodrow Wilson's main rival for the Democratic nomination seemed the embodiment of political caution, compared to the New Jersey governor. (Prints and Photographs Collection, Library of Congress)

veto from Taft. Clark accepted lower duties on wool without seeking complete elimination of that tariff schedule that was infamous for the lobbying and corruption that surrounded it. In May 1911, Bryan denounced the Speaker's strategy and urged him to show real political courage. The ill-feeling between the two men intensified.

Bryan maintained a public neutrality, but in private encouraged the presidential candidacy of Joseph W. Folk, a former governor and Democratic rival to Clark in Missouri. In other venues, the Nebraskan made clear that he lacked enthusiasm for Clark as a standard-bearer. "He was always jealous of Champ," Mrs. Clark wrote a year later, "and never lost an opportunity to knife him in the back." While not openly pro-Wilson, Bryan was happy when Wilson courted him and sought his opinion on Democratic issues and strategy.[18]

For Wilson, the early months of 1912 proved a time of troubles as the Democratic opposition focused on his previous record and some careless statements. He had written a popular American history text that he had dashed off without much original research. It reflected his distaste for immigrants and his scathing opinion of those who had come from Eastern Europe. They were "men of the lower class from the South of Italy and men of the meaner sort out of Hungary and Poland, men out of the ranks where there was neither skill nor energy nor any initiative of quick intelligence." These words naturally stirred anger among the immigrants from these countries, and they besieged Wilson with demands to explain his ethnocentric remarks.[19]

In responding to his critics, Wilson took refuge in assertions that his words had been taken out of context and did not reflect his real feelings toward Americans who had come from Eastern Europe. "My history was written on so condensed a scale," he argued to a Polish immigrant leader, "that I am only too well aware that passages such as you quote are open to misconstruction, though I think their meaning is plain when they are fairly scrutinized." As was Wilson's custom, he indulged in what he termed "grazing the truth" to write his way out of a difficult situation.[20]

Other controversies dogged Wilson and slowed his momentum. He had sought a pension from the Carnegie Foundation after he had left Princeton, a move that for his Democratic critics belied his campaign criticism of large corporations and their donors. More important, a private letter was released that he had written in 1907 when he was still the darling of conservative Democrats. In it he said, "Would that we could do something at once dignified and effective to knock Mr. Bryan once for all into a cocked hat." Borrowing the "cocked hat" phrase from the game of ninepins, Wilson meant that Bryan should be so discredited that he would be forced out of politics. Given Bryan's wide following among Democrats, the letter, released to the press by Wilson's enemies, sought to drive a wedge into an emerging alliance with the Great Commoner.[21]

Bryan knew what his rivals within the Democratic ranks were trying to do. "If the big financial interests think they are going to make a rift in the Progressive ranks of the Democratic party by such tactics," Bryan told the press, "they are mistaken." He looked to Wilson for some reassurance that his words five years earlier did not represent his current thinking. The opportunity to do just that came for Wilson at the annual Jefferson-Jackson Day dinner in New York City on 8 January. When his moment arrived, Wilson took full advantage of the situation. He said to Bryan from the podium: "One of the most striking things in recent years is that with all the rise and fall of particular ideas, with all the ebb and flow of particular proposals, there has been one interesting and fixed point in the history of the Democratic party, and that fixed point has been the character and the devotion and the preachings of William Jennings Bryan." The comment evoked enthusiastic applause. While Bryan was not yet in the Wilson camp, the New Jersey governor had gone a long way toward neutralizing him as a potential roadblock to the nomination.[22]

The newspapers opposing Wilson then became obsessed with a dispute over the end of the political friendship between Wilson and George Harvey, the publisher of *Harper's Weekly*. Harvey had first boomed Wilson for the presidency and then the New Jersey governorship in 1910. As Wilson moved leftward in office, his ties with the conservative Harvey became strained. By late 1911, their alliance was over. Critics of Wilson seized upon the matter as a way of painting him as an opportunist and a hypocrite. But the assaults actually helped confirm the impression of the public that Wilson was a reformer. What the fracas did do was to disrupt the momentum that Wilson had built up in 1911. That development made it unlikely that he would sweep his way to the two-thirds majority in the national convention.[23]

The race for delegates began in late March and early April as the Democrats contested the primaries in the relatively few states where those races were available. Wilson and his rivals had to compete with the attention being lavished on Roosevelt and Taft in the national press. While the Democrats put on an exciting contest, they did not reach the sheer drama of the Republican struggle until the national convention. As the historian J. Franklin Jameson wrote, with more than a little exaggeration by early June, "I believe there is to be an election, though I do not remember to have heard the Democratic party mentioned in the last six weeks unless in some obscure place."[24]

Although the 1912 campaign would become famous for Wilson's program of the "New Freedom," in the quest for the nomination the tariff issue received special emphasis in his speeches. Lowering customs duties remained a subject on which all Democrats could agree. At Boston on 27 January, he said that he knew what "the central question" was because "every road leads to that question, and that is the question of the tariff." In Virginia on 1 February he reiterated that "an absolute readjustment of trade is necessary, and that that is an irresistible battering-ram that is battering at the wall of the tariff." When the campaign entered the spring, he argued that the tariff could not be revised until the people making decisions were changed. "Do you suppose," he asked in Savannah, Georgia, on 20 April, "that any thoughtful man would get up and discuss the tariff again if he thought Mr. Aldrich was going to settle it again?" The next month, however, he called "the whole tariff policy" a "huge scheme of make-believe." On 23 May he concluded that "every business question in this country" came back in the end "to the question of the tariff."[25]

As the primaries unfolded, the process of caucuses and state conventions were also going forward. Wilson did well enough in the early contests with some success in Oklahoma, a split in Kansas, and a positive result in Wisconsin on 2 April. Even so, and despite the generosity of Wilson's wealthy friends, the campaign was now strapped for ready cash. The candidate told the press two days after the Wisconsin voting: "We have no money; our campaign has been bankrupt four times, including the present time, and we must depend altogether on our friends."[26]

Wilson was learning what would become evident in other primary campaigns in the decades that followed. To be a viable national candidate with serious organizations in key states demanded larger amounts of money than had been required under the older system of party conventions. In essence, the campaign was running a dozen statewide elections all over the nation simultaneously. While Wilson was able to manage this feat in 1912 in an age when newspaper coverage still counted for a great deal, the system of choosing presidential candidates through primaries had inherent cost pressures built into it. That condition in turn meant that the need for candidates to turn to well-heeled special interests or wealthy patrons would grow as the twentieth century progressed.

The next big test for Wilson came in the Illinois primary on 9 April. As the assumed front-runner, he felt impelled to challenge Clark in a large midwestern industrial state. If he yielded the delegation to his rival without a fight, it would have seemed an admission of weakness. Since he was from the neighboring state of Missouri, Clark had a substantial following and support from the Democratic leaders in the Chicago area. Wilson campaigned hard in the state with stepped-up rhetoric about the secrecy and inside deals that he said were characteristic of Republicans and some of his own opponents. "What is the use of discussing the tariff until we give the people of the United States a seat inside the committee rooms where the whole game is put up?" he asked at Springfield on 6 April. Clark did not campaign in the state because of his responsibilities in the House. His surrogates made the case for him while the publisher William Randolph Hearst provided intensely negative press coverage of Wilson's candidacy. It became evident that Wilson was likely to be defeated, but few expected a drubbing at the hands of Clark.[27]

The Illinois result was a Clark landslide and a black eye for Wilson. The winner received 218,483 votes to 75,257 for Wilson. The Speaker had shown his strength with midwestern Democrats and given a decided boost to his hopes for winning the nomination. "The Illinois verdict takes Champ Clark out of the favorite son class and places him at once in the lead," said one of his spokesmen. From the presumptive front-runner, Wilson had overnight become the second choice among the Democrats. The candidate said that the outcome was "a great surprise to me. I fully expected to carry the State."[28]

The two main rivals battled through the rest of April. Clark did well in New York on 11 April and made similar gains in Colorado, Nebraska, and Massachusetts. Wilson countered with victories in Michigan and Ohio, but the Wilson camp had to recognize that April had been an excellent month for Clark's hopes of the nomination. Meanwhile, Wilson had to respond to charges that in his writings, while he was skeptical of immigrants from Eastern Europe, he favored allowing the Chinese to enter on the West Coast. Such a position would have been devastating to his chances in California, and he moved to avert such talk. "Democracy rests on the equality of the citizen. Oriental coolieism will give us another race question to solve and surely we have had our lesson." Clark won the California primary by a two-to-one margin despite

Wilson's invocation of ethnocentrism to reassure racist sentiments in the West.[29]

Some racist Democrats thought that Wilson was not bigoted enough. The former Populist, Thomas E. Watson, assailed him for alleged pro-black sympathies, including a tolerance for the African American leader Booker T. Washington, who had been the object of a white assailant's assault in 1911. Enemies of Wilson circulated a broadside entitled "The Nigger and the Governor of New Jersey" that accused Wilson of wiring condolences to Washington when he was injured. Wilson's camp immediately fired off a denial of the charge. These events showed how intense the race was becoming as the Baltimore Convention approached.[30]

May's primary and convention results brought scant consolation for Wilson and more good news for Champ Clark. The House Speaker gathered in delegates from fifteen states such as California, Iowa, and New Hampshire. Wilson did well in New Jersey at the end of the month and he claimed the forty delegates from Texas at the end of May as well. But as the convention neared, he was nowhere close to a majority of the delegates. Even the endorsement of the *New York World*, the country's leading Democratic newspaper, was only a symbolic success. Clark was the clear first-place candidate with, by most estimates, between 400 and 500 committed delegates in his column. Wilson had 248 pledged delegates and probably another 75 or so who were leaning his way.

Wilson's new best friend, Colonel House, told the candidate that he had to make a previously planned trip to Europe and could not be present to assist at the convention. The clever Colonel could thus say, if Wilson won, that he had been confident all along and his presence would not have mattered. If Wilson lost, House would not be associated with the defeat and could look for another political patron. He wrote privately that Wilson had "a good chance, but nothing more." Other Wilson men in and out of Texas would have to take care of the candidate's hopes of a convention victory.[31]

Things were not as bleak as they seemed for the Wilson campaign. The Clark candidacy lacked a strong positive foundation to withstand Wilson at the national convention. Informed observers, many of them already pro-Wilson, believed that the Speaker lacked the brains and character to be president. "He is a dear old boy," wrote the *New York World*, "but his leadership is not the sort of leadership the Democratic party requires in the year 1912 if it is to win the election." The *St. Louis Post-Dispatch* contended from Clark's home state that "he is neither original in his ideas nor stubborn in his convictions." At bottom, the sense that Clark was not up to the job as president pervaded the atmosphere of the convention.[32]

Wilson, in contrast, exuded competence and gave the impression that he would be at home in the White House. His success in managing the New Jersey legislature also seemed to validate his leadership qualities. Few Democrats looked with care at his personal style. There were rumblings about his ingratitude to those who helped his public career get started, only to be abandoned, as happened with the New Jersey political boss James Smith and later with George Harvey. Closer attention to his speeches and campaign tactics might have given hints of his propensity toward arrogance and self-righteousness that would be signal marks of his presidency. But with victory in the air, Wilson seemed the strong candidate, the fresh face that the Democrats had been searching for since the end of the Cleveland era.

Despite the Clark surge, there were some encouraging portents for Wilson in May 1912 as well. His forces carried the Texas county conventions on 1 May and maintained their dominance to insure control of all the state's forty delegates when the Democratic Convention met on 26 May. They pledged "to vote as a unit for Woodrow Wilson as the Democratic nominee for President so long as his name is before the convention." The emergence of Texas as a key Wilson state, along with the growing influence of Colonel House, foreshadowed the major part that the state would play in the Wilson presidency.[33]

By early June, as the convention neared, Wilson had 248 instructed votes, not yet the one-third of the 1086 delegates needed to stop Clark. If he could persuade delegates for Underwood and Harmon to work with him, there was a good chance to block the Speaker. Wilson had an ample amount of second-choice support, especially in the South. It remained to be seen if the Wilson campaign could capitalize on these potential reservoirs of votes. "What we now look forward to with not a little dread are the possibilities of next fortnight in politics," the candidate wrote a friend on 17 June. By that time the story of the Republican Convention and the Taft-Roosevelt rupture had developed. In a sense, the GOP split meant that any Democrat was likely to win, a perception that helped Clark.[34]

More shrewd party members sensed that if they selected a nominee who was not perceived as a progressive, then the Democrat and Taft would split the moderate and conservative vote. Such an outcome might enable Theodore Roosevelt to secure enough reform support to prevail in a three-way contest. The emergence of Roosevelt at the head of a new party helped Wilson, who was recognized as the most progressive figure in the Democratic field. Beside the vote-getting charisma of Roosevelt, both Clark and Underwood seemed uninspiring old-style politicos. As one of Wilson's correspondents put it, the party owed it to the American people "to say plainly whether we are progressives or reactionaries."[35]

The Democratic National Convention in 1912 proved as dramatic and exciting as its Republican counterpart. A reporter who witnessed the week-long spectacle described the Convention Hall as "a giant drum, in which raged hailstorms, and thunder chorus, and strident shriek of wind and tide, raised to ear-shattering force by the hollow echoing of the drum walls." To rouse enthusiasm among the followers of the Speaker, the Clark forces paraded hound dogs on leashes through the streets of Baltimore. The conservative Republican senator, Francis E. Warren of Wyoming, told a friend after the gathering was over that "they have had a great old time in Baltimore, and we here in Washington have been near enough to hear the roar and see the lightning." Out of what the cagy Warren called "a sort of inverse-ratio 'love feast,'" the Democrats produced a winning candidate and a united party, unlike the Grand Old Party and its troubles.[36]

Champ Clark's strategy going into the convention was to obtain a clear majority of the delegates on one of the early ballots. When that development had occurred in previous contested Democratic conventions, the leading candidate usually had little difficulty in securing the necessary two-thirds. To that end, Clark and his aides looked to the large New York delegation with its ninety votes to start a landslide when they threw their support to the Speaker's cause. But making such an entente carried political risks. The New York City machine of Tammany Hall, led by its boss Charles Murphy, had packed the delegation with its allies. The conservative financier August Belmont was a member of the New York slate, and there was a sense throughout the hall among southern and western Democrats that Wall Street, Tammany Hall, and big business determined how the Empire State contingent would vote.

To offset Clark's support, Wilson's backers knew that they had to outorganize the forces arrayed against them. When these men reached Baltimore, however, they perceived that little in the way of serious coordination had been accomplished. The Pennsylvania and Texas delegations, staying at the same hotel, put together committees to track both committed Wilson men and the sentiment within uninstructed delegations. They created a central office to coordinate their work. These steps gave the Wilson camp excellent intelligence throughout the turbulent days that followed. The candidate himself was at his summer home in New Jersey. He had every reason to observe the custom that kept potential nominees away from the convention and no need to emulate the path-breaking tactic that Roosevelt had adopted ten days earlier. Through telephone conversations with McAdoo and McCombs, Wilson was informed of the changing fortunes in the hall. His men on the ground also proved capable in making the deals and bargains that first kept Wilson viable and then enabled him to win the nomination.[37]

The initial key test came on Tuesday, 25 June, when the convention formally opened its deliberations. The delegates had to select a temporary chairman who would have the honor of delivering the keynote address. That oration in turn set the tone for what everyone hoped and expected would be a winning race in the fall. The choice, however, also signaled which faction of the party held control of the convention itself. To demonstrate their hold on power, Clark and the New Yorkers had proposed that the party's nominee in 1904, Alton B. Parker, be the designee for the temporary chair honor. It was an odd choice and showed how out of touch both the Speaker and his allies were with party sentiment. Parker had lost in a landslide to Theodore Roosevelt, in part because of his lack of the slightest trace of charisma or excitement. In 1904 a newspaper said of Parker that he possessed "all the salient qualities of a sphere." Dull, conservative, and a memory of a Democratic debacle, Parker would, said Bryan, "start us off on a reactionary basis that would give the lie to all our progressive declarations."[38]

Bryan decided to fight Parker, with whom he had battled eight years earlier. With his flair for the public gesture, Bryan sent telegrams to all the presidential hopefuls asking them to come out against the Parker choice. The only one who took a clear pro-Bryan stance was Wilson. "You are quite right," he wired to the Commoner, "The Baltimore convention is to be a convention of progressives, of men who are progressive in principle and by conviction." He promised Bryan that he would "find my friends in the convention acting upon clear conviction and always in the interest of the people's cause."[39] Bryan did not win the fight to replace Parker who, once elected, gave an uninspiring keynote address.

Bryan's tactic had wrong-footed Clark and assisted Wilson's perceived viability as a reformer. At this juncture, anything that disrupted Clark's scenario worked to the ultimate advantage of Wilson.

After his initial sally, Bryan further agitated the convention with efforts to put party conservatives further on the defensive. He put forward a resolution that would have ousted delegates who were members of the "the privilege-hunting and favor-seeking class." The proposal was amended and lost its punch. Although it did not assist any repressed desire Bryan may have had for a fourth nomination, it reminded delegates from the South and West of their ties to progressivism.[40]

With the preliminaries out of the way, the convention turned to the nominating speeches and the presentation of the candidates. Clark held on to his lead as the voting began. The question was whether the Speaker could ride his success in the early ballots to a two-thirds victory. The Wilson camp had succeeded in breaking the "unit rule" that enabled a majority in a delegation to cast all the votes of a single state. That change freed up some delegates to endorse the New Jersey governor. But there was no doubt that Champ Clark would break on top when the actual voting commenced.

The trend through the first nine ballots did put Clark ahead. On the first tally he had 440 ½ to 324 for Wilson, with Harmon and Underwood trailing. The results stayed essentially the same through eight more ballots. When the tenth ballot came up, the New York delegation, under the orders of Charles Murphy, switched in dramatic fashion from Harmon to Clark. That move put Clark over 550 votes and gave him a majority of the delegates. He expected, upon hearing the news in his Washington office on Capitol Hill, that he would be swept to the nomination. Wilson told his managers to release his delegates, which would have been the equivalent of a surrender announcement. McCombs sat on the message.

As the tenth ballot continued after a lengthy demonstration for Clark, the Wilson delegations held firm and the expected surge toward the front-runner did not materialize. The Underwood and Wilson delegates refused to yield to the momentary enthusiasm for Clark. Each camp anticipated that a deadlocked convention would make their candidate the eventual nominee. Behind the scenes, the Wilson leaders had been wooing Underwood managers and their delegates. For Wilson, who had fought the combined Democratic field throughout the primaries, it meant that he had now arrayed the remaining candidates against Clark's selection.

A dramatic turn toward Wilson seemed to take place on the four-teenth ballot. As a member of the Nebraska delegation pledged to Clark because of the results in the primary, Bryan told the convention he would now cast his vote for Wilson to protest the Speaker's ties to Wall Street. It was something less than an outright endorsement of Wilson, and raised questions of the motives behind the Commoner's actions. It was a typical Bryan moment, full of heat and controversy, but it had little practical consequence for the convention. No stampede toward Wilson occurred because of what Bryan had done. By the end of Saturday, 29 June 1912, Clark was still in the lead with 463 ½ votes to Wilson's 407 ½ and the rest of the votes scattered among Underwood and minor candi-dates. The delegates took Sunday off for rest, church services, and clan-destine deal making of ever greater intensity.

The tide turned toward Wilson on Monday, 1 July. First, the Indiana delegation, swayed by promises of the vice presidency for its governor, Thomas Riley Marshall, abandoned support of their favorite son. The state's twenty-nine votes went to Wilson. By the thirtieth ballot, Wilson was narrowly in the lead with 460 votes to 455 for Clark. Twelve more ballots left the situation with Wilson ahead and the sense that a break toward him might happen the following day. "I guess my supporters are kind of busy down there," Wilson told reporters from his vacation home at Sea Girt, New Jersey.[41]

On Tuesday, 2 July, the Illinois delegation, under the control of the Democratic boss, Roger Sullivan, broke to Wilson on the initial ballot of the day. He now had a majority of the delegates for the first time. By the forty-third ballot, Virginia and West Virginia moved into the Wilson col-umn, putting the New Jersey governor at more than 600 votes. It looked certain that Wilson would win, but more drama remained. The Illinois delegation was on the verge of switching back to Clark on the forty-sixth ballot, a move that would have revived the hopes of the Speaker and his allies. At that pivotal moment, the Underwood delegates were re-leased. Wilson received 990 votes and became the Democratic nominee for president of the United States. A devastated Champ Clark wired his congratulations to the winner, but he never forgot nor forgave William Jennings Bryan for having frustrated his candidacy.

For his running mate, Wilson first looked to Underwood, who turned down the post. The new presidential candidate then agreed to accept In-diana's Thomas Riley Marshall as part of the deal that had brought the state over to the winner. Indiana had always been an important state in

Democratic calculations. It would not be needed in 1912, but the Democrats could not be sure of that at the convention. Marshall never had a substantive role in the Democratic administration, as Wilson shut him out of all the serious work. There remained the Democratic platform, which was adopted in haste and without much debate. The protective tariff headed the list of major issues. The Democrats called it an unconstitutional use of government power and "the principal cause of the unequal distribution of wealth" in the nation. They promised "immediate downward revision" of the existing rates but, in line with Wilson's thinking, also pledged "the ultimate attainment of the principles we advocate by legislation that would not injure or destroy legitimate industry."[42]

The Democrats also said they would bring down the high cost of living, regulate the trusts, adopt an income tax, and limit presidents to a single six-year term. Wilson did not favor the change, and it never went anywhere once his party took power. The platform reiterated the party's commitment to state rights and what that implied for civil rights, but there was no condemnation of Chinese immigration. There was a plank favoring the demands of organized labor that sought the backing of the American Federation of Labor. It was a progressive platform for the major party that had most fully embraced the ideas of reform within the mainstream of American politics in the Progressive Era.

In the wake of Wilson's victory, the Democrats understood that they had done something unprecedented in their recent history. Faced with a chance to confirm the Republican taunts about the inability to select good candidates and win national elections, the party had managed to select its strongest leader and to do so in a manner that left them united for the fall campaign ahead. In retrospect, Wilson's strengths as a national politician would seem self-evident, but that was not the case in the heat and passion of Baltimore. It would have been simple, once Champ Clark obtained a majority of the delegates, to have done the safe and conventional thing.

What would have happened had Clark been the opponent for Roosevelt and Taft is impossible to know, of course. At best there would have been a sense that the Democrats once again had fallen short of excellence. Certainly Roosevelt and his supporters hoped that someone like Clark, colorless and predictable, would have come out of the Democratic meeting. Instead, both wings of the Republican party recognized that the Democrats had done something shrewd and decisive. To answer the question of Champ Clark's wife a decade later, her husband was not nominated because the Democrats across the spectrum of their party recognized that Woodrow Wilson was their best chance to win the presidency in 1912.

The euphoria of the Democrats spilled over the party's new leader. "Intellectually, Woodrow Wilson is the best-equipped candidate the Democrats have put forward since Thomas Jefferson," wrote the columnist Mark Sullivan in *Collier's*. His words reflected the consensus among Democrats of all persuasions as well as some Republicans disillusioned with Taft and Roosevelt. A flood of congratulatory mail poured into the small town of Sea Girt, New Jersey. "The people looked upon his nomination, not as a political triumph, but as the beginning of a new and better epoch in American life," wrote one of the candidate's aides years later. Wilson himself said that "my nomination was a sort of political miracle," and he struggled to deal with the callers, well-wishers, and eager politicians who flocked to Sea Girt to see him about the campaign. Soon he sought solace from the crowd on the yacht of one of his rich friends as he began to prepare his speech formally accepting the Democratic nomination. The nineteenth-century tradition of telling the candidate weeks after his selection that he had been nominated was still part of the American political scene. During the rest of July politicians across the country pondered what the sudden turn of Democratic fortunes would mean for the election in general.[43]

Wilson's unexpected success and the bitter split within the Grand Old Party brightened Democratic chances of further gains in the congressional elections as well. The party's advantage in the House stood at 228 to 161 after the 1910 elections. The Republicans still controlled the Senate by fifty-one to forty-one, though several progressive Republicans often voted with the Democrats. In a normal presidential election year, the Democrats might have expected to make small gains in the lower house and perhaps come closer to retaking the Senate should their presidential nominee be successful at the polls. But 1912 presented them sudden opportunities. Roosevelt intended to form a third party and run candidates for federal and state offices outside the South. That strategy meant danger for Republican incumbents who faced the prospect of their normal vote being split.

The resurgence of the Democrats in Congress had been building since 1908. Republican divisions within the Senate and House helped the Democrats capitalize on the high cost of living and other issues to win back the House in 1910 and cut the Republican majority in the

The Democrats presented a united front in 1912 as this picture of Wilson,
seated in the middle, with his party's congressional candidates, attested.
(Prints and Photographs Collection, Library of Congress)

Senate. In each body, the Democrats had proved unusually cohesive in 1911–1912. In addition to the leadership of Clark and Underwood in the House, the Democrats in the Senate were also giving the Republicans fits.

John Worth Kern had defeated Albert J. Beveridge in Indiana in 1910 to gain that key seat for the Democrats. The Democratic vice presidential candidate in 1908 with Bryan, Kern proved to be an adroit lawmaker who brought greater unity between the progressive and conservative members of his party in the upper house. Although Kern and his allies could not block the conservative, Thomas S. Martin of Virginia, from becoming the Democratic leader in 1911, the Indiana senator did predict to the press that the number of reform Democrats "will be increased in the natural course until the progressive spirit thoroughly permeates the Democratic minority." The votes of these reform Democrats had helped to pass the constitutional amendment for the direct election of United States senators. In the summer of 1912, it even now seemed possible that the Democrats would win control of the Senate for the first time since 1894.[44]

The task before Kern and his allies would not be an easy one. The Democrats would have to make pickups in such normally safe Republican states as New Hampshire, Kansas, Montana, and Oregon to achieve the desired result. In New Hampshire, there had not been a Democrat elected to the Senate since before the Civil War. While the incumbent, Henry H. Burnham, was not a candidate for reelection, the Republicans expected to retain the seat. In Kansas, where Charles S. Curtis was the incumbent, there had been a Democrat in the Senate for two years during the Populist movement of the mid-1890s, but the state had returned to its normal Republican allegiance in races for the upper house thereafter. Oregon voters had elected a Democratic senator in 1908, but the Republican incumbent in 1912, Jonathan Bourne, retiring after a single term, also expected to have a member of his party continue the GOP's hold on the seat. Montana had been more volatile politically, and the sitting Republican, Joseph M. Dixon, had aroused opposition because of his support for Theodore Roosevelt in the race against William Howard Taft. Since he was serving as Roosevelt's campaign manager and did not campaign, there was a good chance for a Democratic pickup with the party's leading hopeful, Thomas J. Walsh. So there were opportunities for Democrats in 1912 before Roosevelt bolted. Yet not even the most optimistic Senate watchers expected the minority party to gain control. But with the third party in the field, Democratic hopes brightened.

The Democrats in the House did not have to take radical steps during the summer of 1912 to capitalize on their new political advantage. In reliably Republican districts, they did as they had always done and entered candidates who in other years would have been essentially sacrificial offerings. For such Republican stalwarts in Illinois as former Speaker Joseph G. Cannon or Taft leader William B. McKinley, they had routinely won easy races against lackluster challengers. Now these veterans confronted not only the usual Democratic foe but also third-party candidates running to support Roosevelt's presidential bid. When the Democratic House members met with Wilson in July, they came back and told reporters asking about the nominee's chances "that conditions could not be more propitious."[45]

Unlike modern campaigns where House and Senate races are as closely followed in the media as the presidential contest, the congressional decision in 1912 took place in the shadow of the three-way presidential run. With Senate elections decided in the state legislatures for the last time, much depended on what happened with the various races for state houses. That made predicting the outcome of a senatorial contest in advance a chancy business. Nonetheless, Wilson did what he could to assist Democrats running for both houses. He underlined in his speeches that the election of a Democratic Congress was likely to occur and that it thus made sense to choose a Democratic president. In New Jersey, he attacked his old adversary James Smith and championed the progressive Democrat William "Billy" Hughes in the race for a Republican seat. For the first time in memory, the Democratic party had something approaching a coordinated campaign on all levels.

In the Senate, the elections in the one-party South produced changes in Democratic ranks that would shape how Wilson's legislative program would fare if he won as most observers now predicted he would. Joseph Weldon Bailey of Texas, who had served since 1901, left politics because his conservative views were out of step with his party. Morris Sheppard, an ardent progressive and prohibitionist, won the primary to replace Bailey. Joseph T. Robinson of Arkansas, later the majority leader during the 1930s, was elected in early 1913 to replace the deceased Jeff Davis. Ollie James of Kentucky won his party's designation as did Joseph Ransdell of Louisiana, whom Huey Long would oust in 1931. The "White Chief," the racist James K. Vardaman, carried his bigotry from Mississippi to the upper house. Thus, the 1912 elections and their aftermath brought some fascinating Democratic characters to the Senate, but these men did not produce any real change in the partisan balance of that house of Congress. That would occur as a result of the Republican divide.

The Democrats intended to fund their campaign through a system of small donations, and calls went out to loyal party members and the public to contribute modest amounts such as "one honest dollar" to the Wilson canvass. In states such as Texas, Democrats in the various factions of the party competed against each other to raise the most cash. However, these efforts did not provide the funds the campaign needed. Most of the $1,111,000 that the Democrats had available came from millionaire donors such as Charles R. Crane, Cleveland H. Dodge, and banker Jacob H. Schiff. Other contributors found themselves with diplomatic appointments in the new administration in a time-honored tradition of national politics. In 1912, unlike the Republicans and the beleaguered Taft, the Democratic presidential campaign had what it needed to be competitive.

The Democrats also had some organizational problems. William F. McCombs was worn out by the primary campaign. His ill-tempered personality made him a dubious choice to be the public face of the Wilson effort. He gave way reluctantly to William G. McAdoo, whose background in business provided needed expertise about running a presidential canvass. The Democrats were more organized than they had been in the Parker and Bryan campaigns, but to a large extent it did not really matter. As long as Wilson could poll the normal Democratic vote, he was likely to win.

The support of organized labor was another plus for the Democrats as they looked ahead to the fall. The American Federation of Labor (AFL) and its president, Samuel Gompers, had no love for Roosevelt or Taft. Roosevelt had selected the AFL as one of his targets in the 1906 congressional campaigns, and the craft unions that made up the federation had supported Bryan in 1908. Although the AFL did not speak for the mass of unorganized workers, its backing of Wilson would be an important asset in his campaign.

The Wilson forces mobilized women in the summer of 1912. They built on the existing Women's Democratic League of New York and created the National Women's Democratic League in June 1912. Under the leadership of Mrs. J. Borden "Daisy" Harriman, the campaign also set up the Women's National Wilson and Marshall Organization in early August. Harriman came from an aristocratic background but had long been involved in various social justice causes. She and her associates raised money, sent out letters, spoke at rallies, and staged stunts and displays for the Democrats. Harriman believed that "we must get out and make the world better" and thought that the Wilson drive gave her that opportunity.[46]

The presidential candidate himself did not at the outset anticipate much of a speaking tour campaign. He told reporters, "I intend to discuss principles and not men, and I will make speeches only in such debatable States where I accept invitations from the party leaders."[47] But the days of the McKinley style front-porch campaign no longer suited the voters. Bryan and Taft had both toured in 1908, and expectations were that the presidential candidate would be out on the hustings in some form. As the Roosevelt challenge grew, moreover, Wilson recognized that he would have to stump the country to answer his rival's program.

It was up to Woodrow Wilson to set the tone for the Democrats in his acceptance speech, scheduled to be held at Sea Girt on 7 August. Beset by politicians and well-wishers, he escaped from the throng on 23 July to a friend's yacht and returned seven days later with the speech written. "I observe Wilson goes into hiding in order to write his speech," President Taft told his wife, "and I sympathize with him." The notification ceremony itself took place at the Governor's Cottage at Sea Girt before an assembled crowd of Democrats eager to hear what their presidential candidate had to say. It was a hot afternoon, and the crowd displayed some boredom before the candidate had finished his comments.[48]

The extended speech was not one of Wilson's best efforts. He tied his remarks closely to the Democratic platform and did not provide his listeners with much partisan red meat. "There are two great things to do," he said, the first of which was the revision of the tariff downward, "unhesitatingly and steadily downward," regulation of big business, and reform of the banking system. The second phase had to do with labor, conservation, and the expansion of opportunity in areas such as the merchant marine. On the trusts, he was less than specific, accepting the existence of large corporations but promising enforcement of new antitrust laws that went well beyond the Sherman Antitrust Act. He did not, however, anticipate the concept of the New Freedom that he would soon develop in response to Roosevelt and the Progressive Party.[49]

Had Wilson not been well in the lead for the presidency in August 1912, his speech might have been counted a political flop. "Wilson's message is milk and water," concluded President Taft. The Democratic newspapers praised the oration, and the Republicans quibbled about it, but in the end it did not matter much what Wilson said in this archaic ritual. The convention of the Progressive Party and Theodore Roosevelt's presidential chances in 1912, which had ended the day before the Democratic event, upstaged Wilson's debut as a national candidate.[50]

The lineup of the major parties for 1912 would soon be completed once Roosevelt's convention did the expected thing. But the Republicans, Democrats, and Progressives were not the only political organization seeking the votes of the American people in this election. For the fourth time since 1900, the Socialist Party and Eugene V. Debs were on the ballot and making an active canvass for the support of the disgruntled and the downtrodden in society. Debs and his campaign lacked the media attention that the other hopefuls attracted, but in the perspective of history his alternative view of what the United States should do about injustice has proven compelling to many scholars. The possibilities and limits of socialism in the United States, as Debs articulated them in 1912, forms an important phase of the outcome of this crucial election.

A SOCIALIST CELEBRITY
RUNS FOR PRESIDENT

Ripsaw, ripsaw, ripsaw, bang!
We belong to the Gene Debs gang.
Are we Socialists? I should smile.
We're Revolutionists all the while.
—Socialist cheer [1]

As he campaigned for the Democratic nomination for president in the spring of 1912, Woodrow Wilson posed to his audience on several occasions a variation of this question: "Have you noticed the number of intelligent men you have met in your daily intercourse who are becoming subscribers to the Socialistic doctrine?" For Wilson, who disclaimed any love for socialism, the explanation for this rise of interest in the Socialist Party was right at hand. "The great Socialistic vote in this country is not a vote for a programme; it is a protest, a vote in protest against the bitter disappointments that the country has suffered at the hands of both parties."[2]

Theodore Roosevelt also spoke out about the presence of a socialist alternative in the 1912 electoral battle. He noted that his conservative critics often accused him of being a socialist or even an anarchist. As Roosevelt said in a speech to his fellow progressives, "The propositions I make constitute neither anarchy nor Socialism, but, on the contrary, a corrective to Socialism and an antidote to anarchy." Throughout his career, the former president had worried about the potential threat of socialism to the existing order if reforms were not made. In 1912, he saw the progressives as the best answer to the ostensible menace that Eugene V. Debs and his followers posed.[3]

The Socialist Party and its leader would have agreed with Wilson and Roosevelt that the major parties had been disappointing. In contrast to Wilson's tone of condescension, however, the Socialists believed that they had an answer to the excesses of capitalism and the deteriorating plight of the poor in the United States. They saw themselves as a legitimate alternative to the major parties, and they hoped that 1912 would be another step toward the revolution that would change the political and economic system of the country into true socialism.

In the history of socialism in the United States, the election of 1912 stands as the high point of the electoral appeal of the doctrine as the Socialist Party and Eugene V. Debs enunciated it. When the votes came in, Debs and his running mate, Emil Seidel, had collected 900,000 votes, double what he had attained in the ambitious 1908 canvass. With 6 percent of the popular vote, Debs seemed to have made the Socialists a genuine political force in the United States. Over the next four years, however, amid the controversy over the country's neutrality in World War I, the Socialist appeal fell off, and the party entered a long decline. Thus, the 1912 campaign remains the moment when socialism had its best chance during the age of reform to establish itself as a significant aspect of national politics.

The 1912 election forms part of the venerable historical debate about why there was no Socialist left in the United States that approached the power and influence of the Labour Party in Great Britain. Any number of explanations have been put forward to account for the lack of appeal of more radical left-wing approaches than what the Democrats or the Progressives offered during these years. One thesis contends that American workers, the natural constituency for socialism, were more concerned with preserving their own capacity to get ahead in a capitalist nation than opting for class-based appeals. The electoral system itself worked against the interest of third-parties with the winner-take-all voting procedure that made it difficult for Socialists to do well in state or national elections. Since Socialists had the vote in the United States, they did not have to emphasize gaining suffrage as a means of recruiting support. In addition, the conservative mainstream press did not provide extensive or fair coverage of Debs and other Socialist candidates. Factional infighting within the party further crippled its electoral chances in both local and state races.

These considerations did hold the Socialists back, but there was an additional element that came into sharp relief during the 1912 campaign. Eugene V. Debs was not an adroit or successful politician even within the context of the ideologically driven Socialist Party. He approached his task more in the nature of a star turn that kept him in the public eye than as a shrewd politician out to maximize his vote total and the appeal of his party. In his fourth race for the presidency, he followed an old script and the traditional tactics that he had adopted in 1900, 1904, and 1908. The campaign gratified his ego and maintained his celebrity status among Socialists, but it also acted to restrict the gains his party could have made. There were many similarities in personality and approach between Debs and a figure such as Robert La Follette.

Few figures out of the Gilded Age and Progressive Era are more appealing on human terms than Gene Debs. Many reminiscences attest to his kindly nature and abundant human sympathy for the downtrodden and the disadvantaged. Stories of his spontaneous loans made with no expectation of repayment, of clothes given away to strangers, of time and energy spent for his cause run through his life and public career. Even his most virulent enemies recognized that Gene Debs was, in the phrase of a later campaign, "someone you'd like to have a beer with." In fact, there was some dispute about Debs's fondness for alcohol. His family and friends declared that he never had a drinking problem, but there were reports of periodic benders that suggested a different diagnosis was possible.[4]

Debs was also a compelling speaker who was most alive when he stood on the podium before an adoring crowd. "Ink pots have never been inviting to me," he once remarked, "but I cannot say the same of the platform. That is my forte." Once he launched into his set speech about the evils of capitalism, Debs could hold an audience even of those who did not agree with his ideological positions. Along with William Jennings Bryan, Debs was one of the spellbinders of the Progressive Era who could draw a throng who then embraced the communal experience of Debs's oratory.[5]

But how good a politician was the likable Debs? Since he knew that he never had a chance to win the White House, it would be unfair to criticize him for losing his races. His goal was to publicize the ideals of his party and in the process maximize the Socialist vote as evidence of the growing class consciousness of the working class. Holding office as an end in itself never appealed to him. He believed with passionate intensity that capitalism as a political and social system was doomed. If he could only convince his listeners of that simple proposition, he knew that the Socialist commonwealth would soon arrive.

His dream had been evolving ever since he was born in Terre Haute, Indiana, in 1855. He grew up in reasonably comfortable circumstances in the home of the owner of a small grocery store. Not for young Gene, however, were the dry routines of stocking shelves, checking invoices, and sacking produce. Terre Haute, like most midwestern cities, was a railroad hub. When young Gene stood at the depot, he heard the click-ety-clack echo back the call of the rails as a way of life. For five years, until age nineteen, Debs worked on the railroad in a variety of jobs. In time, however, he left that trade and plunged into union work on a full-time basis. His main job was editing the *Locomotive Firemen's Magazine*, a union publication, a post that gave him a large constituency among railroad workers. He held local offices as a Democrat in Terre Haute and even served one term in the Indiana legislature. The bills he introduced were defeated, and his disillusion with the legislative process became profound. His real love, however, was pulling together a union of rail-road men that would safeguard their interests against management.[6]

Debs was the main architect of the American Railway Union which he organized in 1893. With the economy collapsing in the wake of the Panic of 1893, the appeal of Debs resonated with railroad workers fear-ful of lost jobs and no wages. The success of a strike against the Great Northern Railroad in the spring of 1894 seemed a harbinger of further growth for the industrial union that Debs had created.

Then came the Pullman Strike, which made Debs a national figure among union men and a terror to the middle class fearful of social up-heaval. Workers in the town of Pullman, Illinois, where Pullman sleep-ing cars were constructed, went on strike when their wages were cut during the depression. They sought support from the American Railway Union to increase their economic leverage against George Pullman and management. Debs agreed to lead his union in a boycott of the Pullman cars nationwide. The resulting tie-up in rail traffic brought a swift re-sponse from the conservative administration of Grover Cleveland, which sent federal troops to Chicago to break the walkout. At the same time, the government pursued legal action against Debs and the union. Debs and other leaders went to prison, and he was not released until 1895. In the process, Debs became one of the most famous members of the labor movement in the nation. Politicians such as Theodore Roosevelt denounced his actions, but Debs built a base of support among the working people to whom he most appealed.

After supporting William Jennings Bryan and free silver in 1896, Debs moved over the next four years in the direction of the socialists and their more radical assault on American politics. By 1900, as the various factions in the movement came together to form the Socialist Party, Debs seemed the natural choice to run for president. He was the closest thing that the third-party organizers had to a national figure who would be a credible and articulate speaker for the party's message. He argued on the stump that "Democracy and Plutocracy cannot continue to exist together in the State. Democracy must be given new life or cease to be." The initial presidential campaign brought Debs just under 97,000 votes. It was not an inspiring start for the new political organization, but few Socialists blamed Debs for the outcome.[7]

In the years that followed, Debs grappled with a problem that the Socialists never solved. Since they believed that capitalism was doomed and would give way to a socialist commonwealth where the government owned the means of production, they had scant patience with the political institutions that kept the rotten existing system in place. Winning elections and holding government office, some socialists argued, was a betrayal of the party's central ideas. "Voting for socialism," Debs maintained in 1911, "is not socialism any more than a menu is a meal."[8] It was another of the snappy phrases that Debs tossed off in his writings and speeches, but it missed the point. If voters were expected to buy into the message that Debs was preaching, it was only reasonable of them to ask what he would do should the Socialists come to power. A guest at a restaurant would not be much taken with a menu that offered only "food" as its bill of fare. Thus, the Socialists said they would provide the nation with a worker's commonwealth but then turned vague on the details.

Those who agreed with Debs called the exponents of an electoral strategy "slowcialists" and derided them for their willingness to compromise with the nation's power structure and the entrenched order. Adopting such tactics, said Debs and others, meant that the Socialists were becoming just another party that accepted the legitimacy of capitalism. Revolutionaries had to be made of sterner stuff.

The socialists, however, could not just sit around and wait for capitalism to collapse. Americans on the left, like their colleagues in the traditional parties, wanted to see results that indicated the victory was on the way. Debs might proclaim the superior virtues of educating citizens about socialism over holding public office, but it was always hard to measure just how much allegiance to socialism had spread in the abstract. Elections offered a tangible marker of progress toward the better society they were seeking. Getting more votes for president, national, state, and local offices indicated that the movement was gaining momentum.

For those on the left of socialism, such a debate was irrelevant. The important consideration was to destroy the existing order at the earliest possible time through whatever means necessary, up to and including violence. The Industrial Workers of the World (IWW), under the leadership of William D. "Big Bill" Haywood, advocated a confrontational strategy that embraced violent tactics if necessary to win strikes, mobilize public opinion, or exact revenge for capitalist crimes. The "Wobblies," as they were known, were a small percentage of the Socialist movement, but they had an influence out of proportion to their numbers. Their tactics offered a natural target for conservatives in both major parties to label as outside the political mainstream. Theodore Roosevelt, for example, used the tactics of the Wobblies as a major negative theme against both the Socialists and the Democrats in the congressional elections of 1906.

From the founding of the Wobblies through the run-up to the 1912 campaign, the Socialists debated whether to repudiate the IWW as a way of deflecting criticism from their mainstream opponents. Debs admired the underlying principle of the IWW that all workers should be part of "one big union." He had little sympathy for the craft union approach of the American Federation of Labor and its leader, Samuel Gompers. But after an initial brief membership in the IWW, Debs moved away from the group and its violent ideology as counterproductive.

The Socialist movement was more than just Gene Debs. It included such other figures as the New York attorney and unsuccessful congressional candidate Morris Hillquit, whose approach looked to the election of party members to local, state, and national offices. His gradualism put him and his followers on the right of the party. He believed that Americans were "already living at least in the outskirts of the 'Socialist state.'" That statement put him at odds with the left wing of his party who believed that more fundamental change was needed in the United States.[9]

Another major Socialist on the right was Victor Berger of Milwaukee, Wisconsin. In that midwestern city, Berger showed his talents as a political organizer among the German American population. He created the Socialist equivalent of an electoral machine that took him to a seat in the House of Representatives in 1910. Debs told him, "Your election marks the beginning of the end of capitalism and the end of the beginning of Socialism in the United States." That mood of harmony would not last long. Born in Germany, Berger was a gradualist who believed in small, incremental steps toward the ultimate Socialist end. He did not "expect to revolutionize the congress of the United States single-handed." The step-by-step approach had worked for him in Milwaukee where his followers captured local offices such as aldermen and elected a mayor from their party, Emil Seidel, in 1910.[10]

The Socialist campaign in 1912 drew on some of the lessons learned from the effort Debs had made four years earlier. Optimistic regarding the party's chances against William Jennings Bryan for the Democrats and Taft for the Republicans in 1908, the Socialists had decided to have Debs embark on a campaign by train. The cost of such a tour reached $35,000. The party members raised the necessary cash through subscriptions, and the "Red Special" pulled out of Chicago on 30 August 1908. The crowds that gathered to see Debs were large and friendly. As a candidate, he naturally felt more hopeful about the chances of pulling a large vote in November because of the train and the publicity that it generated for the Socialist cause. "The enthusiasm it inspires everywhere is a marvel to me," Debs wrote. "If nothing else it would be worth ten times its cost to the movement."[11]

As they would do again in 1912, Debs and the Socialists confused celebrity with electoral effectiveness. While Debs could always attract an audience, he was dissipating his energies on the cross-country tour. There was little in the way of follow-up directed at the people who came out to see the candidate and his train. In Milwaukee, Berger and his allies did some of the hard electoral work, but elsewhere the effort was spotty. Socialism lacked real organizing techniques nationally and the Debs campaign remained unfocused. Predictions that the Socialist total would exceed 500,000 or even attain 1 million votes proved off the mark. The Socialist ticket reached almost 421,000 votes, an improvement of 20,000 votes over the result in 1904. Nonetheless, it was a major setback to Debs and his comrades since they had expected to achieve so much more.[12]

The Socialists pondered the disappointing outcome in 1908 and blamed the recovery from the Panic of 1907, the competing appeal of

Bryan, and the efforts of the popular Theodore Roosevelt on behalf of Taft. For the radical party, deeply divided about its political mission, presidential elections were not events to analyze in search of lessons. Elections provided a political theater in which the drama of socialism could be played out. That maximizing the vote might involve addressing the regional, interest-group, and historical affiliations of their constituents did not register with Socialists. They saw "the people" as an undifferentiated mass of the oppressed. When they spoke about the "rising tide" of their movement, Socialists relied on the impersonal forces of history to do much of their work for them.

As the Progressive campaigns for reform crested between 1909 and 1913, Socialists witnessed the striking gains their party made at the polls. Republican factionalism and Democratic fealty to limited government, as well as the mounting burden of inflation, made protest votes against the two major parties more attractive. The success of Berger in Milwaukee as a candidate for Congress in 1910, mayoral victories in Schenectady, New York, and other cities, and an increasing number of elected local officials indicated that the party was on the march. The total of dues-paying members mounted, and the party headquarters adopted a capitalist-like budget to manage its yearly income. Stumping in his usual manner during October 1910, Debs reported that "our meetings are jammed and overflowing at almost every point." He added: "It's coming, old man, like a cyclone on the war path."[13]

Amid the excitement of the 1910 election season, socialism suffered a public relations blow that would impede the party's capacity to organize for the presidential contest ahead. In Los Angeles, a bomb exploded at the headquarters of the *Los Angeles Times* on 1 October 1910. The attack grew out of a campaign to unionize the newspaper that the conservative publisher, Harrison Gray Otis, owned. The antiunion Otis had vowed that his business would never be organized. The explosive had been planted by two members of the union, the McNamara brothers, John J. and James, but that, of course, was not known to Socialists at the time. With twenty people dead as a result of the blast, conservatives and even some progressives such as Theodore Roosevelt immediately blamed radicals and labor organizers. The Socialists responded that the guilt lay with the bosses and upper classes who might have set the bomb themselves. Debs charged, for example that "the finger of guilt points steadily in the direction of General Harrison Gray Otis."[14]

Over the next year, Debs and the other members of the Socialist leadership pushed their argument about the Los Angeles episode. It could, Debs wrote an aide, "be made a very great thing if we could only handle it." When the McNamara brothers were extradited to Los Angeles and went on trial in April 1911, Socialists came to their defense as victims of the corruption of the capitalist legal system. Meanwhile, the Socialist Labor Party in Los Angeles ran a candidate named Job Harriman for mayor who seemed to be making a credible race. As he told Morris Hillquit in November 1911, "We are conducting a large campaign and doing it in systematic order. The other people are frightened to death. I believe we will be able to rout them."[15]

In early December 1911, the lawyer for the McNamaras, the famous Clarence Darrow, worked out a plea agreement with the prosecution under which his clients admitted their guilt in exchange for sentences of life in prison. The outcome embarrassed the Socialists and the labor unions who had maintained the innocence of the defendants for so long. Harriman lost his mayoral bid and any prospect of an alliance between the Socialists, and organized labor also was disrupted. As Harriman wrote after the votes were counted, "I, of course, knew that we had no chance of election as soon as the plea of guilty was entered, but, we would have been elected had this not happened. Twenty or twenty-five thousand votes were changed by that act."[16] The case also underlined the problems that socialism had with the issue of violence as a revolutionary weapon in the class struggle. The more that the party and its leaders had to discuss whether they supported extreme measures to pursue their goals, the more they undercut their potential appeal to voters who might be otherwise inclined to vote for socialism.

The outcome of the McNamara trial overshadowed to some degree the real gains that the Socialists had made in local elections in November 1911. In Schenectady, New York, a clergyman named George R. Lunn captured the office of mayor on the party's ticket. A key to Lunn's success was unhappiness with the two major parties and the promise that the Socialists made not to raise city taxes. The winner brought in a majority of the city council with him, and the Socialists also elected one of their candidates to the New York Assembly, the lower house of the state legislature. In his inaugural speech on 8 January 1912, Lunn recognized that capitalism would not disappear from his city, "but we can and will demonstrate to all the spirit of Socialism and the application of Socialist principles insofar as possible with the handicap of laws framed to establish and sustain capitalism." The party also elected a mayor in Berkeley, California. Debs wrote that "the election returns were glorious."[17]

Within the party, however, fissures remained between the proponents of more direct action to bring down capitalism and the reformist faction of Berger and Hillquit, who emphasized political tactics. Personality conflicts and character flaws also impeded Socialist success. One of the key organizing figures for a prospective national campaign was J. Mahlon Barnes, a brewer with the ability to manage Debs's schedule, who served as party secretary. Unfortunately, he was a chronic womanizer, and in 1911 it was revealed that he had harassed several female employees. In one case, the object of his attentions had become pregnant. After a probe within the party, the investigating committee concluded that Barnes had mismanaged office accounts and engaged in sexual relations with three of his employees. Barnes was compelled to resign his position. Despite his misdeeds, sentiment for his return as the manager of the impending Debs campaign persisted among Socialists on the right of the party. As so often happened, Debs did not take a clear stand on the Barnes matter. He did not think it his place to assume an explicit leadership role in the internal politics of the Socialists.[18]

An eruption of labor unrest in the Northeast during early 1912 indicated that the Socialists could achieve further electoral gains in the presidential contest. A strike in Lawrence, Massachusetts, against the American Woolen Company and other textile manufacturers attracted national attention both for the demands of the workers and the violent response of the owners to the walkout. Victor Berger used his influence as a representative to have hearings on the controversy in March 1912 that further dramatized the episode for the public. The presence of William Haywood and the Industrial Workers of the World in Lawrence further intensified the drama surrounding the strike.[19]

Yet for all the optimism that they felt going into the 1912 election, the Socialists, faction ridden as they were, still had to select a presidential candidate. The ruling assumption within the party was that Debs would be making another race. By now he was fifty-six and not in the best of health. He had a breakdown with lumbago and reported to his brother that he "fell on the floor & was helpless & suffered all the tortures of damnation until 2 or 3 days ago." Work with an osteopath and regular exercise restored his health to a degree, but he knew that a protracted campaign would be an ordeal for him. Yet as long as he did not take himself out of the race for the nomination he was likely to be the party's choice. He would say after he was selected that "I did not desire and I did not expect the nomination." He then added, "I did everything I felt that I properly could do to avoid it." But so long as he declined to make an unequivocal statement of withdrawal, he was almost certain to be the Socialist nominee.[20]

The party held its national convention in the middle of May in Indianapolis, Indiana. As the first "chairman for the day," Morris Hillquit welcomed the delegates with the news that the Socialist Party had shown itself to be a "factor in the social, political and public life of the country." He predicted that the party might elect as many as a dozen members of Congress in the fall election. Above all, the Socialists had persuaded "a large portion of the working class" that their party was the only organization "that truly, fully, at all times represents their interests and fights their battles."[21]

Though the gathering was not that far from Debs and his home in Terre Haute, he remained away from the proceedings in the mold of the national candidates of the major parties. That posture made little political sense. If, as he said, he did not want the nomination, he could have easily made an appearance at the conclave, informed the delegates of his wishes, and ended the matter at once. If, however, he craved another race, then a visit to Indianapolis would have enabled him to determine who would run his campaign, influence the content of the platform, and determine the party's stance on key issues. By staying at home, he managed to produce the least attractive result when it came time to make the national campaign.

Indianapolis had been the birthplace of the Socialists a dozen years earlier. For seven days, from 12 May until 18 May 1912, the talkative Socialists debated the issues on which they were divided and their plans for the future. The leading problem was the question of violence in achieving the promised commonwealth. Earlier in the year, Haywood had said publicly that Socialists should use "a little sabotage in the right place at the proper time." Debs disagreed with this controversial approach and said so in the Socialist press. He wanted the national convention to come out against sabotage and terrorism but not to do so in a manner that further split the party. Without the direct intervention of Debs to articulate the party's position, some factional unhappiness could not be avoided.[22]

Berger, Hillquit, and their allies believed that it was imperative for the future of the party to go on record against such tactics. In their view, anarchism "made individual brigandage possible under the cloak of an ideal. I am not willing that our party should stand godfather for any business of that kind." They expected to expel Haywood and the Wobblies if that was what it took to achieve their goals. Better organized than their opponents, the right-wing Socialists (who were all far more radical than Republicans or Democrats) also hoped that they might defeat Debs for the nomination.[23]

The problem for the anti-Debs forces was the lack of a credible candidate with anything like the charisma and fame that Debs possessed. The two alternatives were Emil Seidel, the mayor of Milwaukee, and Charles Edward Russell, a New York journalist who had aligned himself with the Socialists in 1908. In April, Seidel lost his race for reelection in a decisive defeat. That reverse limited Seidel's appeal as a national candidate. As a late convert to socialism who was not a member of the working class, Russell enjoyed little support outside of his home state. Neither Victor Berger nor Morris Hillquit could run since they both had been born in Europe. So Debs it was in 1912.

The nomination came on the fifth day of deliberations. The party deliberately avoided the hoopla and demonstrations characteristic of the major party conventions. Since the rules of the Socialist Party prohibited nominating and seconding speeches for candidates, there was no explicit statement of the claims of each hopeful for the nomination. Hillquit attempted to start a discussion about the suitability of the various potential nominees, but that gambit did not succeed. A roll call vote at once ensued with the final tally showing 165 votes for Debs, 56 for Seidel, and 54 for Russell. The delegates then held another vote and chose Seidel as the running mate for Debs. Debs was the candidate with a national base among the 275 delegates. Seidel was strong in his own state of Wisconsin and three other states. Russell was essentially the candidate of New York. Debs promised those who had voted for him that "I shall now get myself in shape for the campaign and I shall make the fight of my life."[24]

Decisions made at the convention beyond the choice of a presidential nominee set the limits within which the Debs campaign would operate for the rest of 1912. On the day that Debs was nominated, the issue of the party's attitude toward violence as a tactic came up for debate when the delegates decided on amendments to the party's constitution. The key question was expressed in an amendment to Article II, Section 6, of the party's charter:

*Socialist candidate Eugene V. Debs (left) and his running mate Emil Seidel made an aggressive national campaign in what Debs described as "our year" for his party. (*Great Leaders and National Issues of 1912 *[Philadelphia: J. C. Winston Co., 1912])*

Any member of the party who opposes political action or advocates crime, sabotage, or other methods of violence as a weapon of the working class to aid in its emancipation shall be expelled from membership in the party. Political action shall be construed to mean participation in elections for public office and practical legislative and administrative work along the lines of the Socialist party Platform.[25]

Hillquit, Berger, and their allies were the directing forces of this change, and their target was clearly Haywood and the IWW. "That looks like it was aimed at me," Haywood told the press. A debate ensued in which the issue divided the convention. One of the proponents of the amendment said that "it is high time for this convention to take a distinct stand and declare that it is opposed to every form of crime and violence (great cheering)." Another advocate asserted that the convention represented "the high tide of socialism." As a result, the gathering should "put the stamp of its disapproval upon any anti-social, anti-constructive proceeding." Opponents of the language did not defend violence as such. They argued that the change was unnecessary, the word "sabotage" was divisive, and individual labor unions and other organizations should decide when or if violence in a strike or industrial dispute was justified in response to capitalist oppression.[26]

Victor Berger summed up the attitude of the backers of the amendment. "This is the time to draw the line between a real Socialist revolution on one side and anarchy, murder, and sabotage on the other." The decisive vote came on a procedural motion to remove the amendment from the Socialist constitution. It failed by a vote of 90 in favor to 191 opposed. The delegates then adopted the constitution on a voice vote. Non-Socialist publications praised the action of the delegates. The *Outlook*, associated with Theodore Roosevelt, said that the result "will be welcome to Americans without regard to party."[27]

The convention also put forth the platform on which Debs and Seidel would run in the fall. The language denounced capitalism in the United States as "the source of unspeakable misery and suffering to the whole working class." The document called for "the collective ownership and democratic management" of railroads, telegraphs, and "all large-scale industries." Among the specific economic demands were a shorter workday and workweek, an end to child labor, a minimum wage, and old-age and unemployment insurance. An income tax and estate tax would fund "the socialization of industry." The Socialists also sought the abolition of the Senate, an end of the power of the Supreme Court to declare laws unconstitutional, and equal suffrage for men and women.[28]

On issues of race, ethnicity, and gender, the Socialists presented an intriguing blend of innovation and regressive views. As far as African Americans were concerned, the party took a positive stance toward their right to be included in the political process. In practice, currents of prejudice ran through the rhetoric of Berger and others. The most celebrated black Socialist was W. E. B. Du Bois. He would defect to Wilson in 1912 in the vain hope that the Democratic candidate could rise above his party's prejudiced doctrines and attitudes. Since so many Socialists were of immigrant background, the party was hospitable to newcomers from Europe. When it came to Asiatic immigrants, however, the Socialists mirrored the opposition of trade unionists to cheaper competition from China and Japan. Exclusion legislation found support from within the Socialist community.

In the deliberation of the Socialists, women played a significant public part. They were a visible presence at national conventions. In 1912, 10 percent of the delegates at Indianapolis were women. The party created a Women's National Committee in 1908, and state parties followed this precedent in their organization. These tangible gestures, however, did not reflect a strong commitment to enhancing the role of women in the deliberations of the Socialists. Women Socialists complained that the male leadership acted in a patronizing and condescending manner. Their work occurred within a separate party organization, apart from the main activities of Debs and the other leaders.

As the convention wound up its business on the final day of deliberations, Morris Hillquit proposed that a campaign committee be created, along with a campaign manager, to run the Debs canvass in the fall. For that key post, Hillquit nominated J. Mahlon Barnes because "the party has very few men, if any men as efficient, as painstaking, as devoted, and, on the whole, as fit for the position as Comrade Barnes." Hillquit added that Barnes had been the subject "of the campaign of slander instituted against him and the hunting up of matters dead and buried years ago and their publication in Socialist papers." When asked, Hillquit said that the nomination of Barnes was his idea, but he intimated that the general plan of the campaign and the need of a manager came with the unanimous support of the National Executive Committee and the Committee on the Constitution. With these assurances, the selection of Barnes went through.[29]

The Barnes choice displeased Debs and he told the manager that he hoped for a shorter, more focused campaign than in 1908. "I shall want a voice in determining what the program shall be," he informed Barnes on 31 May. He added that "I wish no arrangement made which involves me without being consulted." He asked to have "my dates arranged and program made with the same consideration for the limitations of human capacity and endurance that every comrade expects for himself."[30]

Meanwhile, plans went forward to have Debs deliver his formal opening speech of the campaign in Chicago at Riverside Park on 16 June. The Republican convention was assembling at the same time, and the Socialists hoped to gain favorable attention for their cause from the city's newspapers. While he usually delivered his remarks from memory or with a few notes, Debs told the sizable crowd that gathered on this occasion: "I concluded for obvious reasons to reduce it to writing, in order to prevent my remarks from being garbled or misrepresented by the capitalist papers."[31]

The resulting speech revealed both the strengths and weaknesses of Debs as a national candidate. He was very effective in criticizing the two major parties as representatives of the ruling class and the capitalist system. "There is no longer even the pretense of difference between the so-called Republican and Democratic parties. They are substantially one in what they stand for." He asked the responsive crowd "what difference is there, judged by what they stand for, between Taft, Roosevelt, La Follette, Harmon, Wilson, Clark and Bryan?" For a workingman to join with the major parties "is the badge of his ignorance, his servility and shame." The Socialists, in contrast, identified with the workers whether in Lawrence, Massachusetts, the lumber camps of the Northwest, or among railroad employees striking for their rights. He predicted that "the people, especially the toilers and producers, will be far more receptive to the truth of Socialism than ever before." Voters, said Debs, "are now prepared to cast their fortune with the only political party that proposes a change of system and the only party that has a right to appeal to the intelligence of the people."[32]

Yet when it came down to offering concrete reasons for people to vote for the Socialists, Debs's language turned more vague. Socialists, he went on, are "not in the vote market." The party "wants votes but only of those who want it—those who recognise it as their party, and come to it of their own free will," rather than seeking specific results. He praised the party's platform and the work of Victor Berger in Congress, but he

provided few details as to how voting Socialist would address the immediate needs of undecided voters. The oppressed workers, he said, should
organize themselves into industrial unions that drew in all of the ranks
of labor, not just individual crafts.[33]

Debs did not discuss the provisions of the platform that might advance the agenda of the party or sway potential voters to the Socialist
side. If one of his listeners were to have asked, "What could voting Socialist do for me?" Debs would not have supplied any clear answer. Yet
in the platform were ideas about both procedural changes in how democracy operated and substantive proposals about a minimum wage,
child labor, and old-age insurance that might well have appealed to one
of Debs's listeners. Content with his standard exhortation about the
evils of capitalism, Debs could not move in 1912 to adapt his rhetoric
to the needs of the current campaign. His appearances remained more
in the nature of rhetorical flourishes than political speeches designed to
expand the size of the Socialist electoral coalition.

The Socialist campaign had by this time encountered a persistent distraction that occupied Debs's limited energies for much of the summer.
The selection of J. Mahlon Barnes to run the campaign had produced a
an outpouring of protests from his critics within the party. The charges
of womanizing and corruption were revived amid cries for Barnes's removal. Letters assailing Barnes flooded in to Debs at his home in Terre
Haute, Indiana. "The storm is gathering and is going to break in all its
fury," he wrote to one of Barnes's defenders. For Debs, it was "nothing
less than a calamity to have the party ripped wide open and disembowl
[sic] itself on the eve of a campaign."[34]

The charges against Barnes about sexual transgressions and corrupt behavior took on renewed urgency as the presidential race neared.
"There are thousands now demanding to know if the party is now committed to free love," Debs wrote to John Spargo, a major Barnes backer,
"and you and Hillquit and a few others will be given full opportunity to
answer." As the controversy developed, questions arose about the assurances Morris Hillquit had provided regarding the attitude of the National Executive Committee toward the Barnes selection. Critics charged
that Hillquit had dissembled when he indicated that the committee had
agreed to the Barnes choice. In addition, Hillquit sought to have the
published proceedings of the convention altered to cover up what he
had said. As Debs wrote, "the convention was tricked and deceived by
Hillquit's falsehood and misrepresentation."[35]

The Socialists provided an elaborate mechanism for the members of the party to conduct a referendum on a disputed matter, nomination, or leader. That procedure soon came into play in the Barnes case. As the rhetoric on both sides intensified, the presidential campaign faded in importance. The *Christian Socialist* asked its readers: "Does the party want a convicted adulterer as campaign manager?" Fred Warren, editor of the party journal *Appeal to Reason*, told Debs, "I am at a loss to understand what could have prompted Hillquit and Spargo to put this over on the party unless it was for the purpose, as you so clearly point out to the latter, of humiliating you and placing you on the defensive throughout the campaign."[36]

Although he had talked of a brief campaign, the irrepressible Debs was out on the stump in New England in late June. Meanwhile, the storm over Barnes gathered strength as his critics made their unhappiness ever more public. A full-scale referendum became inevitable. On 20 July, a letter from Debs was released in which he said "that the matter should be settled by a national referendum of the party, and the sooner the better." The Socialists, in the midst of the presidential campaign, thus went forward with an intraparty struggle as well. The final result, released a month before the balloting in October, was that 19,000 members cast votes to keep Barnes as the campaign manager while 11,500 were recorded against him. All the fire and fury had produced no change in the situation.[37]

The published letters of Eugene Debs document how much this controversy occupied his time and energy during the summer of 1912. He could have stood behind Barnes and ended the tumult in a timely manner. Or he could have dumped the campaign manager for someone else to end the unnecessary distraction. Instead, the furor turned into a controversy about Debs and his sense of honor. He became more bitter about the tactics that had been used against him and the demands that were made upon him as a campaigner. His opponents, however, contended that "one thing is sure—the heart has been taken out of the campaign, and the direct Action gang have what they wanted." As he had done before, Debs wanted to be the recognized head of the Socialists without having to dirty his hands with the organizational labors that the party needed at this juncture to broaden its electoral coalition and become a viable alternative to the Republicans and the Democrats.[38]

What the result of the 1912 election could have been had Debs and his fellow Socialists been able to concentrate on the campaign without the distraction of the Barnes affair can never be known. Debs allowed himself to be drawn into the controversy during the summer of 1912 and did not exercise the kind of decisive leadership that a national political campaign required. The time wasted on the Barnes debacle might better have been spent identifying a productive electoral strategy through which the Socialist vote could have been maximized. Nor did Debs seek to achieve party unity through conferences with Berger or Hillquit. But that was not the kind of party direction that Debs provided throughout his public career. He was always a herald of socialism, not its organizer. To a large extent, the Socialists saw the presidential contest as an interruption before they could get back to the serious business of arguing among themselves about the best way to achieve the revolution and the commonwealth that would replace the capitalist state.

While the mainstream press and opinion journals approached socialism in 1912 with some degree of condescension, that posture made sense. The party that Debs led did not pose a serious intellectual challenge to the major political parties because the Socialist nominee did not engage the issues in a manner that compelled Roosevelt, Wilson, and Taft to respond to his critiques. Socialist hecklers might assail Roosevelt, for example, at some of his rallies during his campaign tours, but these were pinpricks that never jostled the candidate or his audiences. Like these operatives, Debs was a gadfly who could irritate and provoke his rivals in the political system. Yet he was not someone whom they had to take seriously because he failed to offer a sustained analysis of where their dominant organizations had come up short in serving the interests of the American people.

The interplay within the Socialist Party did not dominate the headlines during the summer of 1912. The aftermath of the Republican and Democratic conventions attracted continuing press coverage. Most commentators, however, wondered what Theodore Roosevelt would do. Could the former president create a party on the run and make a serious try to regain the White House? The month of July would bring the call for a meeting of the Progressives in Chicago in early August. Out of that gathering would come the third major party and the fourth presidential candidate in a year that few others in the nation's history could match for the quality of the individuals seeking to lead the people of the United States.

6
THE BULL MOOSE CHALLENGE TO THE MAJOR PARTIES

I want to be a Bull Moose,
And with the Bull Moose stand
With Antlers on my forehead
And a Big Stick in my hand.
—Banner at the Progressive Convention[1]

In writing the history of a presidential election, one can easily convey the impression that a majority of the American people felt a passionate interest in the outcome of what now seemed likely to be a four-cornered race for the White House. The activities of President William Howard Taft, Governor Woodrow Wilson, "Colonel" Theodore Roosevelt, and Eugene V. Debs certainly received ample news coverage during the months of July and August. But the picture of what was holding the attention of the average citizen would not be complete without a brief recognition that other stories were in play during that year. To what extent these distractions affected the decisions of Americans to go to the polls in November is still a disputed matter among students of the 1912 election.

During July 1912, Americans read their daily newspapers to learn how their country was faring in the Olympics, held that year in Stockholm, Sweden. One particular member of the U.S. team, Jim Thorpe of the Carlisle Indian School in Pennsylvania, had captured the public's imagination. A collegiate football star, Thorpe was a gifted athlete to whom all sports came easy. He and his teammates had departed for Sweden in late June, and the press cabled back accounts of their preparation for the fourth Olympiad.[2]

THE HUNTERS
The "Special Privilege" Hunters gleefully anticipating the capture of the "Bull Moose."
From the *North American* (Philadelphia)

This cartoon from the Philadelphia North American *showed two hunters from "special privilege" planning how to mount a bull moose head while a giant moose comes out of the forest to smash them. (*American Review of Reviews 46 *[October 1912]: 422)*

When the games began, the American team surprised the experts with a dominant performance. The United States achieved first place in sixteen events and outscored their main rivals, Sweden and England. Thorpe won the decathlon and pentathlon and established himself as "the finest all-around athlete in the world." Parades and accolades greeted the Americans when they returned home. A million people turned out to honor the team in a parade in New York City. Big-time sports had made their way into the national consciousness in a manner that politics could not equal for excitement and general enthusiasm.[3]

While following the Olympics in mid-July, the newspaper-reading public became absorbed in another kind of drama. On 15 July, a New York City gambler named Herman Rosenthal was shot and killed just outside the Metropole Hotel at 43rd Street in what would later become the style for a gangland "hit." In the days leading up to his murder, Rosenthal had promised sensational revelations about police corruption in New York, and there was immediate suspicion that crooked cops had arranged his execution. The New York force was notorious for allegations of bribes and payoffs, and the Rosenthal murder grabbed headlines across the country.[4]

Within two weeks, a police lieutenant named Charles Becker was charged with Rosenthal's murder and arrested. The case soon became one of those "trials of the century" that occurred periodically during the decades after 1900. Aggressive newspaper reporting fed the public's fascination with tales of payoffs and intriguing underworld figures such as "Lefty Louie" and "Gyp the Blood." The prosecution and trial of Lieutenant Becker extended throughout the fall and vied with the political campaign in its coverage. Newspapers as far away as Texas put pictures of the accused on their front pages day after day.[5]

The political campaign, in contrast, had much of its inherent drama drained away with Woodrow Wilson's victory at the Baltimore Convention. The conventional wisdom, which in this instance had a point, said that, if Wilson polled the normal Democratic vote, he would likely defeat both Taft and Roosevelt. As the wife of a Democratic member of the House wrote in late August, "It looks as if nothing but an accident can prevent Wilson's election, not because the country wants him especially, but because of Roosevelt's madness in splitting the G.O.P."[6]

A resolute Roosevelt could count as well as any other politician, but he did not intend to abandon his presidential hopes without at least making a run at another White House term. Much hinged on whether he could sustain interest in his fledgling third-party effort. To that end, he turned to his dependable asset—his gift for excitement and publicity.

When he arrived in Chicago for the Republican National Convention in June 1912, Theodore Roosevelt told reporters that he felt like a "bull moose." It was an image he had used several times before, but on this occasion his words caught the popular fancy. Cartoonists soon depicted a moose with Roosevelt's face in many political situations. The name also stuck and Roosevelt's new political creation was given the nickname "The Bull Moose Party." In the days after the fractured Republicans left Chicago, the nation's attention shifted back and forth between the Democrats in Baltimore and speculation about what Roosevelt would do next. In 1912, there was no summer lull after the political conventions concluded. During this election the continuous campaigning that would arrive later in the century had a kind of preview outing.[7]

For Roosevelt these weeks before his party assembled for its first national convention in early August were filled with crucial decisions about the fate of his new, untried adventure in third-party organizing. The divorce from the Republicans was not an amicable one, and dividing up the property and arranging for custody of the institutional structure of the Grand Old Party led to many intricate partisan battles. Roosevelt's indignation, which had led him out of the Republican ranks, proved easy to sustain as he and Taft vied for control of their political destinies. More difficult was the creation of a new party from the ground up in a few weeks in the middle of an election year. Roosevelt's failure to have thought through his bolt before he made up his mind proved one of the most significant obstacles to the success of his venture.

In the aftermath of the Republican National Convention, Roosevelt could gain some solace from the plight of Taft and the conservatives in the Grand Old Party. The president and his allies were in disarray after Chicago, and their prospects for the fall seemed at best bleak. They agreed that even a drubbing in November would be worth it since their actions had ended "the menace that existed in the possibility of Theodore Roosevelt becoming again President of the United States." Such sentiments pervaded the old guard wing of the party. "It was essential," wrote Vice President Sherman, "both for the life of our party and the continuance of our Government that the Bull Moose and his ilk should be sidetracked." As one senator noted, "The overweening ambition of Roosevelt has upset everything for the republican party."[8]

Having told each other how much they relished beating Roosevelt, Republicans then confronted the formidable task of gearing up to run a national campaign. The overwhelming consensus among professionals was that they faced a hopeless battle. "The present outlook for the Rep. Party is anything but satisfactory," was a typical verdict. Newspapers issued forecasts right after the Democratic convention that predicted Wilson would be the winner. A spirit of defeatism influenced how the Republicans prepared for the campaign. Taft declared that he would follow the precedent, observed by William McKinley in 1900 and Roosevelt in 1904, that an incumbent president should not campaign for reelection. That decision meant for the Republicans that they had no major active public leader making their case to the electorate.[9]

While he had resigned himself intellectually to defeat, Taft did want another four years in the White House. He stayed off the campaign trail and made only a few strategic appearances during the fall before carefully selected audiences. He also gave interviews about his policy positions. The president worked with Charles D. Hilles to set up an organization, raise funds, and make the Republican case in print, through movies and extensive and expensive advertising, and by sending out surrogate speakers. Taft sought to insure that Republicans everywhere had a chance to vote for him and not find themselves with Roosevelt as the only alternative to Wilson. Thus, Taft sought to "make the Republican party solid for conservatism and whatever happens in November we'll swat our enemies later on."[10]

Putting together that kind of campaign taxed the energies of Taft and Hilles throughout the summer. It was difficult to induce important politicians to serve on the Taft campaign committee. The president also had to persuade some of the more conservative figures, such as the scandal-ridden senator, Boies Penrose of Pennsylvania, and William Barnes, the unsavory political boss of New York Republicans, to decline leadership roles that might embarrass the party because of their sins in the past.

Hilles experienced the greatest problem finding a treasurer for the Taft effort. He complained to Taft on 4 August that "the Treasureship, like the poor, we have with us always." Raising money was an unusual problem for the GOP, which had been so well funded in the past. In 1912, with defeat looming, checkbooks closed, corporations withdrew, and money men fled the scene of the GOP disaster. As a result, the Republicans had about $900,000 to spend. For the most part, however, Taft was able to keep the regular Republicans in line behind the ticket.[11]

The major political appearance that Taft made during that summer was his formal acceptance of the Republican presidential nominate on 1 August at the White House. With his wife and several hundred guests listening, Taft laid out the case for his reelection. The president had debated whether to make a defense of his title to the nomination, but decided not to draw more attention to the issue. Instead, he referred to Roosevelt only as a man "whose recently avowed political views would have committed the party to radical proposals involving dangerous changes to our present constitutional form of representative government and our independent judiciary."[12]

Taft went on to enumerate Republican achievements and then spoke of "popular unrest" in which "demagogues have seized the opportunity further to inflame the public mind and have sought to turn the peculiar conditions to their advantage." Wilson and Roosevelt, Taft said, were not socialists as such, "but if their promises mean anything, they lead directly toward the appropriation of what belongs to one man, to another." The confrontation with Roosevelt had emphasized for Taft his conservative leanings, and his acceptance speech continued his party's rightward shift.[13]

Like other Republicans in this difficult year, Taft returned to a familiar party theme, the appeal of the protective tariff. Under the workings of the Payne-Aldrich Tariff, he said, "Prosperity has been gradually restored since the panic of 1907." If the Democrats won, however, the country could "anticipate a serious injury to a large part of our manufacturing industry." He decried the Democratic platform for declaring the tariff unconstitutional and warned that the changes the opposition proposed would "produce a condition of suffering among the people that no reforming legislation could neutralize or mitigate."[14] Henry Cabot Lodge said that the speech showed "a good fighting spirit" and would help to rally "the conservative forces of the country" behind "the maintenance of the Constitution, preservation of representative government, and the independence of the Courts."[15] In fact, the speech did not ignite Taft's candidacy. The country was still watching to see what Roosevelt intended to do with his third-party race.

If Roosevelt as the potential Progressive candidate had expected a surge of support from either mainline Republican progressives or sympathetic Democrats, he was soon disappointed. Many of those politicians who had first encouraged his run against Taft and then worked with him up through the Republican National Convention made clear their dislike for the third-party option. Senator William E. Borah of Idaho was one of the most prominent departures from the Roosevelt camp. Such progressives as Albert B. Cummins and Jonathan Bourne of Oregon, while voting for Roosevelt, stayed in the Grand Old Party. Former Roosevelt stalwarts, including Ormsby McHarg, remained Republicans. The most venomous of the progressives was Robert La Follette, who refused to support Taft, gave Wilson tacit endorsement through favorable mentions in his journal, and was infuriated about Roosevelt. He joined forces with Senator Penrose and other reactionary Republicans in the upper house in devising ways to discomfit Roosevelt's campaign in and out of the Senate.[16]

There was never much real chance that Democrats would defect to Roosevelt even if the party nominated a colorless figure such as Champ Clark. Bryan made noises about doing so, but he was hardly serious. In the end it did not matter. The nomination of Woodrow Wilson, an avowed progressive, produced greater Democratic unity than anyone had anticipated. Roosevelt knew from the action of the Baltimore Convention that his chances of victory were at best slim. As he said the day before Wilson won the prize, "In strict confidence, my feeling is that the Democrats will probably win if they nominate a progressive." But, he added, he intended to pursue his candidacy. "So I hoisted the flag and will win or fall under it."[17]

The big question that confronted Roosevelt during the weeks after the Chicago Convention was the precise nature of the new party that he sought to establish. If he ran simply as an independent candidate for president, then his movement would come down to a personal vendetta against Taft that could be seen as an exercise in egotism. Yet creating a new party in a matter of weeks was a major challenge, especially as it related to the existing machinery of the Republicans in states that were favorable to Roosevelt. In the spring primaries and convention, some presidential electors had been chosen who were favorable to Roosevelt. These individuals, so the argument went, might be left undisturbed on the ballot and cast their votes for Roosevelt if he won the popular vote in the state. The new party, in contrast, could put forward its own electors and candidates for state and local office. Or there could be an effort to incorporate both elements into the mix of what Roosevelt and his new party were trying to accomplish.

There were good arguments for trying to integrate the existing pro-Roosevelt electors into the emerging presidential campaign. In states where Roosevelt was strong, such as Pennsylvania and South Dakota, that would maximize the chances for victory. William Flinn, the Republican leader in Pittsburgh, suggested that a "combined electoral ticket," in which electors agreed to "accept the highest vote, whether Taft or Roosevelt, as binding instructions," would be a good answer.[18]

The problem was that any such half-measure would make it appear that Roosevelt was only trying to take the presidency away from Taft for his own reasons. If, however, the new party ran its own slate of candidates for election at all levels, that would tend to split the Republican vote and hand victory to the Democrats. Adding to Roosevelt's problem was the insistence of Taft and the regular Republicans that adherents of Roosevelt should be expelled from the party organization. The president's allies did just that in Ohio and several other states, where Roosevelt sympathizers were removed from leadership positions. None of the various schemes to mix and match the pro- and anti-Taft forces came to anything, but much infighting in individual states including Kansas, Pennsylvania, and South Dakota lay ahead during July and August. In the end, Roosevelt concluded that "we ought to have a straight-out progressive ticket, on which all progressive Democrats as well as Republicans can vote for me."[19]

The decision to opt for a third party had immediate consequences within Roosevelt's own family. His son-in-law, Nicholas Longworth, was a conservative Republican congressman from Ohio. He had married the former president's daughter in 1906, and their union was already in some difficulty. An accomplished violinist, Longworth also fiddled with other men's wives. The mercurial "Princess Alice" was a passionate supporter of her father's cause, and so her Republican husband was caught. He believed in the Republicans from an ideological perspective but for many weeks could not say so. He prevented his wife from attending the Progressive Convention, and she "cried a few salt tears." Meanwhile, he sought to obtain from his father-in-law a promise that the Progressives would not run a third-party candidate in his district. The relentless demands of the campaign on Roosevelt eventually mandated that Longworth's reelection would face a Progressive challenger. The word was that Longworth, because of the family situation, "had to be quiet and was unhappy about it." The election of 1912 was one of those rare occasions when the passions of the contest divided family members from each other.[20]

The Roosevelt campaign also pressed forward with the case that the nomination at Chicago had been stolen from the former president. A

war of charges and allegations about the four key states and their delegates went on throughout most of the summer. Both sides produced
elaborate statements of the merits of their position. Partisans in each
camp believed that the controversy made a difference. The details of the
dispute, however, were hard to follow and even more difficult to understand. By the time the Progressive Party held its convention in August,
the question of Taft's legitimate title to the Republican nomination no
longer seemed as urgent as it once did. Making the case, however, consumed a good deal of Roosevelt's energy during the month of July in the
prelude to the Progressive Convention.[21]

Once the decision had been made to follow the third-party route, a
national convention at which the delegates could select Roosevelt and
adopt a platform seemed the logical next step. A call for a meeting went
out in July. The first full week in August was selected and Chicago designated for the gathering. The Progressives would return to the scene of
the stolen GOP nomination, and the city could serve as a focal point for
Progressives from all over the country. The *Chicago Tribune* was friendly
to Roosevelt, which insured favorable coverage in the crucial Middle
West. For the Progressives in the summer of 1910, Chicago was their
kind of town.[22]

In these pivotal weeks, the role of financier George W. Perkins became more and more central to the success of Roosevelt's campaign.
The fifty-year-old Perkins had been a partner of J. P. Morgan and an
influential player in Republican politics. More than any other corporate
executive, he had developed an admiration for Roosevelt's ideas about
regulation through a federal commission. The money that Perkins supplied was indispensable to the Roosevelt cause, and the New Yorker
thereby gained a great deal of influence over how the Progressives were
organized. Too much, thought some Progressives, who complained that
Perkins promoted himself even more than Roosevelt. To have such a
prominent exponent of big business close to the presidential candidate somewhat undercut the perception that Roosevelt was pursuing
a radical course. Reformers from states where large corporations were
not popular viewed Perkins with increasing suspicion as the summer
progressed.[23]

During the month of July, the Roosevelt high command made a number of decisions that determined how the fall campaign would be waged.
These judgments reflected Roosevelt's flawed perceptions about his

*George W. Perkins was a major contributor and ideological soulmate for Roosevelt in the Progressive Party campaign. (*Great Leaders and National Issues of 1912 *[Philadelphia: J. C. Winston Co., 1912])*

situation and how best to proceed against Taft and Wilson. By running at all, Roosevelt had pretty well assured the defeat of Taft for reelection. As long as the Republicans were divided, the Democrats would prevail in any number of states that might have been more difficult for them to carry against a single Republican candidate, including New York, Illinois, and Indiana. As a realist, Roosevelt could recognize that his hated enemy was going to lose in November 1912. While satisfying from a personal standpoint, the defeat of Taft was only the first step in Roosevelt's effort to reshape American politics.

The question then became whether Roosevelt could win as a third-party candidate. That task presented greater problems. He would have to put together a coalition of states where he could reach the necessary 266 electoral votes for victory. In the end he would carry six states with eighty-eight electoral votes (California, Washington, South Dakota, Minnesota, Michigan, and Pennsylvania). Three of these states bordered on Canada, and Roosevelt was popular there because of his opposition to the reciprocity treaty of Taft's administration. Pennsylvania and South Dakota, while not contiguous with Canada, shared some of these sentiments. California went into Roosevelt's column because of the actions of Hiram Johnson and his followers in keeping Taft of the ballot.

If he had followed a more overt Canadian border strategy, Roosevelt might have gathered in the electoral votes of Maine, Vermont, and New Hampshire. He campaigned in Rhode Island, Massachusetts, and Vermont early in his canvass but then did not return to New England again. Victory in those three states would have added only fourteen electoral votes to his total, but that result would have edged him over the 100 electoral vote mark.

Where else might Roosevelt have sought support for the Progressive cause with some hope of success? The states of Iowa and Kansas, with another twenty-three electoral votes, would have been good candidates for more attention. Beyond that, there might have been prospects for wins in such states as Illinois and Maryland, where he had done well in the spring primaries, but Roosevelt's campaign would soon have bumped up against the inherent limits of his third-party race. The candidate was correct when he predicted that Wilson would likely win in 1912. The big question was whether Roosevelt was running just to beat Taft or to build a future for the Progressives. Since he tried to do both things at once, he ended up neither creating a base that would endure nor seriously threatening the chances of the Democrats and Wilson to prevail.

The intellectual confusion at the heart of Roosevelt's candidacy emerged first in the campaign strategy that he and his inner circle worked out in July. The program discussed involved a protracted cross-country campaign swing that would take Roosevelt through the Middle West and the Northwest, out to the Pacific Coast, and back across the desert Southwest through the South. The high command then prepared for another swing through the Middle West, ending with a climactic tour through the Middle Atlantic and New England states.

The strategy made little electoral sense. It would have Roosevelt campaigning in states with few votes and place him as well in the South and border states where the Democrats were strong. Moreover, it used up the energy and drive of the candidate to no real purpose. While it exploited Roosevelt's star power to attract crowds, it overlooked the lesson that the former president well understood. At a rally in Cleveland during the Ohio primary in the spring, a British reporter in attendance later talked with Roosevelt and reported that, "afterward at supper, somebody congratulated him on his reception. 'Barnum and Bailey,' he said, his voice rising shrilly, 'Pure Barnum and Bailey. It's my past that brings them; not my future—a trap for politicians like myself." That was the dilemma for Roosevelt in the fall of 1912. He wanted the campaign to be about the future, but his allure resided in his status as a celebrity and former president.[24]

One other decision of that summer's planning underscored the loose thinking that went into the Roosevelt campaign strategy. For his running mate on the Progressive ticket, Roosevelt selected the reform governor of California, Hiram W. Johnson. The choice provided some nice symbolism about the two coasts joining hands to pursue political change. But the selection turned out to be a bust. To be sure, the Johnson organization did deliver California for Roosevelt over Wilson. But that would have occurred even with another vice-presidential candidate since it was predicated on the exclusion of Taft from the ballot. Johnson himself was something of a dud as a campaigner. He resisted the schedule that Roosevelt headquarters mapped out for him and was sometimes late to key events. His leisurely routine of two appearances a day did not come close to fulfilling the demand for his services. For an improvised national campaign that needed everything to go right for an outside chance of victory, Johnson's egotism was a definite political minus.[25]

Facing the daunting electoral odds that he did in July 1912, Theodore Roosevelt determined on a high-risk strategy to make himself competitive in the region that had been the bastion of the Democrats since the Civil War. From the candidate's perspective, if he could mount a serious challenge to Wilson and the Democrats in the South there could be rich returns on Election Day. He was convinced that his new party might appeal to reform Democrats who, if they could get past the issue of race, might find his ideology very attractive. He believed that the Republicans had failed by trying to base their party in the South on black votes. As a result, he said, "there is not and cannot be in the Southern States a party based primarily upon the negro vote and under negro leadership or the leadership of white men who derive their power solely from negroes." The trick, of course, was how to get the status of black Americans out of his way, especially since race was what made the "Solid South" Democratic during this period. Like other Republicans, Roosevelt had engaged this problem for many years and had never found a viable solution that made the GOP a real challenger to "the party of the fathers" in Dixie.[26]

Southerners liked Roosevelt as president, but they never trusted him on racial matters. After all, they contended, he had entertained Booker T. Washington at the White House for a meal with the president's family in October 1901. During his first term, when Roosevelt was courting black Republicans to support his nomination in 1904, he had appointed African Americans to political posts in the South. To denizens of the fever swamp that was Democratic politics at its most racist in the South, these transgressions could never be forgiven or overcome. He had praised Abraham Lincoln and supported the Union victory in the Civil War. Why should they trust him? In fact, Southern Democrats had more confidence in Taft on racial issues without, of course, having any intention of voting for him either.[27]

Roosevelt did not really grasp the intensity of Democratic allegiance in the South. He thought that he could appeal to the logical reasoning of southerners who shared his reformist views on other issues. By so doing, he could, in the words of one of his aides, speed "the development of two white parties in the South" through "a new party that would not be tainted in that section of the country with the negro question, as the Republican party is." Roosevelt's anger at the way black Republicans had treated him at the convention added to his determination to make this move. He believed that the African Americans from Dixie had sold their votes to Taft for cash and favors.[28]

Of course, in embarking on this new course, Roosevelt risked alienating black Republicans in the North. In his electoral calculations, he may have concluded either that he had already lost that black support with his actions in the Brownsville incident of 1906 or that these voters had no place to go, anyway. Whether he might have increased Progressive votes in the North from African Americans with a color-blind policy was not something that crossed Roosevelt's mind in July 1912. Like Wilson and Taft, Roosevelt believed that blacks were inferior and accordingly they assumed a lesser role in his plans than did southern whites. As he told reporters, he was now pleased "that I have been able to fearlessly state my views on great questions, such as the trusts, the negroes, and the tariff." His position on blacks in the South had become that they should remain out of the politics of his new party.[29]

As the date for the Progressive convention neared, Roosevelt had to resolve the problem of race when competing black and white delegations from Alabama, Florida, Georgia, and Mississippi presented themselves for seating as legitimate participants in the new party's councils. These were all pro-Roosevelt slates, of course, but the presidential candidate would have to choose what to do about them. His white supporters in the South told him "that this should be a white man's party" that recognized "the superior ability of the white man and his superior civilization" in contrast to "the negro" who, in the judgment of white politicians, "has been perfectly content to remain the ignorant savage devoid of pride of ancestry or civic ambition." If Roosevelt hoped to carry one or more southern states, he told himself that he had to acknowledge the logic of the "lily-white" stance of his followers.[30]

To get his message out, Roosevelt composed a lengthy letter to Julian Harris, the son of Joel Chandler Harris, the author of the "Uncle Remus" stories. The document was also made public and formed the basis for the ensuing debate about Roosevelt's racial policies. In this extended treatment of how the Progressives would approach race, Roosevelt asserted that he would encourage black participation in Northern politics while barring them from the new party's councils in the South. He concluded that, "by appealing to the best white men in the South, the men of justice and of vision as well as of strength and leadership, and by frankly putting the movement in their hands from the outset we shall create a situation by which the colored men of the South will ultimately get justice as it is not possible for them get justice if we are to continue and perpetuate the present conditions."[31]

The reaction among black Republicans in the North was public dismay at what they regarded as Roosevelt's betrayal of their interest. "We've been with the Colonel because we expected fair play. If we don't get it the Colonel don't get our votes," said G. B. Ellis, a black politician from Chicago. The issue threatened to disrupt the Progressive convention as unfriendly newspapers wrote of "a widespread revolt among negro voters on both sides of the Mason-Dixon line." The incipient protests from his black supporters provided one more problem that Roosevelt confronted as he prepared to leave for the Progressive conclave.[32]

There were happier developments for Roosevelt as the opening day of the convention approached. He received endorsements from the community of settlement house workers and intellectuals interested in social justice. Those who opposed child labor, advocated city planning, and spoke out for charitable causes found in Roosevelt a receptive audience for their priorities. These activists liked Roosevelt's program of greater government involvement to address social inequities. From Jane Addams to Colorado juvenile court reformer Benjamin B. Lindsey (who was so small he was dubbed "the Bull Mouse"), they responded to Roosevelt's call. His platform, one of them observed, "embodies all the dreams and aspirations which have been a large part of our lives."[33]

Jane Addams of Hull House became the most visible embodiment of the large role that social justice advocates played in the new Roosevelt coalition. These individuals did not quite qualify as the "Brains Trust" of another Roosevelt two decades later, but they went a good distance down that road. Knowing a publicity coup when he saw one, Roosevelt embraced the idea that Addams should second his nomination at Chicago. At that moment, she would be introduced as "America's most eminent and most loved woman." Despite her enthusiasm for the candidate's domestic program, she had to swallow hard to accept the platform's call to add more battleships to the navy and to exclude southern blacks from the party's deliberations.[34]

The enhanced role of Addams and other women at the Progressive Convention included another policy commitment that Roosevelt adopted as his reform sentiments intensified during the summer of 1912. He had not been an advocate of woman suffrage and in February had proposed that women nationally should have a special election to decide whether they wanted suffrage or not. Once the Progressive Party came into being, the platform committee sensed a chance to appeal to women in states such as California. They wrote language proclaiming "that no

The Progressive National Convention assembled reformers from around the country who infused religious enthusiasm into their deliberations. (Prints and Photographs Collection, Library of Congress)

people can justly claim to be a true democracy which denies political rights on account of sex." Therefore, the Progressives stood for "equal suffrage to men and women alike."[35]

Roosevelt adopted this new doctrine at the Chicago Convention and in the campaign that followed. He had learned, he said, that "the women from whom I received most aid in endeavoring to grapple with the social and industrial problems of the day were themselves believers in woman suffrage." So he came to believe that women did not present the dangers that its opponents often advanced. "I see no reason why voting should interfere with women's home life any more than it interferes with the everyday work of the man which enables him to support the home." Not all proponents of suffrage were convinced at Roosevelt's sudden conversion to their cause, and the ensuing debate about his sincerity would persist during the fall campaign.[36]

While race, suffrage, and social justice were important aspects of Roosevelt's appeal in 1912, the core premise of the Progressive candidate's program stood on the issue of greater corporate regulation and the expansion of national power to accomplish that task. In keeping with his long-standing views, which his close ally George W. Perkins reinforced, Roosevelt accepted big business as an accomplished fact. The issue for the national government was how to manage the activities of these corporate giants in the public interest. Perkins believed that it was not "possible for this country in the twentieth century to ... maintain its commercial supremacy under a technical enforcement of the Sherman [antitrust] law." Roosevelt did not put the question in such a controversial way, but he stood with Perkins on the substance of the matter.[37]

Other Progressives from the Middle West, where anticorporate sentiments ran strong, believed that the Sherman Act remained important and should be affirmed. They also distrusted Perkins and his motives. The core of Roosevelt's support in states such as Kansas and Iowa told him that the new party should endorse the principles of trust busting. As Senator Joseph L. Bristow of Kansas argued, "In this scheme of regulation is there not a grave danger that 'big business' will more likely control the government than the government controlling big business?" This fault line in the Progressive ideology would surface in the convention and then influence the party's subsequent history.[38]

For those who came to Chicago in August 1912 for the Progressive Convention, the experience represented one of the transcendent moments of their public lives. Even the subsequent loss in November 1912 and the tawdry end of the party during the summer of 1916 did not diminish the memory of the euphoria that gripped those in the hall. "The occasion had all of the psychological trappings and habiliments of a crusade," wrote William Allen White decades later. "We were indeed Christian soldiers 'marching as to war'—and rather more than mildly mad."[39]

Four decades after the Bull Moose conclave, historians would assert that a biographical profile of the delegates revealed that white, middle-class Protestant professionals predominated in the membership of the new party. From that judgment came a theory that a decline in status and anxiety about their place in a new industrial society prompted these men and women to rally to Roosevelt's banner. Subsequent research disclosed, however, that conservative Republicans (and Democrats) shared many of these same traits. Progressive Party loyalists were somewhat younger and had less experience in politics than conservative Republicans did. What seems to have divided them most from their former Republican allies was an ideological commitment to Roosevelt's policies for a larger role for the government and more social reform.[40]

The religiosity of the convention dominated the press coverage of the event. One reporter called the hall "a vast patriotic picture." The correspondent for the *New York Times*, a newspaper that opposed Roosevelt, admitted that the tone of the proceedings impressed him: "It was not a convention at all. It was an assemblage of religious enthusiasts." Comparisons with the convention that nominated Abraham Lincoln in 1860 also appeared. Spontaneous singing of the "Battle Hymn of the Republic" echoed several times, as did "Onward Christian Soldiers." Another hymn provided a Roosevelt theme:

Follow, follow,
We will follow Roosevelt,
Anywhere, everywhere,
We will follow on![41]

Before the convention, a clever songster matched new words to the melody of "Maryland, My Maryland:

Thou wilt not cower in the dust, Roosevelt, O Roosevelt!
Thy gleaming sword shall never rust, Roosevelt, O Roosevelt!
In thee we hail a leader just,

In thee repose a sacred trust,
To crush the powers of greed and lust, Roosevelt, O, Roosevelt.[42]

Roosevelt arrived in Chicago on 5 August to find a comparatively small crowd of 700 admirers at the train station. By the time he reached the Congress Hotel, 1,000 people heard him say: "I am glad to be with you in Chicago again, and this time at the birth of a party and not at the death of a party." He faced at once the reaction to his "lily-white" policy toward the South and, behind the scenes, emerging disputes over the content of the Progressive platform.[43]

On the issue of blacks in the new party, the Provisional National Progressive Committee met to address the problems of competing delegations from three southern states. The panel endorsed Roosevelt's wishes and rejected the claims of black politicians to seat representatives from Alabama, Florida, and Mississippi. A white member of the National Association for the Advancement of Colored People failed in his campaign to secure a plank stating that "distinctions of race and class in political life have no place in a democracy." There were no words about blacks in the platform, and Roosevelt reaffirmed his own views in his acceptance speech. By that time, Roosevelt's vague dream of making electoral inroads in the South was clearly doomed. White Democrats rallied behind Woodrow Wilson. Roosevelt and the Progressives had shown their true indifference, if not hostility, to black Americans and gained nothing from their prejudices.[44]

Within the ranks of the delegates to the convention, the problem of corporate regulation posed more intense concern. The debate became acute within the platform committee. That panel started its discussions on 5 August. The drafters did not achieve a finished product until two days later, when the convention was nearly over. During the course of their discussions, committee members decided not to urge the recall of judges. They did, however, provide language asserting that, when a state court ruled a regulatory law unconstitutional, the people "shall have an opportunity to vote on the question whether they desire the Act to become law, notwithstanding such decision." The recall of judicial decisions, so controversial in the spring of 1912, was thus reduced to general language in the Progressive charter.[45]

The greatest backstage controversy turned on the part of the platform that dealt with big business and the proper means of supervising large corporations. The dispute remained out of sight in August 1912

This image of the committee that "notified" Roosevelt of the nomination by the Progressives indicates something of the moral earnestness that permeated the party's convention in August 1912. (George Henry Payne, *The Birth of the New Party* [*n.p.: H. E. Rennels, 1912*])

as Roosevelt pursued a consensus position that maintained party unity within his new organization. In the platform deliberations that went on behind the public hoopla at Chicago, the proponents of the Sherman Act wanted to include wording that said: "We favor strengthening the Sherman law by prohibiting agreements to divide territory or limit output; and refusing to sell to customers who buy from business rivals and sell below cost in certain areas by maintaining higher prices in other places; using the power of transportation to aid or injure special business concerns or other unfair business practices."[46]

This approach of prescribing what business could not do under the Sherman Act did not suit either George W. Perkins or Roosevelt. Working in tandem, the two men compelled the platform committee to agree to delete the wording about the Sherman Act. Through a mix-up at the convention itself, the dropped wording was read out. Perkins jumped up from his chair and proclaimed that an error had been made. The offending language was removed and the press persuaded not to mention the mistake. The episode did not become public until after the election was over. Without that distraction, Roosevelt's views on corporate regulation would become a major element in the campaign against Wilson in the fall.[47]

The convention itself, once the delegates had assembled, provided a series of oratorical highlights to the enthusiastic throng. At first, Roosevelt wanted to give his "Confession of Faith" on the day the proceedings opened. Since that option would upstage all the other speakers, the presidential candidate agreed to speak on the second day. For the keynote address, the organizers enlisted Albert J. Beveridge of Indiana to perform the warm-up duties for the expectant crowd.

Just two and a half months short of his fiftieth birthday, Beveridge still looked like the youthful Indiana senator who had burst on to the national scene in 1899 with a spread-eagle defense of American imperialism in the upper house. In his two terms from 1899 to 1911, the ambitious and conceited politician had moved toward progressivism. He sought regulation of child labor and opposed the Payne-Aldrich Tariff Act. Beveridge lost his reelection bid in 1910 in the Democratic tide of that year. With some trepidation, he followed Roosevelt out of the Republican Party. Indiana Progressives nominated him to run for governor in the days before the Chicago Convention. For the grandiloquent Beveridge, the keynote address offered him another taste of national fame.[48]

In remarks that he called "Pass Prosperity Around," Beveridge asserted that "this party comes from the grass roots. It has grown from the soil of the people's hard necessities." He assailed "the invisible government which is the real danger to American institutions," the union of reactionary politicians in both older parties. Beveridge told his audience that "there ought not to be in this Republic a single day of bad business, a single unemployed workingman, a single unfed child." The task of the new party was to "protect womanhood, save childhood, and restore the dignity of manhood." He labeled the Sherman law outdated and advocated "honest protection" for his tariff policy. In his conclusion, he said that the Progressive Party proclaimed for women "the chivalry of the state," including a minimum wage, old-age pensions, and suffrage. Above all, Beveridge thundered, the Progressives saw the Constitution as "a living thing, growing with the people's growth, strengthening with the people's strength, aiding the people in their struggle for life, liberty and the pursuit of happiness, permitting the people to meet all their needs as conditions change."[49]

A conservative man at heart, Beveridge would soon recede from these innovative positions, as would many in the hall who applauded his statement of Progressive values. In the words of Beveridge and later Theodore Roosevelt, the Progressive Party looked forward to greater power for the national government, a broader program of social justice, and policies of the welfare state that took generations to put into operation. The salience of the 1912 election and the sense of its substantive importance derives to a large extent from the ideas that the Progressives advanced in that religion-tinged, socially conscious political revival meeting in Chicago during August.

Beveridge scored an oratorical triumph, but the expectant crowd knew that the headline attraction had yet to appear. Theodore Roosevelt saw this speech to his adoring followers as his moment to rivet the nation's attention on the ideas that he had summed up in New Nationalism two years earlier. For the first time he could say what he really thought about major issues absent the constraints of being a Republican. Once again, for a brief hour or two, he could be back in his bully pulpit preaching to a congregation ready to imbibe every word. No wonder he called his oration "A Confession of Faith." Beyond the walls of the Coliseum lay his bigger audience. Could he convert them to the Progressive cause and achieve the goals of his personal crusade?

Roosevelt's big moment came on 6 August. That afternoon he appeared in the Coliseum for his own keynote speech. An hour-long demonstration greeted his presence as "the convention voiced out of lusty lungs its adulation of its third-term candidate for president." After thirty-five minutes of cheering and hat waving, the band played, as it had done several times earlier, the "Battle Hymn of the Republic." Delegates jumped onto their chairs and the Civil War anthem boomed through the hall. "Onward, Christian Soldiers" followed with delegates and audience all standing and singing. Women moved toward the platform to shake hands with Roosevelt. First was Jane Addams and then other female Progressives, including Rebecca Felton of Georgia who would, ten years later, serve briefly as the first female U.S. senator. Following fifty-eight minutes of tumult, the hall fell silent. Roosevelt was introduced, and his keynote address, political manifesto, and rationale for the new party began.[50]

Roosevelt's two-hour address did not break new ground. He restated and elaborated the themes that he had been articulating since the New Nationalism speech two years earlier. "The old parties are husks," he began, "with no real soul within either, divided on artificial lines, boss-ridden and privilege-controlled, each a jumble of incongruous elements, and neither daring to speak out wisely and fearlessly what should be said on the vital issues of the day." Now "there must be a new party of nation-wide and non-sectional principles" that would represent "the cause of human rights and of governmental efficiency." He then went on to discuss first measures such primaries and reforms of the courts, which he saw not as radicalism but as a means of preventing more radical social change.[51]

While Roosevelt spoke for a number of social justice measures in his oration, the central point of his program was the idea of a national industrial commission to act as a regulatory agency. That body would have "complete power to regulate and control all the great industrial concerns engaged in interstate business—which practically means all of them in this country." Roosevelt added that "we promise nothing which will jeopardize honest business. We promise adequate control of all big business, and the stern suppression of the evils connected with big business, and this promise we can absolutely keep."[52]

For all of its innovative quality, Roosevelt's speech had to take into account the protectionist sentiment within the new party and among the disenchanted Republican voters he was trying to win over. In his formal prepared text, he said that "the American people favor the principle of a protective tariff, but they desire such a tariff to be established primarily in the interests of the wage-earner and the consumer." He wanted a sci-entific commission in this area, too, that would make the key decisions for Congress, and he assailed the Democratic platform for having called the tariff unconstitutional.[53]

When it came time to deliver the long-running address, however, the candidate tried to cut short his remarks after seventy-five minutes. The crowd told him that he "had forgotten to discuss the tariff." Roosevelt asked to be excused from going into the protection issue. The crowd, aware of the political risk if Roosevelt did not address the protection is-sue, insisted on hearing what he had written. Roosevelt had never been comfortable with the tariff as an issue, and he displayed uneasy loyalty to it as a Progressive candidate. The persistence and salience of the mat-ter, not to mention Wilson's emphasis on it, meant that Roosevelt had to keep coming back to the tariff in the fall campaign.[54]

There was another awkward moment when a black delegate inter-rupted the speech to ask about race. Roosevelt broke away from his text to review his position on the South and African Americans in politics. He assailed "the ignorant and debased kind of people" that had served as delegates to Republican national conventions from among southern blacks. By the end of the meeting, newspapers unfriendly to Roosevelt were reporting the defection of African American leaders who were turning back to Taft's candidacy.[55]

How forward-looking was Roosevelt's personal platform for his new party in 1912? In terms of social justice, he would have provided the most extensive protection for citizens in the workplace and in their homes. He advocated a minimum wage for women, protection of child labor, a system of "social insurance" that anticipated Social Security, and the ratification of the then-pending income tax amendment to the Con-stitution. "Our aim" Roosevelt said, "is to promote prosperity, and then see to its proper division." As he said in his summation, "I believe in a larger use of governmental power to help remedy industrial wrongs, because it has been borne in on me by actual experience that without ex-ercise of such power many of the wrongs will go unremedied."[56]

In the context of American politics as it existed in 1912, Theodore Roosevelt had taken the most advanced position toward a modern ver-sion of the regulatory state. He acknowledged that large corporate power was an accomplished fact. He believed that the authority of the national government must be increased as a result. He was comfortable with the idea that an expanded bureaucracy should oversee an important sector of the economy. Since Roosevelt hoped that he would be in charge of picking the individuals to staff such a bureaucracy, he saw little danger from that development.

The Progressive Party was not the New Deal in 1912. In its platform and ideology the new organization provided scope for action in the states and was not simply a nationally oriented program. Nonetheless, the Progressives and Roosevelt had put at the center of the public agenda a group of ideas that would concern American politics throughout the rest of the twentieth century. That was the most important legacy of the quixotic political venture that Roosevelt launched during this phase of his life.

Roosevelt's "Confession of Faith" marked a high point of the third-party convention, but there remained the task of a presidential nomination, the selection of a running mate, and the adoption of a platform. Then the candidate would accept in a formal way the designation of his party. All that took place on 7 August. Earlier in the day, Woodrow Wilson had completed the ritual of accepting the Democratic nomination. Now it was Roosevelt's turn. There was no doubt about what would happen in the final session of the convention. The organizers set up the event so that the platform would be adopted first. The flap over the antitrust plank did not get in the newspapers. Then the delegates turned to what they had come for in the first place. They nominated Roosevelt. In the seconding speeches for Roosevelt, Jane Addams said that the new party "has become the American exponent of a world-wide movement toward juster social conditions, a movement which the United States, lagging behind other great nations, has been unaccountably slow to embody in political action." Roosevelt, she said in supporting his nomination, was one of the few leaders "who has caught the significance of the modern movement."[57]

After the seconding speeches were over and Roosevelt nominated, the convention selected Hiram Johnson for his running mate. Some thought had been given to naming a Democrat, even one from the South, but that would have sparked defections from Progressives with Republican roots who wanted one of their own on the national ticket. Johnson was thought to be an outstanding campaigner, he did not have to give up his office as governor of California to run, and the symbolism of candidates from New York and the West Coast seemed attractive from a public relations perspective. A banner was unrolled that said:

Roosevelt and Johnson
New York and California
Hands Across the Continent.

The makers of the banner added a verse from Rudyard Kipling:

For there is neither East nor West
Border, nor breed, nor birth,
When two strong men stand face to face,
Though they come from the ends of the earth.[58]

As for Roosevelt himself, he told the crowd "of course I accept," and he called the nomination an even greater honor than being president. He pledged to "put every particle of courage, of common sense, and of strength that I have at your disposal." With the convention behind him, Roosevelt laid his plans for several national tours, which a friendly journalist called "one of the most extensive and arduous political trips ever attempted by a candidate for the presidency." The proposed junket, however, did not reflect a coherent electoral strategy for the new party. Roosevelt seemed to have still thought that he could break into the Solid South and thus wasted time with forays into Dixie.[59]

In mid-August, Roosevelt made his first campaign swing into New England with speeches in Providence, Rhode Island, and then in Boston. His opening speech and the ones that followed provided a good sense of the assets and liabilities of Roosevelt as a national candidate. The Progressives were, he said, "a permanent party, a new party." The old parties had failed to meet the challenges of the time, and "in their essence the Republican and Democratic machines are alike." Only the Progressives could achieve the "social justice" that Roosevelt sought. The new party stood "for the elemental rights not only of American citizenship but of human kind." In one of his Boston speeches, Roosevelt himself expressed some surprise at how the election of 1912 had evolved from the conventional expectations: "This contest has developed into a far greater contest than any of us thought of when it was begun six months. I had not an idea what it was going to turn out to be." But now that the decisive race to achieve his vision had started, he was intent on seeing it through to the end.[60]

In protectionist Rhode Island, Roosevelt mentioned the tariff where "we wish to see the benefits of the protective tariff get into the pay envelope of the working man." He said that "instead of decreasing we wish to increase the amount of the prize money which is rightly due those who work hard in industry, but we want a more equitable division of the prize money." Reading these comments, Woodrow Wilson and the Democrats knew an opening when they saw one, and the Democratic candidate would needle Roosevelt about the "prize money" quote in the weeks ahead. Following appearances in Boston the next day, Roosevelt spent most of the next two weeks at Oyster Bay preparing for the campaign swing that would commence at the end of the month and extend through September.[61]

Vermont was holding state elections, and that was seen as a key test of Progressive strength at the polls. Roosevelt went back to New England to buttress his party's chances in that region. Roosevelt spoke at Saint Johnsbury, Vermont, on 30 August and promised the six-day workweek and the eight-hour day "in continuous twenty-four-hour industries," the ending of night work, and the eight-hour day for women. He defended his support for woman suffrage, and credited Jane Addams, Frances Kellor, and Florence Kelley for instructing him about why women needed the vote to secure social justice. "I do not believe," he said, that "there is identity in functions between men and women, but I do believe there should be equality of rights." Roosevelt's speeches were inspiring to his followers, but these orations were lengthy, filled with details, and not yet focused into a simple, compelling message.[62]

While Roosevelt began his canvass with this trip through New England and then headed westward, his political foes on the right and left sought to put him in an embarrassing position about his personal and political friendship with George W. Perkins. Robert La Follette, still smarting about his failed candidacy, roamed the corridors of the U.S. Senate. He told reformist colleagues that they should resist Roosevelt's allure. Battle Bob's hatred of Roosevelt drew him into an unlikely entente with a Republican stand-patter, Senator Boies Penrose of Pennsylvania. The political odd couple decided to hit the Progressive candidate about his campaign contributions and Perkins's role in financing the Republican presidential campaign in 1904.[63]

In August, the newspaper publisher William Randolph Hearst revealed that Penrose had received a $25,000 contribution for the 1904 election from Standard Oil. The fat, dissipated Pennsylvania lawmaker argued that the money had really been meant for Roosevelt's campaign coffers. He and La Follette proposed in the waning days of the congressional session that there be a probe of campaign spending in 1904, 1908, and 1912. The charge of the inquiry was to examine "all correspondence and financial transaction between John D. Archbold [of Standard Oil], George W. Perkins, Theodore Roosevelt, and members of the United States Senate from 1900 to the date of the investigation."[64]

Moses E. Clapp of Minnesota chaired the panel, which moved with unaccustomed speed to hear testimony from Penrose and his reported benefactor, John D. Archbold of Standard Oil. When Roosevelt asked if he could testify before the panel, he learned that several senators on the committee had already left Washington with the adjournment of Congress. His chance, if any, to appear in person would have to occur later. As the press noted, the effect would be to "break into" Roosevelt's series of campaign engagements in September and October."[65]

An outraged Roosevelt fired off one of his lengthy public letters to Senator Clapp on 28 August. In the document, he denied any wrongdoing in 1904 and produced extensive evidence from his files to make his case. To the press he said that his enemies have "picked up the wrong end of the poker, by George!" In the invective contest, Roosevelt probably won the day. But the controversy over campaign funding did not help the Progressives. Whatever momentum the Chicago convention might have achieved in early August was dissipated in the battle over who had given how much to Roosevelt and when they had done so. The *Wall Street Journal* identified the real winner. "Democratic campaign managers ought to pay for the space occupied by the Roosevelt-Penrose controversy at advertising rates—both wings of the Republican party are equally compromised."[66]

That was the main problem that the Roosevelt campaign and his new party confronted as the last phase of the 1912 presidential election began around Labor Day. The former president had been able to split his party after the Republican National Convention and establish the structure of a third party built around his own personality and program. He had failed during the summer to win over Democratic voters and put himself in a position to secure the White House. The Progressives, for all of their innovations in terms of their policy ideas, remained a splinter of the Republicans. They were a larger faction than their conservative counterparts within the Grand Old Party, but it seemed improbable that they could win the election based on their own electoral resources.

As a shrewd politician, Roosevelt recognized his predicament and admitted in private that he would likely lose. He had two choices. He could base a campaign on his personal appeal and public record. That strategy would assure him of second place ahead of Taft. Or he might use the election as a building effort to make the Progressives a viable organization for the longer-range goal of transforming American politics. It was understandable that he chose the first direction, but that meant that his third-party candidacy would have less sustained effect once the 1912 election was over. The fall campaign did produce, however, a confrontation between Roosevelt and Wilson over the direction that progressivism should take in the future. Their clash between the New Nationalism of Roosevelt and the New Freedom of Wilson gave the election of 1912 its lasting place in the history of American reform.

THE CLASH OF IDEAS

Wil-son, that's all, Wil-son, that's all!
Who strikes the pub-lic sen-ti-ment?
Say, who will be our next Pres-i-dent?
It's Wil-son, that's all.
—*Wilson campaign song*[1]

On the surface, the presidential election campaign that raged during the autumn of 1912 resembled the similar contests that had preceded it for the past three decades. After the national conventions, both Woodrow Wilson and William Howard Taft had been "notified" in formal ceremonies and made their speeches of acceptance. At the same time, the two parties had issued their "campaign textbooks," mobilized speakers, and prepared for the round of candidate speeches in September and October. Theodore Roosevelt and the Progressives followed the same overall rituals as September opened. Meanwhile, the Socialists conducted their campaign according to their own schedule. For newspapers of the day, it must have seemed that a familiar ritual was unfolding.

Observers of campaign practices, however, noted significant alterations in how voters were now being wooed. Two years earlier, the editors of the *Outlook* magazine wrote that "the country has passed from the emotional to the intellectual stage" in campaigns. Gone were the "processions, parades, bands of music, and red fire" that had marked the military style of politicking during the Gilded Age. Theater owners found that box office receipts remained strong despite the competition from rallies and speeches during the early fall. The major changes came from newspapers and to a lesser degree the automobile. Newspapers reached a wider audience in a time before movies and radio had attained mass penetration. Campaigning with cars to get to rallies and promote candidates could now reach more of the electorate in a day or a week than had been possible with railroad swings through a district or state.[2]

The 1912 election saw the first signs of how these innovations would affect national politics. All three major-party candidates made audio recordings of their speeches, a process that Woodrow Wilson found uncomfortable and demeaning. Movies had also advanced to a sufficient degree that camera operators followed Wilson and Roosevelt around to catch them in informal moments and on the stump. The Democrats produced a movie to show the cost of the protective tariff with melodramatic touches about the "High Tariff Boss" who displayed his ill-gotten gains in a cash-filled safe. The Republicans, at the behest of Charles Hilles, spent part of their very limited funds on motion pictures. The effect of these rudimentary media efforts on the campaign has not been established. Four years later in 1916 Wilson would be more friendly to the camera's presence.[3]

One thing the press did agree on in its coverage of the 1912 race was the novel presence of women in the campaigns of the Democrats, Republicans, and Progressives. As the *Dallas Morning News* put it in somewhat breathless terms, "With a suddenness and force that has left observers gasping women have injected themselves into the National campaign this year in a manner never before dreamed of in American politics."[4]

What Jane Addams, "probably the most noted settlement worker in the world," had done in seconding Theodore Roosevelt's nomination at the Progressive Party convention made her the leading symbol of the heightened role of women in 1912. As a result, she faced criticism from opponents of Roosevelt. Mabel Boardman chided her for taking a partisan stance and said her own affiliation with the American Red Cross would preclude such a gesture. A week later Boardman said she would circulate a fund-raising letter for Taft. Charles William Eliot, the former president of Harvard University, chimed in about Addams: "Women have no proper share in a political convention." What she did in seconding Roosevelt was "a very spectacular proceeding, but it was in very bad taste." Roosevelt countered that the Progressives were "the one Party which since the [Civil] War has dealt with real issues, and these real issues affect women precisely as much as men."[5]

Mabel Boardman, one of the leading female supporters of President Taft, exemplified the enhanced role for women in politics that marked the 1912 election. (Prints and Photographs Collection, Library of Congress)

Roosevelt's endorsement of woman suffrage in the Progressive platform and on the stump also attracted criticism from within the movement to get women the vote. Ida Husted Harper argued that Roosevelt
had used tricky language to lure suffrage supporters, a claim that his
female supporters rebutted. The novelist Gertrude Atherton wrote in a
sarcastic vein that "in wedding the Suffrage party" Roosevelt had "ac-
cumulated a harem which will henpeck him day and night to translate
his words into deeds." While there was a certain amount of expediency
in Roosevelt's conversion on woman suffrage, the change represented a
recognition of what female supporters had meant to his campaign.[6]

Despite the partisan bantering, the role of women in the 1912 campaign foreshadowed greater participation and acclimated men to the
presence of females in a wider variety of roles. The general consensus
was that the visibility of women boosted the chances of suffrage as well.
Four years later both the Democratic and Republican platforms endorsed
suffrage on the state level, but it took another four years, as well as the
impetus from World War I, when women contributed to the war effort,
for the national suffrage amendment to be adopted.

For African Americans, the 1912 election posed a choice among three
candidates who had scant sympathy for black aspirations. Theodore
Roosevelt had rejected African Americans in the South as part of his
new party, and several black leaders, including W. E. B. Du Bois, abandoned their earlier support for the Progressives as a result. Northern
blacks seem to have split their votes between Roosevelt and Taft in the
November balloting.

So despairing were some African Americans of their electoral choices
that they looked with hopeful expectation toward Wilson and the Democrats. On the surface, it was an improbable choice. Since the Civil War
the Democrats, especially in the South, had stood for state rights, segregation, and white supremacy. There had been some muting of these
positions in the North during the Gilded Age, but the fundamental ori-
entation of the Democracy was against civil rights for blacks.

Despite this discouraging record, blacks such as Du Bois wondered if
they might wield their votes in northern industrial states to move Wilson
toward a greater recognition of their rights and needs. Seeing an opportunity to pick up support from a community long loyal to the Grand Old
Party, Wilson's managers were willing to talk to blacks and even make
some encouraging signals. In fact, Wilson kept his own racist views
under cover. He had discouraged African Americans from attending

Princeton while he was president, and he believed in segregation of the races, as he assured Texas supporters during the primary campaign. As a presidential candidate, Wilson was prepared to make some conciliatory gestures toward blacks as long as no substantive steps were involved. He promised to "speak out against lynching" but at the same time "did not wish the colored people to get the impression that he could help them in that matter as President, as the President had no power."[7]

From the start of the campaign, the assumption among political observers was that Wilson was going to win in November. For the first time in twenty years the electoral map favored the Democrats. Despite Roosevelt's attempt to penetrate the South for the Progressives, the unity of Democrats in the region indicated that Wilson would have the 126 electoral votes from the states of the Confederacy. Added to that were the votes of Oklahoma, Kentucky, and West Virginia for an additional thirty-one electoral votes. With the Republicans split, New York and Wilson's home state of New Jersey were conceded to the Democrats for another fifty-nine electoral votes. That put Wilson at 216 electoral votes of the 266 needed to win. He was deemed ahead in such former Republican bastions as Ohio, Indiana, Illinois, and Iowa, not to mention a lead in Missouri and Kansas. Unless the Democrats imploded or Wilson made some unforeseen gaffe of monumental proportions, his victory seemed assured.

While the 1912 election had been an exciting contest through the two major-party conventions, by the first of July the suspense had thus been drained from the ultimate result. Informal polls and newspaper surveys reported many undecided voters perhaps to maintain interest in the proceedings. The four candidates would campaign because that was what politicians did during a presidential election. Much of interest from an ideological standpoint remained to be discussed. The 1912 election had more to say about the future direction of the country and the nature of progressive reform. For the watching electorate, however, the result of their votes was not really in doubt. To some degree, Americans were now more spectators than participants in the operation of this presidential race.[8]

In this four-way race, there were in effect two tiers of candidates. President Taft and Debs commanded less attention amid the campaign clashes between Roosevelt and Wilson. With Taft having opted for the sidelines, the Republican canvass struggled to gain traction. Charles D. Hilles took the party through its tested rituals of speakers and press releases with the usual skill, but GOP strategists found that the press and the voters did not have their usual response to the Republican effort. "The difficulty," Hilles wrote on 31 July, "is that the party has not the momentum it has had in the past. One who tried to summon the 'mighty hosts' finds that they do not respond."[9]

The Republican leadership still could not find a treasurer to collect funds for many weeks, and the campaign had problems simply paying its running expenses. "Our big men all seem either to be stunned or to have lost their courage," reported the Republican assistant treasurer to Hilles on 11 October 1912, and the financial woes persisted down to Election Day. A congressional investigation of fund-raising practices, aimed largely at Theodore Roosevelt and his war chest, deterred many regular givers from being exposed to the resulting publicity.[10]

With President Taft's role limited to an occasional speech such as one at Beverly, Massachusetts, on 28 September, the burden of the Republican campaign would in ordinary circumstances have fallen on Vice President James S. Sherman. The two politicians did not like each other much, and Sherman had been well removed from Taft's inner circle. In late August Hilles wrote to Sherman to ask, "When and where do you think the speaking campaign should be opened?" Suffering from the heart condition that would kill him by late October, the vice president replied that he was too sick to campaign.[11]

The Republicans had to rely on such senators and representatives as they could induce to rally to mobilize the faithful. The resulting lack of star power on the stump limited the party's appeal to voters. Cabinet members also stayed mute. Attorney General George Wickersham asked Secretary of Commerce Charles Nagel on 19 September: "Have you done any campaigning yet? Is there any campaign except that which the Colonel & Wilson are conducting?"[12]

For many conservative Republicans, the key judgment became that, as one senator put it, "we can't elect Taft & we must do anything to elect Wilson so as to defeat Roosevelt." Anger at Roosevelt trumped all other considerations among these GOP members. "T. R.'s attitude toward political morality," wrote one, "is like that of a tom-cat toward a marriage license." The hope of rallying the Republican base against the Progressives was Taft's main resource, and he looked for encouraging signs that defectors were coming home all throughout October. That the economy was in good shape added to the faint Republican hopes as September moved into October.[13]

In their attacks on Woodrow Wilson, the Republicans took their cue from Taft's acceptance speech and stressed the protectionism that still bound the party together. "The Governor," wrote Hilles, "is essentially a free-trader and is running on a tariff-for-revenue only platform." Wilson's election and a Democratic Congress "would result in an attack on the tariff which would cause merchants and manufacturers to drift until they learned the worst." Such time-honored pressure groups as the American Protective Tariff League warned of the alleged dire consequences of a Wilson triumph. The political and economic claims of imminent disaster that had resonated with voters for so many years had lost their power at a time of inflation. The fears over the high cost of living drained protectionism of its previous clout. The GOP hoped that the general economic prosperity of the country would carry them to victory despite the odds against them.[14]

For the Republicans, it was one of those election years when anything that could go wrong for them did. On 30 October, Vice President Sherman died. The Republican National Committee replaced him before Election Day in hurried fashion with Nicholas Murray Butler, the anti-Roosevelt president of Columbia University. Everyone realized that it did not matter by that time who was on the ticket with Taft. As the candidate himself wrote to his wife on 1 November 1912, "It would seem as if all the ill luck possible were crowded into the cup of the Republican party. The death of Sherman is very discouraging because it may induce many not to vote for the ticket. Why this should be so I do not know but the voter seems to be regarded as a natural born fool unable to understand anything."[15]

Eugene V. Debs and the Socialist Party had no expectations of winning the 1912 election. Their goal was to maximize the number of popular votes and to gain far more than the 420,00 votes they had compiled in 1908. Their campaign strategy, such as it was, consisted of sending Debs around the country to speak to as many audiences as would pay to listen to him. His canvass was self-financing. Those who attended his rallies paid in about $15,000 toward the ultimate campaign fund of $66,000. The party raised other funds through the sale of its literature and donations from members and the public. These moneys represented only a fraction of what even the losing Republicans were able to pull in. Still, it was more than the party had possessed in 1904 and 1908.[16]

There was no Red Special train in 1912. Debs used the regular rail lines to get around the country, which sometimes made him late for his engagements. Like Roosevelt, he turned first to the western states where his party had gained ground since the last presidential contest. The problem was that, while he could pile up large percentage gains over his 1908 totals at the polls in these states, they were more thinly populated than their eastern counterparts. As a result, Debs was spending valuable time in places like Texas and Arizona, where he could have only a marginal effect on the overall national vote total for the Socialists. His presence built party morale among the activists in these areas, but his appearances diverted energies that might have been better spent elsewhere in amassing votes in larger cities on a sustained basis.[17]

Debs and the Socialists resented the extent to which the Progressives and Roosevelt appropriated many of their ideas on labor, government regulation, and the courts. As his associate, Fred Warren, wrote Debs after attending the Bull Moose meeting, "I sat within twenty feet of Roosevelt and there were times when I could have shut my eyes and readily believed that I was listening to a Socialist soap boxer! In the decorations, red predominated and the red bandana was very much in evidence. My prediction that Roosevelt would steal our platform bodily has been fulfilled." Warren and Debs recognized that Roosevelt was identifying with some Socialist causes while at the same time presenting himself as the best agent of the middle class to stave off violent societal revolution.[18]

Debs attempted to fight back in the mainstream press with letters that pointed out what he believed Roosevelt was doing to steal ideas from the Socialists and how he was deceiving the electorate about his true role. "At bottom," Debs wrote to the *New York Times* in mid-August, "the Progressive Party is a capitalist class party. It stands for the present capitalist system, aiming only to mitigate some of its most glaring evils." Throughout the fall, Debs denounced Roosevelt's new party as a sham and urged his audiences to support the real source of potential change, the Socialists.[19]

During September and October, Debs followed his now familiar routine as a presidential campaigner. He attracted large audiences to his rallies as he moved around the country. After his opening address in Chicago on 16 June, he became embroiled with the Barnes controversy and did not use that time to the best advantage in preparing a focused appeal to the voters. In contrast to the ceremonies of the major parties,

Debs on 26 August simply released his printed address of acceptance to the newspapers and started out on his campaign swing. "The Socialist party," he wrote, "is the one party which stands squarely and uncompromisingly for the abolition of industrial slavery; the one party pledged in every fiber of its being to the economic freedom of all the people."[20]

For the next month, Debs toured the nation, giving his standard speech about the appeal of the Socialists. His schedule took him to Texas in mid-September where he told an audience of tenant farmers that "these are stirring days. The old order can survive but little longer. The swelling minority sounds the warning of impending change. Soon the minority will become the majority and then will come the Co-operative Commonwealth." Democrats in Oklahoma worried about the appeal of Debs and his party in that agrarian state.[21]

The big moments of the Debs campaign, however, came in his sold-out individual appearances in major cities where he could draw the crowds that infused him with energy. On 29 September there occurred an official notification meeting at Madison Square Garden in New York City. So sizable was the throng, "the largest Socialist demonstration ever held in the United States," that it spilled outside of the hall. When Debs was introduced, a protracted ovation ensued. He told his audience the election was between the Socialists and the "capitalistic class party" from which the Republicans, Democrats, and Progressives drew their supporters. The Progressives, he added were just "a fifth party which has stolen the planks of the Socialist platform."[22]

Three weeks later on 18 October Debs took his campaign to Washington, D.C. Before an audience of 3,000 people, "many of them waving red flags," Debs attacked Woodrow Wilson, by then the presumed winner of the presidential contest. He called Wilson's effort to restore economic competition "absolutely foolish." The world, he argued, "is in the midst of a wave of discontent, and a change is at hand." When the American people awoke, Debs concluded, "they will then vote the Socialist ticket, and then, and then only, will the people of the United States begin to be really happy." But these occasions were onetime events without a follow-up to build on whatever momentum Debs had created.[23]

The Socialists made a prodigious effort in 1912. The newspapers allied with the party provided extensive coverage of Debs' tours. There was enough in the campaign treasury for an ample supply of pamphlets and literature. The Socialists got their message out despite harassment of speakers and sporadic arrest of sympathizers on flimsy charges. Debs seemed on the stump, as one Socialist wrote, "the greatly beloved comrade of old and the entire trip is a continuous ovation." Debs had always been able to draw a crowd. The suspense for the Socialists lay in how many votes their energized and hopeful party might obtain when the electorate went to the polls in November. It was to be the last time Debs campaigned as the party's presidential nominee. Eight years later he would be in prison when the party selected him as its candidate.[24]

As the election season got under way in September 1912, the two most active contenders, Wilson and Roosevelt, jockeyed for the vote of Progressives as the key to victory. The Democratic candidate soon demonstrated a deft ability to get under the skin of his Progressive opponent. Of the lengthy Progressive platform Wilson said, "It is a Sabbath's day's journey through that program." Wilson also twitted Roosevelt about describing the tariff as "prize money" in his Providence speech. His rival's words, said Wilson, admitted "the absolute failure of the protective policy as Republicans had always advocated it."[25]

From the start of the campaign, there was an air of victory around the Wilson campaign. In late September, on a train ride through Massachusetts, crowds "stretched their hands upward to him, wishing him success. Cries for buttons were insistent, and the governor himself helped toss them from the train." Along the way, Wilson crossed paths with President Taft at the Copley Plaza Hotel in Boston. "I hope the campaign has not worn you out," said Taft. "It hasn't done that," replied Wilson, "but it has nearly done so. It has been quite a hard week."[26]

Wilson knew that he had to counter Roosevelt's appeal in his stump speeches. In his address to the Progressive Convention, the former president had laid out a very ambitious program of social change. He had spoken out for social justice for women and minors, regulation of the way corporations issued stock, government supervision of the condition of the workplace, and improved marketing techniques for farmers. Absent an effective Democratic rebuttal to his extensive agenda, Roosevelt might create an outside chance to win a three-way race against Wilson and Taft. An electoral victory for the Democrats was still the most probable outcome, but the Wilson campaign concluded that their candidate had to respond. As Bryan told Wilson, "Our only hope is in *holding our progressives* and in winning progressive Republicans."[27]

Wilson and Roosevelt had known each other for a decade and a half before their 1912 confrontation. They had met in 1896 and had some

HYMN TO PALLAS
DEMOCRÁTHÈNE

Woodrow Wilson's academic background was much emphasized in popular culture during the campaign. In this image from the cover of Life, Wilson is depicted as a Roman consul with the owl of learning perched nearby. The Latin words praise him as an executive, teacher, and spokesman of the people. (Life, 19 September 1912) personal contacts during the years that followed. While they were not intimate friends in any sense, there was a perception of shared purpose in their letters about academic and governmental matters. When Wilson was named the president of Princeton University in 1902, Roosevelt wrote that "Woodrow Wilson is a perfect trump."[28]

The rapport, such as it was, between the two men soon broke down during Roosevelt's second term. Wilson criticized Roosevelt's personal style as chief executive. "I have not seen much of Mr. Roosevelt since he became President," Wilson told a reporter in 1907, "but I am told he no sooner thinks than he talks, which is a miracle not wholly in accord with an educational theory of forming an opinion." A year later Roosevelt wrote to a friend about Wilson that he "felt rather impatient with his recent attitude on certain matters, notably the effort to control corporations." As Wilson ventured more into politics, the differences between the two men grew. "Down at bottom," Roosevelt wrote in December 1911, "Wilson is pretty thin material for a President."[29]

The political fight between the two men was conducted on a high level in 1912. There were whispers about Wilson's relationship with Mrs. Mary Ann Hulbert, some of which reached the candidate's ears. He inquired of his friend whether she knew anything about such rumors, which, if they became public, would "put an end to my candidacy and to my career." She seems to have reassured him there was nothing to worry about.[30]

In the meantime, Republicans learned of "a sheaf of letters" from Wilson to Hulbert and declined to accept them. They were then taken to the Roosevelt camp, which also refused to purchase them. When Roosevelt was told that had happened, he said to his campaign manager, Senator Joseph M. Dixon of Montana, that the senator had done the right thing: "Joe, those letters would be entirely unconvincing. Nothing, no evidence would ever make the American people believe that a man like Woodrow Wilson, cast so perfectly as the apothecary's clerk, could ever play Romeo!"[31]

The confrontation between Wilson and his rival came on the level of political philosophy and their contrasting ideas. The conceptual problem for Wilson lay with Roosevelt's program of the New Nationalism. The Progressive nominee, long an advocate of an active national government, had no philosophical qualms about employing federal power to supervise corporations and pursue social justice. Indeed, he thought that the duty of the president was to wield his authority to produce just such results. As for state rights, he saw that theory as an obsolete idea.

A strong federal government, relying on an expert bureaucracy to make wise policy decisions, should pursue regulation in the public interest. That was what Roosevelt believed he had done as president before and what he could now do again if he should return to the White House.

Democratic ideas hemmed in Wilson about effective answers. The party still believed that Jeffersonian precepts regarding small, limited, and inexpensive government were valid. Especially in the South, Democrats saw state rights as a bastion in defense of segregation and white supremacy. While there was support within the party for more government regulation along the lines that Bryan had put forward, a Democratic presidential candidate could not identify himself with anything like the activism that Roosevelt embraced. Wilson did not wish to go far in the direction of the New Nationalism, in any case. His reform impulse was cautious and limited. He wanted tariff reform and procedural innovation at most. But he knew that he had to provide an alternative to his rival that confirmed his own progressive credentials.

At the end of August, Wilson found his response in the person of Louis D. Brandeis. A Boston attorney known as the "people's lawyer," Brandeis believed that big business was both immoral and inefficient. He had seen what business could do to influence government when he represented Gifford Pinchot during the congressional hearings over the Ballinger dispute. Brandeis had been for Taft in 1908 and had then endorsed Robert La Follette. He could not abide Roosevelt's support of corporate size and government regulatory power. When Wilson was nominated, Brandeis saw an opportunity to advance ideas to which he had devoted his public life. He met with Wilson on 28 August, and the two men hit it off at once. Brandeis told reporters that he had found Wilson "to be entirely in accord with my own views of what we need to do to accomplish industrial freedom."[32]

Out of his practice representing small businesses in Massachusetts, especially the manufacturers of boots and shoes, Brandeis had concluded that big business could not attain the efficiency that Roosevelt, Perkins, and others attributed to industrial growth. In his mind, "The very large unit is not as efficient as the smaller unit." The issue boiled down to a single question: "Shall we have regulated competition or regulated monopoly?" What Brandeis thus told Wilson was to enforce competition in an effort to prove that monopolies could not survive. If a federal commission of any kind were to be created, its main task should be to enforce the Sherman antitrust law.[33]

From Wilson's perspective, these suggestions were ideal. Roosevelt had outlined a federal policy that accepted consolidation and wielded regulatory power to change corporate behavior. Instead, Wilson and Brandeis sought a restoration of competition and the use of the government first to create and then to sustain a competitive balance among various businesses. Soon the concepts that Brandeis had provided to him showed up in Wilson's campaign speeches. On 2 September, in a Labor Day address, Wilson said that "unregulated competition" had created monopolies. Where Roosevelt wanted to accept the existence of big business, Wilson promised that "remedial legislation will so restrict the wrong use of competition that the right use of competition will destroy monopoly. In other words, ours is a program of liberty and theirs is a program of regulation."[34] Wilson had identified an effective line of criticism against Roosevelt's New Nationalism. He could accuse his rival of accepting the existence of monopoly and therefore helping its spread. Roosevelt was thus part of the system of private corruption that had infected politics. After allowing monopoly to spread with his leadership of the Republicans, Roosevelt would now seek to regulate the force he had unleashed. By proposing an industrial commission to oversee business, Roosevelt was offering the nation, as Wilson put it, "a government of experts," a tolerance of paternalism, and "a legitimized continuation and perpetuation of the existing alliance between the government and big business."[35]

Brandeis and Wilson had selected a middle position that allowed the Democratic candidate to portray Roosevelt not as a reformer but as the agent of big business. At the same time, Wilson could speak to the Democratic doubts about the wisdom of Roosevelt's proposals for a bigger federal government. The Democratic nominee could endorse the goals of the Progressive Party for social justice but raise questions about the wisdom of the means that Roosevelt proposed to address such problems. Wilson was very adroit in conveying the sense of empathy for ideals while holding off from adopting the methods that would be required to implement the objectives. When he spoke of "a great pulse of irresistible sympathy which is going to transform the process of government among us," he carefully left vague just how these societal emotions were going to manifest themselves.[36]

A month after he met with Brandeis, Wilson put a label on his program. In a speech at Indianapolis, Indiana, he said that "there will be no greater burden in our generation than to organize the forces of liberty in our time to make conquest of a new freedom for America." The name "New Freedom" stuck as a way of describing what Wilson had in mind in contrast to Roosevelt and the New Nationalism and as the approach of the subsequent administration in both foreign and domestic affairs. The term was liberating for Wilson, too, since it imparted a degree of coherence to his general critique of Roosevelt's candidacy.[37]

By September, the Progressives had assembled the makings of a national political organization. They had gubernatorial candidates of credible stature with Albert J. Beveridge in Indiana and Oscar S. Straus in New York. Congressional nominees contested seats across the North, Middle West, and Far West. Though the party sought money from small donors, most of its $596,000 in campaign funds came from a few wealthy contributors. Roosevelt maintained that the third party was more than just the sum of his personality and career. "If this was a one man party," he said at Des Moines, Iowa, on 4 September, "I would not be in it."[38]

As he started out on his cross-country tour in early September from one state convention of the Progressives to another, Roosevelt kept track of what Wilson was saying in his speeches. He now saw the Democratic candidate as his main rival. As one of his staff put it, "It was Wilson, Wilson, Wilson, all the time in the private car, and nothing but Wilson and his record in the Colonel's talks." On his train, Roosevelt could relax between demanding events as his party crossed the continent. A reporter in Portland, Oregon, caught a glimpse of a tired candidate reading a book after a hard day of campaigning and handshaking. "Never once did he raise his head, and the old genial smile was missing."[39]

When Wilson delivered his Labor Day address in Buffalo, New York, and spoke again that evening in the same city, Roosevelt was ready with an attack on Wilson's tariff views. He assailed the Democrat for "the utter folly of any assertion that free trade or a tariff for revenue only will make even the smallest beginning toward solving the great industrial problems of the day." As for the Democratic platform that called the tariff unconstitutional, Roosevelt responded, "I cannot imagine anything that would bring more disaster to the country than the abolition of the tariff."[40]

During the ensuing campaign, Wilson and Roosevelt spent a good deal of time on the issue of business regulation and how large a role the government should play in that process. At the same time, the question of the tariff was never far below the surface of their interchanges. Wilson

A Progressive Party membership certificate from 1912. The efforts of the Progressives and the Democrats to raise money from small contributors did not prove notably successful. (Lewis L. Gould Personal Collection)

argued in New York City on 9 September, for example, that "radical reductions in our tariff schedules" would for the workingman "double and treble his prosperity." Roosevelt responded that Wilson should compare the experience of free-trade Great Britain, burdened with labor unrest, and protectionist Germany with its vibrant economy. While they often talked past each other, the two candidates did revisit many of the themes and issues of the tariff campaigns that dominated previous elections for twenty-five years.[41]

As the Wilson-Roosevelt exchanges became more intense during early September, politicians marked the results in Vermont, where state elections on 3 September showed the impact of the Progressive-Republican split. Despite Roosevelt's efforts, the Democrats made gains over their performance in 1910, and the Republican vote was down. The state seemed likely to go Republican in the November election but with a reduced majority. Happy Democrats called the result "a political barometer" and predicted that the outcome in November would be "the most decisive victory at the polls in our history."[42]

While the professionals read these electoral tea leaves, the two major candidates pressed on with their rhetorical struggle. On the campaign trail in 1912, there was no mechanism for a formal debate between Wilson and Roosevelt. The two campaigns existed in separate bubbles that interacted only through the newspapers. So the ideological battle between the New Nationalism and the New Freedom was not a tidy affair of dueling position papers with focus groups and modern polling thrown into the mix. Instead, Roosevelt and Wilson reacted to what each other reportedly said in the previous day's speeches.

One dramatic moment came on 9 September when Wilson spoke in New York City. He was discussing Roosevelt's industrial commission program, which he contrasted with his idea of regulating competition. Social betterment, he continued, did not arise from government power but from the resistance to such authority. He then added: "The history of liberty is the history of the limitation of government power, not the increase of it."[43]

Roosevelt read the newspaper reports of the address, which did not include what Wilson said before the last quoted sentence. Basing his conclusions on what he had seen in the press, Roosevelt responded in a lengthy San Francisco speech on 14 September to what Wilson had argued: "This is a bit of outworn academic doctrine which was kept in the school room and the professorial study for a generation after it had been abandoned by all who had experience of actual life." For Wilson to say that about the United States, Roosevelt went on, "means literally and absolutely to refuse to make a single effort to better any one of our social or industrial conditions." All of the regulatory legislation that Roosevelt sought would be impossible if Wilson had his way, or so his Progressive challenger alleged.[44]

Roosevelt had a point about Wilson's Democratic ideology, and his opponent sought to address that issue in a speech nine days later in Pennsylvania. "America is not now and cannot in the future be a place for unrestricted individual enterprise," Wilson told his audience. "I am not afraid of the utmost exercise of the power of the government of Pennsylvania or of the Union, provided they are exercised with patriotism and intelligence and really in the interest of the people who are living under them." Roosevelt, said the Democratic candidate, proposed "not to take you out of the hands of the men who have corrupted the Government of the United States, but to see to it that you remain in their hands and that that government guarantees to you that they will be humane to you."[45]

Wilson then added that "the most corrupting thing in this country has been this self-same tariff." He predicted that "the workingmen of America are not going to allow themselves to be deceived by a colossal bluff any longer." For his part, Roosevelt often returned to the tariff issue. The Progressives would maintain the protective system but use a series of commissions and "scientific" studies to insure that workers and not the industrialists got a fair share of what the existing tariff arrangements had produced.[46]

By the end of September, Wilson had articulated his "New Freedom" ideas and had not succumbed to Roosevelt's taunts about his conservative views. He proved to be a disciplined campaigner who could, in the modern phrase, stay "on message." Unless the Progressive candidate found a way to throw his Democratic opponent off-stride, there was almost no chance that Roosevelt could win the election. Even if Wilson made a slip, which he did not, the Democratic loyalty to him and the favorable electoral map would have cushioned any such blow to his campaign. Roosevelt had not found a winning strategy, and there may not have been one available to him in the political world of 1912.

Despite his short-range political problems, which hampered his third-party bid in 1912, Roosevelt's race represented a significant broadening of the national agenda. Because his speeches have not been as closely

PROGRESSIVE PARTY

DEMOCRATIC BLIND ALLEY

REPUBLICAN BLIND ALLEY

WORKER FOR WOMAN SOCIALIST

PATRIOTIC CITIZEN

DESERVING OLD AGE

ILL-PAID LABOR

CHILD LABOR

DEMOCRATIC BOSS

REPUBLICAN BOSS

POVERTY

ROBERT CARTER

LIBERTY JUSTICE EQUALITY

THE "OPEN ROAD"

"I suppose you know the force that is behind the new party that has recently been formed—the so-called Progressive party. It is a force of discontent with the regular parties of the United States. It is the feeling that men have gone into blind alleys and come out often enough, and that they propose to find an open road for themselves."—WOODROW WILSON

This cartoon illustrates the appeal the Progressive Party made to those dissatisfied with the Republicans and Democrats. It shows a number of Americans walking toward Liberty, Justice, and Equality, disdaining the "blind alley of the Republicans and Democrats." (American Review of Reviews 46 [October 1912]: 423) studied as Wilson's, historians have missed the innovative quality of what the Progressive candidate was saying. He spoke about on-the-job safety long before such concerns penetrated other national campaigns, he gave a speech on the development of the Mississippi River basin that looked forward to the Tennessee Valley Authority, and he advocated social justice measures such as a minimum wage for women and restrictions on child labor that would not come to pass for a quarter of a century. In his party's platform and on the stump, Roosevelt pushed the boundaries as much as any major-party candidate did during the first four decades of the twentieth century.[47]

Before Roosevelt could get back on the campaign trail, he had to take time out to testify before the Senate committee investigating the issue of business funds donated to the Grand Old Party in previous elections. He appeared in early October and, as he had done in his earlier public letter, rebutted the charges that he had known about and accepted corporate contributions to the 1904 campaign from Standard Oil. He complained as well regarding the timing of the probe that had interfered with his own canvass. He had frustrated his adversaries, including Boies Penrose and La Follette, when the charge that he had taken money from corporations fell flat. However, the episode had disrupted whatever momentum Roosevelt had gained from his cross-country tour.[48]

Roosevelt's campaign swing took him to Michigan and the upper Middle West before moving across the rest of the nation. By this time, Roosevelt was showing the strain of his exertions with a persistent sore throat. In a speech at Houghton, Michigan, on 10 October, he said that Wilson had not yet reached "as advanced a position as I took eleven years ago in my first message to Congress. I congratulate him upon having gotten so far, but this fact does not entitle him to leadership, and in many respects he has still a long way to go."[49]

Knowing that he was behind with less than a month to go in the campaign, Roosevelt hoped to turn his fortunes around with more intense attacks on his Democratic rival. The momentum of the campaign, however, seemed to be running in favor of the Democrats. In a speech on the trusts at Chicago on 12 October, for example, Roosevelt spent much of his time replying to Wilson's charges that he was too friendly with the trusts. The detailed discussion indicated how defensive Roosevelt had become about his program of government regulation.[50]

The presidential election of 1912 had one more surprise in store for the voters. Roosevelt's tour of the Middle West included a stop in Milwaukee, Wisconsin. There on 14 October as he got out of his car to wave to the crowd an assassin shot Roosevelt in the chest. The bullet struck his glasses case and a copy of his speech before entering the right side of his body where it broke a rib. The shooter, a man named John Schrank, had stalked Roosevelt for some time. The assailant was demented and believed that the ghost of William McKinley had instructed him to kill the Progressive candidate lest there be a third term. The wounded Roosevelt insisted that he could deliver his speech on schedule and went to the auditorium. He told the crowd, "I don't know whether you fully understand that I have just been shot; but it takes more than that to kill a Bull Moose." He went on to speak for eighty minutes before he stopped and received more medical attention.[51]

Roosevelt recuperated for the next ten days as others made the campaign for him. Some of his supporters believed that a wave of sympathy surrounding the shooting "has insured his election." In deference to his opponent's wounds, Wilson made no public appearances while Roosevelt was in the hospital. While the shooting disrupted the pace of Roosevelt's canvass for votes, it also froze the election in place with Wilson well ahead of his rivals. Several newspapers reported a large undecided vote still remained, and one journal said, "there has been confusion of issues, confusion of thought, and confusion of purpose on the part of the voters." As long as Wilson secured the bulk of Democratic support, however, the result of the contest was not really in doubt. The result was, said a Baltimore newspaper, "This is not a campaign which has aroused the passions of men."[52]

At the time Roosevelt was shot, other events once again distracted Americans from attention to the election campaign. Two days after the attempt on Roosevelt's life, the concluding game of the World Series took place in Boston. The Red Sox and the Giants were tied at three games apiece. In the bottom of the tenth inning, the favored Giants held a slim 2–1 lead with their ace Christy Mathewson on the mound. The first batter lifted a high fly ball to right-center field where Fred Snodgrass settled under what seemed to be a routine out. The reporter for the *New York Times*, recounting the play, imagined what the impact of the impending catch would be: "A campaign which may mean a change in the whole structure of the nation's Government has been put into the background. What happens will be flashed by telegraph the length and breadth of the land, and thereby carried over and under the sea, and millions will be uplifted or downcast."[53]

Snodgrass muffed the catch; the Red Sox scored two runs and won the World Series. The unlucky fielder had dropped a world championship, and the mishap stayed with him until his death. Half a century later, writing about the 1960 election, Theodore H. White would say, "There is a politicians' rule of thumb, particularly hallowed by Democratic politicians, that no election campaign starts until the World Series is over." To the extent that was true in 1912, the Snodgrass muff and the Red Sox victory on 16 October could have been a moment when Americans engaged in full the issues of that election year.[54]

There were, however, media distractions that competed with the election for public involvement. The trial of Lieutenant Charles Becker for the murder of Herman Rosenthal had opened in New York on 7 October. A parade of colorful and sordid witnesses provided the nation with a first look at the emerging culture of organized crime. The New York City police seemed to have Manhattan, the Bronx, and Staten Island, too, in their corrupt grip. The *New York Times* and other papers in the city devoted their front pages to copious coverage of the Becker proceedings. Only the shooting of Roosevelt bumped the mobsters off the front pages for a day or so.[55]

Another event, involving the intersection of race and sports, also grabbed the spotlight in the last two weeks of October. The African American heavyweight boxing champion, Jack Johnson, had been in the news a month earlier when his wife committed suicide. Their interracial marriage had been much criticized in the racist newspapers of 1912. When the news broke that Johnson was about to get married again and to an eighteen-year-old white girl, controversy flared anew. The girl's mother pressed authorities in Chicago to arrest Johnson while the federal government explored whether to charge the fighter for alleged criminal behavior. The controversy stayed in the news well past the election. Events that pushed Roosevelt off the front page or even below the fold meant that the publicity his campaign needed so much simply dried up. The media furor meant less time and attention for the last stages of the presidential race.[56]

Roosevelt convalesced in Chicago for a week and then returned to his home in Oyster Bay, New York. He saved his strength for one major campaign appearance on 30 October at Madison Square Garden in New York City. Wilson would follow him the next evening while Taft remained away from big rallies, as he had done throughout the campaign.

Roosevelt's speech came before 15,000 people with an estimated 20,000 more outside. To entertain the crowd before Roosevelt spoke, movies of the campaign depicted the candidate in a variety of situations across the country. One witness said of these scenes: "Everywhere people stretched out eager yearning hands toward their leader as plants reach up towards the sun for help to grow!" When Roosevelt came into view, the crowd exploded. "He stood for forty-three minutes, while the people sang the campaign songs, waved the flag and applauded." In his own remarks, the Progressive candidate, still weary from his wound, took a lofty tone and did not name his rivals. "We war against the forces of evil, and the weapons we use are the weapons of right." His ideas were not new, he said, but reached back to biblical times. "We are for human rights and we intend to work for them in efficient fashion." He renewed his call to rise above partisan and sectional divisions. "We recognize no differences of class, creed, or birthplace. We recognize no sectionalism." As he neared the end, he summed up the new party's philosophy: "We Progressives are trying to represent what we know to be the highest ideals and the deepest and most intimate convictions of the plain men and women, of the good men and women, who work for the home and within the home."[57]

Roosevelt was tired and did not perform at his best despite the enthusiasm of the crowd. Two days later, in a speech to the New York Progressives, he was more animated. "We stand for the two National principles of American good citizenship—the right of the people to rule themselves, and their duty to so rule, as to bring nearer the day when social and industrial justice shall be done to every man and woman within this great land of ours."[58]

Roosevelt made one last attack on Wilson's record on the trusts at Oyster Bay the next day. In his conclusion, Roosevelt returned to a familiar theme that had influenced the election all year long. Of the tariff, he said that the Progressives "propose to reduce all excessive duties while maintaining the principle of protection through the action of a tariff commission like that which in actual practice has worked so admirably in Germany." With that last bow to the most persistent issue of the 1912 election, the extended campaign that Roosevelt had launched at Columbus, Ohio, in February was over. "No one seems to think he can win," wrote James Bryce, "but he may get a large vote in some regions, especially in the West."[59]

On 31 October, Wilson had his turn. Before an audience similar in size to that of Roosevelt, the Democratic candidate received a one-hour demonstration. The enthusiasm was genuine, but Tammany Hall, determined to accentuate the positive, choreographed the applause so that it went longer than Roosevelt's reception. When this artificial pandemonium came upon the scene, a stirred Wilson forgot his prepared text. Instead, he improvised around his general themes for the campaign. He asked for a "united government" and said that "the only possible chance of having a great united organization after the fourth of March next is to vote the Democratic ticket." He promised that Democratic tariff policy would not disturb "honest business" in the country but that "it is going to upset dishonest business in the United States." He added that he was "ready to accept the verdict" of the voters, "whether it is for me or against me." In a message to Democratic rallies, Wilson stressed that the "the tariff question must be solved in the interest of those who work and spend and plan and struggle." There were a few more statements by Wilson and Roosevelt, but as 5 November approached the campaign had finally come down to the voters.[60]

There were no polls in the modern sense in 1912, though newspapers surveyed public opinion in their areas. Political observers did not believe that the dynamics of the race had changed much as Election Day neared. With the Republican-Progressive split, if Wilson received the normal Democratic vote, he was likely to be elected. President Taft, while still clinging to some hope of victory, caught the conventional assumption when he wrote his brother on 1 November. While the Republicans were still the majority party, that edge was not "sufficiently great to divide the total vote of the Republican party into anywhere near equal parts and give a plurality to either of those parts."[61] Professional gamblers set odds at 6–1 that Wilson would be the winner.

On election night, crowds gathered in Times Square in New York City at the headquarters of the *New York Times*. Similar scenes occurred in other cities since newspapers were the only source for up-to-date results. An electric bulletin carried the totals across the *Times* tower on both sides. The news of the Democratic electoral success soon came across the building to the throng clustered below. In Princeton, New Jersey, at Woodrow Wilson's home, the verdict was in by ten o'clock in the evening. Mrs. Wilson kissed her husband and told him he was the president-elect.[62]

In the electoral vote, Wilson had achieved a historic landslide for a Democratic presidential candidate. He carried forty states with 433 elec-

Cartoon showing candidates Taft, Roosevelt, and Wilson as optimistic in public and apprehensive in private about the outcome of the voting. The artist, Clifford K. Berryman, was a rising cartoonist during the 1912 election. In fact there was little suspense about the likely result as the voting drew near. (Clifford K. Berryman collection, National Archives)

toral votes and gained 2 electoral votes in California. Roosevelt won six states with 88 electoral votes, and Taft triumphed in Vermont and Utah with 8 electoral votes. The Democrats won a sweeping victory in the House races with a pickup of sixty-three seats. The Republicans saw their numbers fall by forty-six while the Progressives elected seventeen House members. The new House of Representatives would have 291 Democrats, 127 Republicans, and the 17 Progressives. In the Senate, the Democrats gained control with fifty-one seats to forty-four for the Republicans and one Progressive. The Democrats had achieved the united government that Wilson had stressed in his campaign speeches.

The result in the popular vote reflected a closer race among the four presidential candidates. Wilson had 6,293,454 popular votes to 4,122,721 for Roosevelt, and 3,486,242 votes for Taft. Debs improved his performance over 1908 in a substantial way with 901,551 votes. Wilson had achieved 41.9 percent of the popular vote and was thus a minority president in that sense. Republicans told themselves that a united party could have defeated the Democrats once again.[63]

For President Taft, the result was about what he had expected in terms of the popular vote. "I hoped against hope, but in my heart was making preparations for the future to be lived outside the White House," he told a friend three days after the voting. He warned against "a spirit of compromise" among Republicans that might let Roosevelt back into the affairs of the GOP. Taft had run second to Wilson in seventeen states. He lost narrowly in Idaho and Wyoming and was competitive in Massachusetts, New Hampshire, and Rhode Island. Although he came in second as well in his home state of Ohio, he trailed Wilson badly there. Had Taft been running on his own against Wilson, even with a reasonably united Republican party behind him, he would have been an underdog going into the race.[64]

Roosevelt and the Progressives had some reason for optimism based on their showing in the first presidential election they contested as a third party. The six states in Roosevelt's column included eleven of thirteen electoral votes from California, where the margin over Wilson was very narrow and Taft was not on the ballot, and South Dakota, where Taft was also not on the ballot. In Washington, Michigan, and Minnesota, where the issue of Canadian reciprocity helped him, Roosevelt achieved solid pluralities. With the help of the machine of William Flinn in Pennsylvania, Roosevelt rolled up a 50,000 vote margin over Wilson and the Democrats.[65]

Roosevelt finished second to Wilson in twenty-three states, seven of which were southern states where his percentage exceeded Taft's but did not threaten Wilson's lead. Roosevelt came within 19,000 votes of Wilson in Illinois, 3,000 votes in Maine, 6,000 votes in Montana, and 4,000 in North Dakota. He also lost Vermont to Taft by 1,000 votes. Winning those states would have improved his electoral vote total but would not have gotten Roosevelt within any distance of a majority in the electoral college.

The Progressives failed to elect any of the gubernatorial candidates they had nominated with such optimism earlier in the fall. Beveridge came in second to the Democratic candidate in Indiana and even ran ahead of Roosevelt. Still, he lost by more than 100,000 ballots. Oscar Straus lost to a Democrat in New York. The party's candidates for governor came up short in Ohio and Illinois as well. On the state level, the Progressives elected some 260 members of state legislatures. It all added up to a good start, but no more, for the third party.

Wilson was the only candidate to demonstrate genuine strength in all regions of the country. That was not because he brought new voters into the Democratic party; rather, his success rested on his ability to win the votes of all elements of his party.

The president-elect and his associates recognized that he was the choice of a minority of the voters, but they understood that his electoral landslide attested to his legitimacy as an incoming president. Rather than analyzing the election results, Wilson turned at once to forming his cabinet and preparing to engage the issues now associated with the New Freedom.

The campaign, of course, had not defined what the New Freedom meant to any greater degree than elections usually clarify such matters. Wilson benefited most from the loose phrasing of his slogan. Beyond a promise of tariff reform and some effort to control corporations through antitrust laws, the Democrats had not been all that specific. This situation gave Wilson a good deal of latitude in the White House. He could characterize his positions as carrying out aspects of the New Freedom, confident that from the contradictions, vague language, and noble goals of his speeches he could find what he needed to justify his actions. As it turned out, Wilson during his two terms would implement government programs such as farm loans, child labor laws, and prolabor legislation in ways that many Democrats would not have anticipated during 1912.

In Congress, the Democratic sweep produced some notable Republican casualties. Two of the most prominent Republican members of the

House of Representatives to lose were former Speaker Joseph G. Cannon and Roosevelt's son-in-law, Nicholas Longworth. Cannon lost his seat for the first time since the Democrats controlled Congress after the 1890 election. He wrote to a friend that "the party landed in Purgatory, from which place according to orthodox teaching there is an escape. We have to be thankful we didn't land in that other place from which it is said there is no escape." The Republican contingent in the House was at its lowest number of members in twenty years. There would be little they could do to block the Democrats from implementing the Wilson program.[66]

That the Senate would be Democratic was evident as the election returns flowed in. The Republicans lost seven seats as the Democrats established a 51–44 margin over their opponents. The elections in state legislatures took some time to accomplish, and it was not until early 1913 that all the new members of the upper house had been identified. New Democratic senators came from such usually Republican bastions as Montana, New Hampshire, Illinois, New Jersey, and Kansas. In an ironic twist, these seats would be vulnerable to Republican pickups six years later in the 1918 election, when Democrats lost control of the Senate. That change in turn helped frustrate Wilson's dream of a League of Nations.[67]

The most decisive effect of the Republican split in 1912 was the reshaping of Congress. What would have been a difficult struggle for the Democrats to expand their majority in the House and regain control of the Senate turned instead into a Republican rout. For Woodrow Wilson, that meant during his first year in office that he had the capacity to see the elements of the New Freedom through the legislative process with relative ease. In turn, the new president and his congressional colleagues refuted the traditional Republican notion that the Democrats could not govern.

The Republicans and Progressives soon assessed their future prospects. For the Grand Old Party, there was talk of rewriting their rules to address the issues of fairness that had arisen at the national convention and the delegate-selection process. These produced little result. The dominant sentiment among conservatives was to insure that Roosevelt and his followers did not regain a place in the party. "All that is necessary," wrote one conservative, "is a complete separation of the sheep from the goats and the Republican Party will again be doing business at the old stand." Another contended that the GOP "must be the great conservative party of the nation." To the degree that was the lesson of the election of 1912, the Taft defeat set the Republicans on a more rightward course that they followed during the twentieth century.[68]

Taft took his loss with humorous grace that won him public respect. The people had rendered an "emphatic verdict" against him but he still felt "deep gratitude" at having held the office, he said in a public address. In private, he concluded that "the fight was not altogether fruitless and I am quite content to await history's verdict as to my administration," as he told a friend. Similarly, Hilles complained that, "with one or two exceptions, all of the devoted friends of the President disappeared in the crisis, after they saw no satisfaction in contemplating the outcome." He pointed out that Taft did not campaign, Vice President Sherman was fatally ill, and no Republican governors took to the stump. Republicans defected to Wilson to insure that Roosevelt lost. The problems about the lineup of state electoral tickets further depressed the GOP effort. All in all, Hilles wrote "it was a crushing defeat."[69]

Republicans in 1912 and historians since that time noted that the combined Roosevelt-Taft vote united on a single candidate would have given victory to the Grand Old Party. The problem was that neither Roosevelt nor Taft, assuming they were nominated on their own, would have had a cohesive Republican organization behind them. In a Wilson-Taft race, with Roosevelt on the sidelines, the Democratic candidate would have been the favorite. Pitting Wilson against Roosevelt in an imaginary match-up would probably have been closer, but the Democrat would still have had the advantage. Disgruntled conservative Republicans would likely have stayed home if Roosevelt headed the ticket. These what-ifs, while fascinating to contemplate, were only suppositions based on what the voters had actually done in 1912.

Roosevelt professed to be encouraged with the result of his party's first presidential race. "It was a phenomenal thing to be able to bring the new party into second place and beat out the Republicans," he told a friend. Now his task was "to keep the Progressive Party in such shape that it will be ready to serve the Nation in any way that the Nation's needs demand." That would be easier to pledge than to do. Almost as soon as the votes were in, the Progressives bickered about the role of George W. Perkins in the campaign and in the party's councils as chair of the Executive Committee. Roosevelt was able to maintain Perkins's position in December 1912, but the internal strains of the party, submerged during the election, soon demonstrated that the prospects for continued success were not very good. Roosevelt seemed to sense the problems his improvised candidacy had faced. He quipped to a British visitor in January 1913, "I got more bullets than ballots this time."[70]

The Socialists had done well, from their point of view, with nearly 6 percent of the total vote. They believed that they had gained from the popular mood for reform but had preserved their own integrity against the competing claims of Wilson and Roosevelt. "For the first time in years," said one party journal, "the Socialist party vote was a clear-cut Socialist vote." The big states for the party were Ohio, Pennsylvania, Illinois, California, and New York, which cast 373,000 votes, or more than 40 percent of Debs's total tally. The bigger percentage gains for Debs and his party came in the West in states such as Oklahoma, Montana, Arizona, and Washington. Perhaps the Socialists would have done better by concentrating their efforts in the states where there were more potential voters. In any case, Debs was going to campaign nationwide no matter what.[71]

Internal warfare among the Socialists had abated during the campaign. By early 1913, the splits within the party over the tactic of violence had reappeared. Nonetheless, the Socialists made some gains in the 1914 elections. Then came World War I and its effects, which devastated the Socialists. The onset of the Russian Revolution in 1917 further crippled the party with an association to a foreign, radical ideology. The election of 1912 did not prove to be a time of optimism for Debs and the Socialists. It was the highest percentage of the popular vote that the Socialist Party ever achieved. But they could have done better. Gene Debs was wrong. It was not their year after all.

What did 1912 mean for the long sweep of American politics? Going into the balloting there had been a tacit assumption that the fervor of the 1912 race, the presence of four creditable presidential candidates, and the heightened role for women would result in greater voter interest overall. Postelection analyses, however, soon revealed that the 1912 campaign had not brought a flood of voters to the ballot boxes. The total vote was slightly higher than what had been cast in 1908, but estimated turnout in the North fell some 8 percent. Wilson received almost 120,000 votes fewer than the total for Bryan four years earlier. Roosevelt and Taft together garnered almost 71,000 fewer votes than Taft's tally in 1908. Debs saw the only increase, with 480,000 additional ballots over his 1908 performance. Based on these results, the initial impression would be that the 1908 election, usually regarded as one of the more dull contests in political history, attracted more involvement from the electorate than did the famous 1912 confrontation.

Placing the electoral results in 1912 in context means understanding the change in American politics that had taken place since the McKinley-Bryan race in 1896. At the end of the nineteenth century, the United States had a political system that mobilized large numbers of eligible voters to come out to the polls and to participate in campaigns and caucuses as well. In the 1896 election, for example, some 86 percent of eligible voters in the North came out to vote in the McKinley-Bryan contest. The total for the nation stood at almost 80 percent. Then over the next three elections, turnout slacked off. Turnout slipped to around 74 percent in 1900 and then fell to 65.4 percent in 1904. In 1908, turnout did not continue to slide; it went up slightly to 65.5 percent. In the North, however, turnout reached 75 percent.[72]

Rather than rising as a result of interest in the election of 1912, turnout declined once again to 66.8 percent for the North and 58.8 percent for the nation as a whole. Of all the sections of the country, only New England experienced a rise in turnout of about 1 percent. In such areas of presumed strength for Theodore Roosevelt as the North Central States and the West, turnout fell about 8 to 9 percentage points. Turnout improved some 3 percent in the 1916 election, which pitted Wilson against Charles Evans Hughes. So the 1912 election does not stand out as an interruption of the trend of declining voter turnout. It was, rather, one of the moments when this process accelerated.

Historians and political scientists are still debating the causes for these changes in how American elections worked. The rise of the mass media and popular entertainment after 1900 provided citizens with an alternative to participation in incessant political campaigns. The style of campaigning shifted from mobilizing voters to educating them about the issues through print and film. In the process, the taste for politics ebbed. The emergence of these cultural diversions affected how Americans viewed public life, but there were other forces at work too.[73]

In the late nineteenth century, partisanship had been seen as a virtue among many Americans. That changed as the Progressive Era commenced after 1900. Political parties no longer seemed the embodiment of democracy. To their critics, parties provided a means for unscrupulous leaders to frustrate the democratic will. Reforms designed to curb the power of politicians gained adherents and became an answer to the excesses of partisanship. As a result, the progressives set about hampering the capacity of the parties to bring voters to the polls. That in turn led to a decline in participation.[74]

Another interpretation contends that the parties themselves sought to restrict the role of the electorate. In this view, the Democrats and Republicans imposed limitations on voting that turned potential voters, especially from the lower classes, away from the act of casting ballots. Measures to bar blacks from voting in the South, techniques to curb voter fraud, tighter registration requirements, all these changes cut down on voter turnout. Power shifted to government bureaucrats and regulatory agencies, offices that politicians staffed with their allies. People saw less reason to take part in elections that often produced meaningless results.[75]

Whatever the causes of a relative lack of interest in the 1912 election, several elements seem clear. This election did not impel Americans to vote because of their involvement with the candidates and the issues. The results did not signal any long-term shift in partisan allegiance. This election was not one that realigned or left enduring marks on the way Americans selected their leaders. Its true significance lay elsewhere. With it modern American politics commenced.

The campaign in 1912 marked the last time that the tariff issue played a significant role in the selection of a president. In 1913, the Democrats adopted an income tax as part of the Underwood Tariff Law. That change in how the United States raised its revenue diminished the importance of customs duties as a source of political debate. The role of tariffs and trade remained an important subtheme in national politics, but protectionism, once so salient in partisan debate, gave way to questions of the income tax, government regulation, and foreign policy from 1916 onward.

The 1912 election was most important because of Theodore Roosevelt. First, he challenged Taft and then split the Republican party. That shift turned a likely Democratic victory into a certainty for whoever the party nominated as their candidate. The desire to have a real progressive alternative to Roosevelt led in turn to the fortunate success of Woodrow Wilson at Baltimore. The Democrats had selected their best possible candidate. Had he been nominated, Champ Clark might well have become president, but his capacity to deal with the domestic problems of the day and the challenges of World War I would have been in doubt.

In the fall campaign, Roosevelt and Wilson discussed in an imperfect debate the future of American reform. Roosevelt lost in the exchanges with Wilson and, of course, did not gain the White House, either. But in the long run, Roosevelt's New Nationalism proved to be more useful as a way of meeting society's problems than did Wilson's more limited New Freedom. Wilson himself adopted many aspects of Roosevelt's ideas to gain reelection in 1916. In 1912, it turned out that, for a moment, political philosophy and principles really did matter. That is why this election has remained so fascinating and thought-provoking for Americans ever since.

In that sense, 1912 also saw the emergence of modern politics with its primaries, continuous campaigning throughout the entire year, influence of the media, and the competition from other athletic and cultural events for voter attention. The decline in interest among Americans, even for a contest as exciting as the one Roosevelt and Wilson waged, indicated that choosing national leaders would be done in a different context than had existed since the Civil War. Americans would be less politically mobilized, participation would recede, and the nature of government itself would become more bureaucratic and removed from the people. All these trends were only starting in 1912, and the sense that this contest marked a turning point in how the people of the nation chose to live together also accounts for the enduring relevance of this race for the White House.

On 1 January 1913, newspapers in Washington and New York reported that the end of 1912 had been marked with the customary din. "Mingled with the chatter and the laughter of the celebrators," noted the *Washington Post*, "were the distant sounds of horns and whistles." In New York, Theodore Roosevelt's friend Jacob Riis led his associates in an effort to have "a safe and sane" New Year's celebration. On the political side, the editor of the *New York Tribune* lamented the defeat of the Republican Party in the year just past. That sad outcome was blamed on "the personal ambitions and popularity of a single man." Within two years, the newspaper suggested, the Republicans would be back in power in Congress.[1]

Outside of politics, the controversial figures who had attracted attention away from the election during the preceding months found more sadness, pain, and punishment than new beginnings with the New Year. Lieutenant Charles Becker of New York City was convicted of the murder of Herman Rosenthal and then received a new trial. Found guilty a second time, he went to the electric chair in 1915. Jim Thorpe had the triumph of the Olympics snatched away in early 1913 when it was revealed that he had played professional baseball several years earlier. He had to return his medals. Jack Johnson fled to Europe after he was convicted in 1913 on charges of transporting his future wife across state lines for immoral purposes. Thorpe and Johnson remained in the public eye, but they never again attained the athletic heights they had reached before 1912.

For those politicians who had failed to win the White House in 1912, the future held redemption for one and disappointment for the others. President William Howard Taft left office on 4 March 1913 and taught law at Yale for several years. When the Republicans regained power under Warren G. Harding in 1921, Taft was named chief justice of the United States Supreme Court, the post he had coveted more than the presidency. He served there until his death in 1930.

Robert La Follette remained in the Senate with his hopes for the presidency undimmed. He opposed American entry into World War I and faced censure from his colleagues when he spoke out in 1917. The move to rebuke him failed. He got his chance to run for the White House in

1924 as a third-party candidate but went down in the landslide for Calvin Coolidge. La Follette died the following year.

Champ Clark held on to the post of Speaker of the House but was not a consequential player in the politics of the Wilson years. His bitterness toward William Jennings Bryan never dimmed with the passage of time. Before his death in 1921, he wrote two large, uninformative volumes of memoirs.

Oscar W. Underwood supported Wilson's policies, first in the House and then in the Senate after 1914. Underwood made another run for the White House in 1924. At the Democratic National Convention, the Alabama delegation cast its votes for him on more than 100 ballots. That was not enough, and John W. Davis became the party's nominee. Underwood died in 1927.

In 1916, Eugene V. Debs was not the Socialist candidate for president. He sought a seat in the House of Representatives from his Indiana district but did not succeed in that conservative constituency. When the United States entered World War I, Debs attacked the nation's role in the conflict. A speech he gave in 1918 led to his arrest and conviction for having violated the wartime Sedition Act. While serving his sentence in federal prison, Debs ran for president in 1920. He received 919,000 votes, more than in 1912. Because of the increased size of the electorate, his percentage of the vote was smaller. Pardoned by President Harding in 1921, Debs died in October 1926.

Theodore Roosevelt experienced bouts of depression after his loss in 1912, but his energy and vitality soon returned. A British visitor to the United States found him in January 1913 with " 'l'elan vital' in greater degree than any man I have ever met."[2] The last six years of his life brought Roosevelt recurrent disappointments. His health faltered from an unwise trip to the Brazilian jungle in late 1913. The Progressive Party did poorly in the 1914 elections, and the third-party dream collapsed. Roosevelt opposed Wilson's foreign policy over neutrality during World War I from 1914 to 1917. His attempt to win the Republican nomination in 1916 failed, and with it the remnants of the Progressive cause disappeared. The president rejected Roosevelt's request to take a division to France in 1917 after the United States entered the war. By late 1918, Roosevelt's strength had worn out from overexertion and obesity. He died on 6 January 1919.

Roosevelt had failed to regain the White House in 1912, but his Progressive campaign had imparted a shock of reforming energy to the nation's political system. It took decades for some of the ideas he had advanced to be adopted. Democratic presidents, beginning with Wilson and continuing through Franklin D. Roosevelt, Harry Truman, John Kennedy, and Lyndon B. Johnson, brought Roosevelt's initiatives to completion. In that sense, Roosevelt's campaign in the fall of 1912 resonated through American politics long after he had passed from the scene.

Following his eloquent inaugural address on 4 March 1913, Woodrow Wilson proved in his first term that the Democrats could govern. He persuaded Congress to lower the tariff and enact an income tax. Lawmakers established the Federal Reserve System, and enacted antitrust legislation during 1913–1914. Black Americans who had supported Wilson's candidacy learned of his racism when the federal government was segregated during his administration. When his reelection seemed in doubt, Wilson moved in 1915–1916 to adopt many elements of the New Nationalism to woo progressives. That deft strategy and the claim that he had kept the nation out of the war produced a narrow victory and a second term.

Then Wilson's political fortunes soured. The nation emerged victorious in World War I, but the president's domestic policies weakened and then fractured the Democratic coalition. His dream of a League of Nations encountered Senate rejection in 1919–1920. The Republicans surged back into power in 1918 and 1920. A crippling stroke left Wilson a broken man by the time he stepped down as an unpopular and repudiated executive in March 1921.

As Wilson lived out his last years in a house on S Street in Washington, D.C., did his mind ever drift back to the sights and sounds of the summer and fall of 1912:

The happy Democrats introducing him as "the next president of the United States"; the people gathered around the back of the train as the whistle-stopping Wilson leaned forward to make a point; the fun of throwing buttons to the friendly crowds as the train chugged through Massachusetts; the tang of the autumn air as the open cars took the candidate to the next event in the heartland cities of Omaha, Topeka, and Kokomo; the sense of impending victory that made Wilson's limericks funnier, his arguments more pointed, his perorations more moving to the rapt audiences; the intoxication of a winning campaign that could be felt and inhaled and always remembered.

Lonely and enfeebled, did Wilson ever wonder if it had been only nine or ten years ago when he stood on the verge of power during that magical autumn? Did nostalgia for those vanished moments flicker across his mind before he died in February 1924?

Every presidential election carries with it the promise of expectation and hope for some Americans. Afterward scholars come to appraise how human frailty and inescapable disappointment confounded these fragile electoral aspirations. Almost a century later, the election of 1912, so near the guns of August 1914 and so far from the squalor of modern politics, seems a poignant moment. Four distinguished citizens actually sought the presidency in a campaign of serious ideas and elevated discourse. That such an outcome now seems inconceivable in contemporary America attests to why 1912 will always remain an election rich in possibility and historical meaning.

APPENDIX A
DEMOCRATIC PRIMARY RESULTS 1912

		Wilson	Clark	Underwood	Harmon	Other
Mar. 19	North Dakota (No Democratic primary was held in the state)					
Apr. 2	Wisconsin	45,945	36,464		148	
Apr. 9	Illinois	75,527	218,483			
Apr. 13	Pennsylvania	97,585		710		394
Apr. 19	Nebraska	14,289	21,027		12,454	3,499
Apr. 19	Oregon	9,588	7,857			
Apr. 30	Massachusetts	15,002	34,575			627
Apr. 30	Florida	20,482		28,343		
May 1	Georgia	57,267	692	71,410	189	
May 6	Maryland	22,816	34,510	7,157		
May 14	California	17,214	43,163			
May 20	Ohio	85,054	2,428		96,164	
May 28	New Jersey	48,336	522			
June 4	South Dakota	4,694	4,275			
Totals:		513,829	401,568	136,673	116,294	4,274

Source: Louise Overacker, *The Presidential Primary* (New York: Macmillan, 1926), 236; Arthur S. Link, ed., *The Papers of Woodrow Wilson,* vol. 24, *Jan.–Aug. 1912* (Princeton, N.J.: Princeton University Press, 1977), 382, for Florida and Georgia results.

APPENDIX B
REPUBLICAN PRIMARY RESULTS 1912

		Roosevelt	Taft	La Follette
Mar. 19	North Dakota	23,669	1,876	34,123
Apr. 2	Wisconsin	628	47,514	133,354
Apr. 9	Illinois	266,917	127,481	42,692
Apr. 13	Pennsylvania	282,853	191,179	
Apr. 19	Nebraska	45,795	13,341	16,785
Apr. 19	Oregon	28,905	20,517	22,491
Apr. 30	Massachusetts	83,099	86,722	2,058
May 6	Maryland	29,124	25,995	
May 14	California	138,563	69,345	45,876
May 20	Ohio	165,809	118,362	15,570
May 28	New Jersey	61,297	44,034	3,464
June 4	South Dakota	38,106	19,960	10,944
Totals:		1,164,765	768,202	327,357

Source: Louise Overacker, *The Presidential Primary* (New York: Macmillan, 1926), 236; John A. Gable, *The Bull Moose Years: Theodore Roosevelt and the Progressive Party* (Port Washington, N.Y.: Kennikat Press, 1978), 14, for the Ohio result.

APPENDIX C
POPULAR AND ELECCTORAL VOTE FOR PRESIDENT IN 1912

State	Wilson	Roosevelt	Popular Vote Taft	Debs	Electoral Vote W	R	T
Alabama	82,439	22,689	9,731	3,029	12		
Arizona	10,324	6,949	3,021	3,163	3		
Arkansas	68,838	21,674	24,297	8,153	9		
California	283,436	283,640	3,914	79,201	2	11	
Colorado	114,223	72,366	58,386	16,418	6		
Connecticut	74,561	34,129	68,324	10,056	7		
Delaware	22,631	8,886	15,1998	556	3		
Florida	35,343	4,555	4,279	4,806	6		
Georgia	93,171	21,985	5,191	1,058	14		
Idaho	33,921	25,527	32,810	11,960	4		
Illinois	405,048	386,478	253,593	81,278	29		
Indiana	281,890	162,007	151,267	36,931	15		
Iowa	185,325	161,819	119,805	16,967	13		
Kansas	143,663	120,210	74,845	26,779	10		
Kentucky	219,484	101,766	115,510	11,646	13		
Louisiana	60,871	9,283	3,833	5,261	10		
Maine	51,113	48,495	26,545	2,541	6		
Maryland	112,674	57,789	54,956	3,996	8		
Massachusetts	173,408	142,228	155,948	12,616	18		
Michigan	150,751	214,584	152,244	23,211	15		
Minnesota	106,426	125,856	64,334	27,505	12		
Mississippi	57,324	3,549	1,560	2,050	10		
Missouri	330,746	124,375	207,821	28,646	18		
Montana	27,941	22,546	18,512	10,885	4		
Nebraska	109,008	72,681	54,226	10,185	8		
Nevada	7,986	5,620	3,196	3,313	3		
New Hampshire	34,724	17,794	32,927	1,981	4		
New Jersey	178,289	145,510	88,835	15,948	14		
New Mexico	20,437	8,347	17,733	2,859	3		
New York	655,573	390,093	455,487	63,434	45		
North Carolina	144,407	69,135	29,129	987	12		
North Dakota	29,555	25,726	23,090	6,966	5		
Ohio	424,834	229,807	278,168	90,144	24		
Oklahoma	119,156	——	90,786	41,674	10		
Oregon	47,064	37,600	34,673	13,343	5		
Pennsylvania	395,637	444,894	273,360	83,614	38		
Rhode Island	30,412	16,878	27,703	2,049	5		
South Carolina	48,357	1,293	536	164	9		

State	Wilson	Roosevelt	Popular Vote Taft	Debs	Electoral Vote W	R	T
South Dakota	48,942	58,511	——	4,662	5		
Tennessee	133,335	54,041	60,475	3,564	12		
Texas	221,589	28,853	26,755	25,743	20		
Utah	36,579	24,174	42,100	9,023		4	
Vermont	15,354	22,132	23,332	928	4		
Virginia	90,332	21,776	23,288	820	12		
Washington	86.840	113,698	70,445	40,134	7		
West Virginia	113,097	79,112	56,754	15,248	8		
Wisconsin	164,230	62,448	130,596	33,476	13		
Wyoming	15,310	9,232	14,560	2760	3		
Totals:	6,293,454	4,122,721	3,486,242	901,551	435	88	8

The Prohibition Party candidate, Eugene Wilder Chain received 208,157 votes, and Arthur Elmer Reimer, the candidate of the Socialist Labor Party, received 29,324 votes. Roosevelt was not on the ballot in Oklahoma, and Taft was not on the ballot in South Dakota.

Source: New York Times, 29 December 1912; David Leip, *Dave Leip's Atlas of U.S. Presidential Elections,* http://www.uselectionatlas.org/.

There has been a change of government. It began two years ago, when the House of Representatives became Democratic by a decisive majority. It has now been completed. The Senate about to assemble will also be Democratic. The offices of President and Vice-President have been put into the hands of Democrats. What does the change mean? That is the question that is uppermost in our minds to-day. That is the question I am going to try to answer, in order, if I may, to interpret the occasion.

It means much more than the mere success of a party. The success of a party means little except when the Nation is using that party for a large and definite purpose. No one can mistake the purpose for which the Nation now seeks to use the Democratic Party. It seeks to use it to interpret a change in its own plans and point of view. Some old things with which we had grown familiar, and which had begun to creep into the very habit of our thought and of our lives, have altered their aspect as we have latterly looked critically upon them, with fresh, awakened eyes; have dropped their disguises and shown themselves alien and sinister. Some new things, as we look frankly upon them, willing to comprehend their real character, have come to assume the aspect of things long believed in and familiar, stuff of our own convictions. We have been refreshed by a new insight into our own life.

We see that in many things that life is very great. It is incomparably great in its material aspects, in its body of wealth, in the diversity and sweep of its energy, in the industries which have been conceived and built up by the genius of individual men and the limitless enterprise of groups of men. It is great, also, very great, in its moral force. Nowhere else in the world have noble men and women exhibited in more striking forms the beauty and the energy of sympathy and helpfulness and counsel in their efforts to rectify wrong, alleviate suffering, and set the weak in the way of strength and hope. We have built up, moreover, a great system of government, which has stood through a long age as in many respects a model for those who seek to set liberty upon foundations that will endure against fortuitous change, against storm and accident. Our life contains every great thing, and contains it in rich abundance.

But the evil has come with the good, and much fine gold has been corroded. With riches has come inexcusable waste. We have squandered a great part of what we might have used, and have not stopped to conserve the exceeding bounty of nature, without which our genius for enterprise would have been worthless and impotent, scorning to be careful, shamefully prodigal as well as admirably efficient. We have been proud of our industrial achievements, but we have hitherto not stopped thoughtfully enough to count the human cost, the cost of lives snuffed out, of energies overtaxed and broken, the fearful physical and spiritual cost to the men and women and children upon whom the dead weight and burden of it all has fallen pitilessly the years through. The groans and agony of it all had not yet reached our ears, the solemn, moving undertone of our life, coming up out of the mines and factories, and out of every home where the struggle had its intimate and familiar seat. With the great Government went many deep secret things which we too long delayed to look into and scrutinize with candid, fearless eyes. The great Government we loved has too often been made use of for private and selfish purposes, and those who used it had forgotten the people.

At last a vision has been vouchsafed us of our life as a whole. We see the bad with the good, the debased and decadent with the sound and vital. With this vision we approach new affairs. Our duty is to cleanse, to reconsider, to restore, to correct the evil without impairing the good, to purify and humanize every process of our common life without weakening or sentimentalizing it. There has been something crude and heartless and unfeeling in our haste to succeed and be great. Our thought has been "Let every man look out for himself, let every generation look out for itself," while we reared giant machinery which made it impossible that any but those who stood at the levers of control should have a chance to look out for themselves. We had not forgotten our morals. We remembered well enough that we had set up a policy which was meant to serve the humblest as well as the most powerful, with an eye single to the standards of justice and fair play, and remembered it with pride. But we were very heedless and in a hurry to be great.

We have come now to the sober second thought. The scales of heedlessness have fallen from our eyes. We have made up our minds to square every process of our national life again with the standards we so proudly set up at the beginning and have always carried at our hearts. Our work is a work of restoration.

We have itemized with some degree of particularity the things that ought to be altered and here are some of the chief items: A tariff which cuts us off from our proper part in the commerce of the world, violates the just principles of taxation, and makes the Government a facile instrument in the hands of private interests; a banking and currency system based upon the necessity of the Government to sell its bonds fifty years ago and perfectly adapted to concentrating cash and restricting credits; an industrial system which, take it on all its sides, financial as well as administrative, holds capital in leading strings, restricts the liberties and limits the opportunities of labor, and exploits without renewing or conserving the natural resources of the country; a body of agricultural activities never yet given the efficiency of great business undertakings or served as it should be through the instrumentality of science taken directly to the farm, or afforded the facilities of credit best suited to its practical needs; watercourses undeveloped, waste places unreclaimed, forests untended, fast disappearing without plan or prospect of renewal, unregarded waste heaps at every mine. We have studied as perhaps no other nation has the most effective means of production, but we have not studied cost or economy as we should either as organizers of industry, as statesmen, or as individuals.

Nor have we studied and perfected the means by which government may be put at the service of humanity, in safeguarding the health of the Nation, the health of its men and its women and its children, as well as their rights in the struggle for existence. This is no sentimental duty. The firm basis of government is justice, not pity. These are matters of justice. There can be no equality or opportunity, the first essential of justice in the body politic, if men and women and children be not shielded in their lives, their very vitality, from the consequences of great industrial and social processes which they can not alter, control, or singly cope with. Society must see to it that it does not itself crush or weaken or damage its own constituent parts. The first duty of law is to keep sound the society it serves. Sanitary laws, pure food laws, and laws determining conditions of labor which individuals are powerless to determine for themselves are intimate parts of the very business of justice and legal efficiency.

These are some of the things we ought to do, and not leave the others undone, the old-fashioned, never-to-be-neglected, fundamental safeguarding of property and of individual right. This is the high enterprise of the new day: To lift everything that concerns our life as a Nation to the light that shines from the hearthfire of every man's conscience and vision of the right. It is inconceivable that we should do this as partisans; it is inconceivable we should do it in ignorance of the facts as they are or in blind haste. We shall restore, not destroy. We shall deal with our economic system as it is and as it may be modified, not as it might be if we had a clean sheet of paper to write upon; and step by step we shall make it what it should be, in the spirit of those who question their own wisdom and seek counsel and knowledge, not shallow self-satisfaction or the excitement of excursions whither they can not tell. Justice, and only justice, shall always be our motto.

And yet it will be no cool process of mere science. The Nation has been deeply stirred, stirred by a solemn passion, stirred by the knowledge of wrong, of ideals lost, of government too often debauched and made an instrument of evil. The feelings with which we face this new age of right and opportunity sweep across our heartstrings like some air out of God's own presence, where justice and mercy are reconciled and the judge and the brother are one. We know our task to be no mere task of politics but a task which shall search us through and through, whether we be able to understand our time and the need of our people, whether we be indeed their spokesmen and interpreters, whether we have the pure heart to comprehend and the rectified will to choose our high course of action.

This is not a day of triumph; it is a day of dedication. Here muster, not the forces of party, but the forces of humanity. Men's hearts wait upon us; men's lives hang in the balance; men's hopes call upon us to say what we will do. Who shall live up to the great trust? Who dares fail to try? I summon all honest men, all patriotic, forward-looking men, to my side. God helping me, I will not fail them, if they will but counsel and sustain me!

NOTES

AUTHOR'S PREFACE

1 George E. Mowry, *Theodore Roosevelt and the Progressive Movement* (Madison: University of Wisconsin Press, 1946).

2 Arthur S. Link, *Wilson: The Road to the White House* (Princeton, N.J.: Princeton University Press, 1947).

3 John Morton Blum, *The Republican Roosevelt* (Cambridge, Mass.: Harvard University Press, 1954).

4 William H. Harbaugh, *Power and Responsibility: The Life and Times of Theodore Roosevelt* (New York: Farrar, Straus, & Cudahy, 1961).

5 Arthur S. Link, *Wilson*, 5 vols. (Princeton, N.J.: Princeton University Press, 1947–1965), vol. 1, *The Road to the White House;* vol. 2, *The New Freedom;* vol. 3, *The Struggle for Neutrality;* vol. 4, *Confusions and Crises, 1915–1916;* vol. 5, *Campaigns for Progressivism and Peace, 1916–1917.*

6 Frank K. Kelly, *The Fight for the White House: The Story of 1912* (New York: Thomas Y. Crowell, 1961), 296.

7 Ibid., 297.

8 Francis L. Broderick, *Progressivism at Risk: Electing a President in 1912* (New York: Greenwood Press, 1989).

9 James Chace, *1912: Wilson, Roosevelt, Taft and Debs—The Election That Changed the Country* (New York: Simon & Schuster, 2004).

PROLOGUE: THE NEW YEAR—1912

1 "New Year Begins Well, Business Men Say," *New-York Daily Tribune*, 1 January 1912.

2 *Chicago Daily Tribune*, 1 January 1912.

3 "Taft Peace Talk Ends Republican Hope of Harmony," *Chicago Daily Tribune*, 1 January 1912.

4 "Ohio Insurgents to Convene Today," *Atlanta Constitution*, 1 January 1912.

CHAPTER 1 PROGRESSIVE POLITICS, 1909–1910

1 Mark Sullivan, *Our Times*, vol. 4, *The War Begins* (New York: Charles Scribner's Sons, 1940), 441, reprints this verse, which originally appeared in *Life* magazine.

2 Elihu Root to Theodore Roosevelt, 12 September 1908, Theodore Roosevelt Papers, Manuscript Division, Library of Congress, Washington, D.C. (hereafter LC).

3 Lawrence F. Abbott, ed., *The Letters of Archie Butt* (Garden City, N.Y.: Doubleday, Page, 1924), 153; Roosevelt to George O. Trevelyan, 19 June 1908 (third quotation), Roosevelt to Sydney Brooks, 20 November 1908 (second

quotation), in Elting E. Morison, ed., *The Letters of Theodore Roosevelt*, 8 vols. (Cambridge, Mass.: Harvard University Press, 1951–1954), 6:1085, 1369.

4 William Howard Taft to Theodore Roosevelt, 7 November 1908, William Howard Taft Papers, LC.

5 Lucius B. Swift to Mrs. Swift, 8 July 1910, Lucius B. Swift Papers, Indiana State Library, Indianapolis.

6 Elihu Root to Whitelaw Reid, 20 December 1909, Whitelaw Reid Papers, LC.

7 Lawrence F. Abbott, *Impressions of Theodore Roosevelt* (Garden City, N.Y.: Doubleday, Page, 1920), 267; Theodore Roosevelt, "Progressive Nationalism; or What?" in *Social Justice and Popular Rule*, vol. 17 of *The Works of Theodore Roosevelt*, ed. Hermann Hagedorn, national ed., 20 vols. (New York: Charles Scribner's Sons, 1926), 49.

8 *New York Times*, 4 April 1905, quotes Roosevelt.

9 For Taft's reservations about Roosevelt's administrative style, see Taft to Helen Herron Taft, 3 October 1909, Taft Papers.

10 George von Lengerke Meyer Diary, 4 January 1909, LC; Henry F. Pringle, *The Life and Times of William Howard Taft*, 2 vols. (New York: Farrar & Rinehart, 1939), 1: 394, 396.

11 *The Autobiography of William Allen White* (New York: Macmillan, 1946), 426.

12 Dave Von Drehle, *Triangle: The Fire That Changed America* (New York: Atlantic Monthly Press, 2003).

13 Henry L. West, "The Present Session of Congress," *Forum* 32 (December 1901): 428.

14 There is no systematic treatment of the Republican ideology about the tariff during the Gilded Age and Progressive Era. Richard Cleveland Baker, *The Tariff under Roosevelt and Taft* (Hastings, Neb.: Democrat Printing Co., 1941), still has much of interest to say on the subject for the era of Theodore Roosevelt.

15 Milton W. Blumenberg, comp., *Official Report of the Proceedings of the Fourteenth Republican National Convention* (Columbus, Ohio: Press of J. F. Heer, 1908), 117.

16 The legislative struggle over cattle hides can be followed in, e.g., Charles H. Jones to Charles E. Hoyt, 23 July 1909, 26 July 1909, Commonwealth Shoe and Leather Company Papers, Baker Library, Harvard Business School, Cambridge, Mass. See also Lewis L. Gould, "Western Range Senators and the Payne-Aldrich Tariff," *Pacific Northwest Quarterly* 64 (1973): 49–56.

17 Joseph L. Bristow to Harold T. Chase, 27 May 1909, Joseph L. Bristow Papers, Kansas State Historical Society, Topeka.

18 Lewis L. Gould, *Reform and Regulation: American Politics from Roosevelt to Wilson* (Prospect Heights, Ill.: Waveland Press, 1996), 119.

19 James A. Tawney to Taft, 18 August 1909, series 5, case file 3727, Taft Papers; William Howard Taft, *Presidential Addresses and State Papers* (New York: Doubleday, Page, 1910), 222. For progressive reaction to the speech,

see Thomas Thorson to Jonathan P. Dolliver, 20 September 1909, Jonathan P. Dolliver Papers, Iowa State Historical Society, Iowa City.

20 Joseph L. Bristow to Kate J. Adams, 27 September 1909, Bristow Papers, mentions Roosevelt's renewed appeal. For an assessment of Taft's situation and the interest in Roosevelt, see Oscar King Davis to James T. Williams Jr., 11 October 1909, James T. Williams Jr. Papers, Duke University Library, Durham, N.C.

21 The best treatment of this episode remains James L. Penick Jr., *Progressive Politics and Conservation: The Ballinger-Pinchot Affair* (Chicago: University of Chicago Press, 1968).

22 See ibid., 165–180, for the outcome of the controversy.

23 Henry Wallace to Horace Plunkett, 4 February 1910, *American Letters of Sir Horace Plunkett, 1883–1932* (East Ardsley, Yorkshire: Micro Methods, 1963); Chester H. Rowell to William Kent, 12 January 1910, Chester H. Rowell Papers, Bancroft Library, University of California, Berkeley; Theodore Roosevelt Jr. to Warrington Dawson, 15 February 1910, Warrington Dawson Papers, Duke University Library, Durham, N.C.

24 Roosevelt to Gifford Pinchot, 17 January 1910, Roosevelt to Henry Cabot Lodge, 10 April 1910, 5 May 1910, in Morison, ed., *Letters of Theodore Roosevelt*, 7:45, 73, 80.

25 "The Situation in Congress," *Independent* 68 (February 1910): 324.

26 "One Year of Taft," *Literary Digest* 46 (19 March 1910): 525.

27 James S. Clarkson to Grenville M. Dodge, 11 April 1910, Grenville M. Dodge Papers, Iowa State Department of History and Archives, Des Moines.

28 Claude E. Barfield, "The Democratic Party in Congress, 1909–1913" (Ph.D. diss., Northwestern University, 1965), 1.

29 National Democratic Campaign Committee, *Democratic Campaign Textbook for 1910* (Baltimore: National Democratic Campaign Committee, 1910), 92.

30 Ray Stannard Baker, "What about the Democratic Party?" *American Magazine* 70 (June 1910): 160.

31 Taft to Helen Taft, 3 October 1909, Taft Papers.

32 Worthington Chauncey Ford, ed., *Letters of Henry Adams (1892–1918)* (Boston: Houghton Mifflin, 1938), 520.

33 H. J. Haskell to William Allen White, 21 July 1910, William Allen White Papers, LC.

34 George Wickersham to Charles Nagel, 3 July 1910, Charles Nagel Papers, Sterling Memorial Library, Yale University, New Haven, Conn.

35 *Minneapolis Journal*, 9 July 1910.

36 Roosevelt to Fremont Older, 18 August 1910, in Morison, ed., *Letters of Theodore Roosevelt*, 7:118–119.

37 Theodore Roosevelt, *The New Nationalism* (New York: Outlook Co., 1910), 38–39, 40–42.

38 Herbert Croly, *The Promise of American Life* (New York: Macmillan, 1909).

39 Roosevelt, *The New Nationalism*, 11–12. For Herbert Croly's impact on Roosevelt, see George E. Mowry, *Theodore Roosevelt and the Progressive Movement*

(Madison: University of Wisconsin Press, 1946), 146–147. Roosevelt scholars believe that he had developed most of his reform ideas before he read Croly's book in 1910.

40 Roosevelt, *The New Nationalism*, 28.

41 Esmond Ovey to Mitchell Innes, 20 September 1910, U.S Political Correspondence, FO 371/1020, British National Archives, Kew; Henry Field to Henry Cabot Lodge, 26 September 1910, Henry Cabot Lodge Papers, Massachusetts Historical Society, Boston.

42 Robert S. La Forte, "Theodore Roosevelt's Osawatomie Speech," *Kansas Historical Quarterly* 32 (1966): 199; Henry Cabot Lodge to William E. Chandler, 19 October 1910, Lodge Papers.

43 Ray Stannard Baker to Robert M. La Follette, 30 September 1910, La Follette Family Papers, LC.

44 Arthur S. Link, *Wilson: The Road to the White House* (Princeton, N.J.: Princeton University Press, 1947), 109.

45 Ibid., 167; Wilson to Mary Allen Hulbert Peck, 5 September 1909, in Arthur S. Link, ed., *The Papers of Woodrow Wilson*, vol. 19, *1909–1910* (Princeton, N.J.: Princeton University Press, 1975), 358.

46 *Dallas Morning News*, 5 November 1910.

47 Geoffrey Morrison, "A Political Biography of Champ Clark" (Ph.D. diss., Saint Louis University, 1972), 203; *The World Almanac and Encyclopedia* (New York: Press Publishing Co., 1910), 212.

48 Thomas B. Love to Wilson, 8 November 1910, Woodrow Wilson Papers, LC.

49 J. Sloat Fassett to James S. Sherman, 19 November 1910, James S. Sherman Papers, New York Public Library; Gifford Pinchot to J. L. Houghteling Jr., 29 November 1910, Gifford Pinchot Papers, LC; Roosevelt to William Allen White, 24 January 1911, in Morison, *Letters of Theodore Roosevelt*, 7:231–214.

50 Taft to Mrs. Aaron F. Perry, 3 November 1910, Taft to Lafayette Young, 25 November 1910, Taft Papers; Knute Nelson to Soren Listoe, 24 December 1910, Knute Nelson Papers, Minnesota Historical Society, Saint Paul.

CHAPTER 2 PRELUDE TO THE PRESIDENTIAL RACE, 1911

1 Oscar King Davis, *Released for Publication: Some Inside History of Theodore Roosevelt and His Times, 1898–1918* (Boston: Houghton Mifflin, 1925), 215. The parody was of the popular song "Has Anybody Here Seen Kelly?"

2 Frederic C. Howe to Robert M. La Follette, 14 December 1910, La Follette Family Papers, box B64, Manuscript Division, Library of Congress, Washington, D.C. (hereafter LC).

3 *The Campaign Text Book of the Democratic Party of the United States, 1908* (n.p., 1908), 237.

4 *Fort Worth Record*, 3 March 1912, quoting Democrat Jacob F. Wolters.

5 Rome G. Brown, "The Judicial Recall: A Fallacy Repugnant to Congressional Government," Senate Document no. 892, 62nd Cong., 2nd sess. (Washington, D.C.: U.S. Government Printing Office, 1912), 23.

6 Theodore Roosevelt, "A Charter of Democracy," in *Social Justice and Popular Rule*, vol. 17 of *The Works of Theodore Roosevelt*, ed. Hermann Hagedorn, national ed., 20 vols. (New York: Charles Scribner's Sons, 1926), 139.

7 William Howard Taft to Helen Taft, 19 August 1911, William Howard Taft Papers, LC; Howard Roberts Lamar, *The Far Southwest, 1846–1912: A Territorial History* (New Haven, Conn.: Yale University Press, 1966), 502–504.

8 Lewis L. Gould, *The Most Exclusive Club: A History of the Modern United States Senate* (New York: Basic Books, 2005), 53–55. For a full treatment of the Lorimer case, see Joel Arthur Tarr, *A Study in Boss Politics: William Lorimer of Chicago* (Urbana: University of Illinois Press, 1971).

9 "California Voters Give Votes to Women: Sees Beginning of the End," *New York Times*, 13 October 1911.

10 "Women as a Factor in the Political Campaign," *New York Times*, 1 September 1912, quoting Frances Kellor.

11 "Want Federal Labor Board," *New York Times*, 30 December 1911. Jo Freeman, "The Rise of Political Women in the Election of 1912," 2003, http://www.jofreeman.com/polhistory/1912.htm, is an excellent and well-documented survey of the role of women in the election of 1912.

12 Richard B. Sherman, *The Republican Party and Black America from McKinley to Hoover, 1896–1933* (Charlottesville: University Press of Virginia, 1973), 78–82, 88–95.

13 Ibid., 100–101.

14 *Campaign Text Book of the Democratic Party, 1908*, 17.

15 David Sarasohn, *The Party of Reform: Democrats in the Progressive Era* (Jackson: University of Mississippi Press, 1989), 17–34, is good on the sources of Democratic voting strength.

16 Arthur S. Link, *Wilson: The Road to the White House* (Princeton, N.J.: Princeton University Press, 1947), 212.

17 Ibid., 211–237, covers the fight over Smith in detail. *Dallas Morning News*, 22 December 1910.

18 *San Antonio Express*, 24 April 1911.

19 John E. Lathrop to Henry S. Breckinridge, 1 March 1911, Woodrow Wilson Papers, LC.

20 Judson Harmon to George A. Harmon, 23 October 1911, Judson Harmon Papers, Cincinnati Historical Society; Oscar W. Underwood to J. C. Hemphill, 10 May 1912, Hemphill Family Papers, Duke University Library, Durham, N.C. Sarasohn, *The Party of Reform*, 126–127, examines the strengths and drawbacks of the Harmon and Underwood candidacies.

21 Claude E. Barfield, "The Democratic Party in Congress, 1909–1913" (Ph.D. diss., Northwestern University, 1965), 353.

22 Clark to J. C. Hemphill, 3 September 1911, Hemphill Family Papers. Geoffrey F. Morrison, "A Political Biography of Champ Clark" (Ph.D. diss., Saint Louis University, 1972), 231, has the quotation about Canada.

23 Ray Ginger, *The Bending Cross: A Biography of Eugene Victor Debs* (New Brunswick, N.J.: Rutgers University Press, 1949), 307.

24 "The Tide of Socialism," *World's Work* 23 (January 1912): 252.

25 H. Wayne Morgan, *Eugene V. Debs: Socialist for President* (Syracuse, N.Y.: Syracuse University Press, 1962), 117; Nick Salvatore, *Eugene V. Debs: Citizen and Socialist* (Urbana: University of Illinois Press, 1987), 242.

26 James Bryce to Alfred Henry George Grey, 5 June 1911, James Bryce Papers, FO 800/334, British National Archives, Kew. The president's success in getting Canadian reciprocity through Congress can be followed in L. Ethan Ellis, *Reciprocity 1911: A Study in Canadian-American Relations* (New Haven, Conn.: Yale University Press, 1939), 110–140.

27 "Nothing to Stop Taft Renomination," *New York Times*, 20 August 1911, outlined the confidence that the Taft camp displayed at this point.

28 Robert M. La Follette to William Kent, February 15, 1912, William Kent Papers, Sterling Memorial Library, Yale University, New Haven, Conn. The best biography of La Follette is Nancy C. Unger, *Fighting Bob La Follette: The Righteous Reformer* (Chapel Hill: University of North Carolina Press, 2000).

29 Mark Sullivan to George S. Loftus, 27 December 1911, James Manahan Papers, Minnesota Historical Society, Saint Paul; Herbert Parsons to Joseph Deutsch, 22 March 1911, box 10, Herbert Parsons Papers, Columbia University Library, New York.

30 Gifford Pinchot to George C. Pardee, 24 February 1911, George C. Pardee Papers, Bancroft Library, University of California, Berkeley.

31 Roosevelt to James R. Garfield, 8 June 1911, Theodore Roosevelt Papers, LC. Charles D. Hilles to Melville E. Stone, 29 July 1911, Charles D. Hilles Papers, Sterling Memorial Library, Yale University, New Haven, Conn., discussed the circumstances around the leaked story. See also Roosevelt to Edwin A. Van Valkenburg, 14 June 1911, in Elting E. Morison, ed., *The Letters of Theodore Roosevelt*, 8 vols. (Cambridge, Mass.: Harvard University Press, 1951–1954), 7:286–287.

32 Taft to Philander Knox, 9 September 1911, Philander C. Knox Papers, LC.

33 George Wickersham to Albert H. Walker, 28 February 1911, author's collection.

34 Roosevelt to Richard Wilson Knott, 6 June 1911, in Morison, ed., *The Letters of Theodore Roosevelt*, 7:277–278.

35 Roosevelt to Herbert Parsons, 6 December 1911, in Morison, ed., *The Letters of Theodore Roosevelt*, 7:452–453, provides Roosevelt's explanation for why the third-term tradition did not apply in his case. For the circumstances surrounding the decision on Election Night of 1904 to make this declaration, see Lewis L. Gould, *The Presidency of Theodore Roosevelt* (Lawrence: University Press of Kansas, 1991), 143–144, quoted at 144.

36 Eustace Percy to James Bryce, 5 September 1911, Bryce Embassy Papers, Bodleian Library, Oxford.

CHAPTER 3 ROOSEVELT VERSUS TAFT IN 1912

1 The verses about Roosevelt appear in the speech by John Sharp Williams (D-Mississippi) in the U.S. Senate, *Congressional Record*, 62nd Cong., 2nd

sess. (22 August 1912), 11535. Senator Williams received the verses in the mail from an unknown author as he mentions on the page cited.

2 The pivotal role of the Republican National Committee in 1908 is discussed in Victor Rosewater, *Backstage in 1912: The Inside Story of the Split Republican Convention* (Philadelphia: Dorrance, 1932), 13–20.

3 Lewis L. Gould, "Theodore Roosevelt, William Howard Taft and the Disputed Delegates in 1912: Texas as a Test Case," *Southwestern Historical Quarterly* 80 (1976): 33–56.

4 Charles D. Hilles to Charles P. Taft, 24 September 1911, Charles D. Hilles Papers, Sterling Memorial Library, Yale University, New Haven, Conn.. Norman Wilensky, *Conservatives in the Progressive Era: The Taft Republicans of 1912* (Greenville: Florida State University Press, 1965), is excellent on Hilles's role.

5 For the reciprocity issue and the Canadian election, see L. Ethan Ellis, *Reciprocity 1991: A Study in Canadian-American Relations* (New Haven, Conn.: Yale University Press, 1939), 183–186.

6 "Taft Denounces Tariff-For-Politics," *New York Times*, 27 August 1911.

7 Roosevelt to Arthur Lee, 22 August 1911, in Elting E. Morison, ed., *The Letters of Theodore Roosevelt*, 8 vols. (Cambridge, Mass.: Harvard University Press, 1951–1954), 7:338. Oscar King Davis to Roosevelt, 5 June 1911, Theodore Roosevelt Papers, Manuscript Division, Library of Congress, Washington, D.C. (hereafter LC).

8 Fred Greenbaum, "Teddy Roosevelt Creates a 'Draft' in 1912," in *Theodore Roosevelt: Many-Sided American*, ed. Natalie Naylor, Douglas Brinkley, and John Allen Gable (Interlaken, N.Y.: Heart of the Lakes Publishing, 1992), 433–442, maintains that La Follette's campaign would have been a winning one had not Roosevelt preempted him. Herbert F. Margulies, "La Follette, Roosevelt and the Republican Presidential Nomination of 1912," *Mid-America* 58 (January 1976): 54–76, is more attuned to the inherent weakness of the La Follette canvass.

9 Medill McCormick to Walter L. Houser, 22 November 1911, box 112, Houser to Gifford Pinchot, 24 October 1911, box 85, National Progressive Republican League Files, La Follette Family Papers, LC; James R. Garfield to Truman Newberry, 11 December 1911, James R. Garfield Papers, box 117, LC.

10 John D. Fackler to Houser, 22 November 1911, National Progressive Republican League Files, box 72, La Follette Family Papers.

11 Roosevelt to Theodore Roosevelt Jr., 22 August 1911, in Morison ed., *The Letters of Theodore Roosevelt*, 7:336.

12 James C. German Jr., "Taft, Roosevelt, and United States Steel," *Historian* 34 (1972): 598–613, remains the best study of the case.

13 Ibid., 605.

14 Roosevelt to James R. Garfield, 31 October 1911, Roosevelt to Benjamin B. Lindsey, 5 December 1911, in Morison, ed., *The Letters of Theodore Roosevelt*, 7:431, 451; Theodore Roosevelt, "The Trusts, the People, and the Square Deal," *Outlook* 99 (1911): 655; Frank Trumbull to Grenville M. Dodge, 24

November 1911, Grenville M. Dodge Papers, Iowa State Department of History and Archives, Des Moines. Ralph M. Easley to Seth Low, 16 November 1911, National Civil Federation Papers, box 79A, New York Public Library.

15 Roosevelt to Edward Sanford Martin, 8 February 1912, in Morison, ed., *The Letters of Theodore Roosevelt*, 7:498.

16 Roosevelt to Charles Dwight Willard, 11 December 1911, in Morison, ed., *The Letters of Theodore Roosevelt*, 7:455.

17 "Taft Men Victors in First Skirmish," *New York Times*, 13 December 1911.

18 *Taft and Roosevelt: The Intimate Letters of Archie Butt: Military Aide*, 2 vols. (Garden City, N.Y.: Doubleday, Doran, 1930), 2:802; James R. Garfield to W. R. Stubbs, 2 January 1912, box 90, Garfield to Dan Casement, 3 January 1912, box 109, James R. Garfield Papers, discussed the outcome of the Columbus meeting.

19 Roosevelt to Henry Beach Needham, 9 January 1912, in Morison, ed., *The Letters of Theodore Roosevelt*, 7:475.

20 Roosevelt to William L. Ward, 9 January 1912, Roosevelt to Ormsby McHarg, 4 March 1912, in Morison, ed., *The Letters of Theodore Roosevelt*, 7:474. For McHarg's activities, see McHarg to Dear Friend, 20 March 1912, Charles D. Hilles Papers, and A. R. Jones to Gifford Pinchot, 20 April 1912, Gifford Pinchot Papers, LC.

21 Root to Roosevelt, 12 February 1912, Theodore Roosevelt Papers. On the letter from the progressive governors, see Herbert S. Hadley to Chester H. Aldrich, 22 January 1912, Herbert S. Hadley Papers, Western Historical Manuscripts Collection, University of Missouri, Columbia.

22 J. Cal O'Laughlin to Frank B. Kellogg, 5 February 1912, Frank B. Kellogg Papers, Minnesota Historical Society, Saint Paul. For La Follette's view of what happened at Philadelphia, see La Follette to Josephine Siebecker, 5 February 1912, series A, box B12, La Follette Family Papers.

23 La Follette to George Keenan, 12 February 1912, box B107, La Follette, "An Open Letter to the Progressives of North Dakota," 1912, J-National Progressive Republican League, box 112, La Follette Family Papers.

24 Butt, *Taft and Roosevelt*, 1:38; Maud Howe Elliott, *Three Generations* (Boston: Little, Brown, 1923), 349.

25 "Taft Denounces Recall of Judges," *New York Times*, 21 January 1912; Henry F. Pringle, *The Life and Times of William Howard Taft*, 2 vols. (New York: Farrar & Rinehart, 1939), 2:766; Roosevelt to Augustus Everett Wilson, 14 February 1912, in Morison, ed., *The Letters of Theodore Roosevelt*, 7:504. R. W. Patterson to Elihu Root, 15 May 1912, Elihu Root Papers, LC, reported that Patterson had offered in December 1910 to give $1,000 to charity if Roosevelt "on examination, was not found to be insane, 'non compos mentis' and a dangerous character to be at large among the peaceful citizens of the United States." In this letter Patterson raised his offer to $5,000.

26 Henry L. Stimson to Roosevelt, 23 January 1912, copy in Charles D. Hilles Papers; Butt, *Taft and Roosevelt*, 2:834–835.

27   Roosevelt to Amos Pinchot, 15 February 1912, in Morison, ed., *The Letters of Theodore Roosevelt*, 7:505.

28   "Roosevelt Indorses Recall of Judges," *New York Times*, 22 February (first quotation), "Roosevelt Back to Storm Boston," 23 February 1912 (second quotation).

29   Theodore Roosevelt, "A Charter of Democracy," in *Social Justice and Popular Rule*, vol. 17 of *The Works of Theodore Roosevelt*, ed. Hermann Hagedorn, national ed., 20 vols. (New York: Charles Scribner's Sons, 1926), 137–138, 139.

30   Theodore Roosevelt, "Judges and Progress," *Outlook* 100 (6 January 1912): 42. Roosevelt to Hiram Johnson, 27 October 1911, in Morison, ed., *The Letters of Theodore Roosevelt*, 7:421.

31   For the response of the American Bar Association, see Frank. B. Kellogg to Rodney A. Mercur, 4 March 1912, author's collection; Hadley to Roosevelt, 3 March 1912, Herbert S. Hadley Papers; Harry Daugherty to Hilles, 23 February 1912, Charles D. Hilles Papers; "Alarms His Own Followers," *New York Times*, 22 February 1912. Steve Stagner, "The Recall of Judicial Decisions and the Due Process Debate," *American Journal of Legal History* 24 (1980): 257–272, is excellent on the whole controversy.

32   Henry Cabot Lodge to Brooks Adams, 5 March 1912, Henry Cabot Lodge Papers, Massachusetts Historical Society, Boston.

33   Roosevelt to William Ellsworth Glasscock and Others, 24 February 1912, Roosevelt to Joseph M. Dixon, 8 March 1912, in Morison, ed., *The Letters of Theodore Roosevelt*, 7: 511, 523; Louise Overacker, *The Presidential Primary* (New York: Macmillan, 1926), 13–14.

34   J. J. Hannan to Walter L. Houser, 21 March 1912, box J111, La Follette Family Papers; Hiram Johnson to Benjamin B. Lindsey, 27 March 1912, Hiram Johnson Papers, Bancroft Library, University of California, Berkeley.

35   Taft to William B. McKinley, 12 March 1912, Charles D. Hilles Papers.

36   James Bryce to Arthur, Duke of Connaught, 1 April 1912, Bryce Embassy Papers, Bodleian Library, Oxford; Hilles to J. A. O. Preus, 6 April 1912, J. A. O. Preus Papers, Minnesota Historical Society, Saint Paul.

37   "Roosevelt Rules out Third Party Report," *New York Times*, 29 March 1912.

38   Nicholas Murray Butler, *The Supreme Issue of 1912: Speech of the Temporary Chairman at the Republican State Convention, Rochester, N. Y., April 9, 1912*, author's collection; "Roosevelt Denies Taft Is Progressive," *New York Times*, 4 April 1912; Pringle, *Taft*, 2:771.

39   "Roosevelt Jubilant, Seeks New Victory," *New York Times*, 11 April 1912.

40   "Taft To Fight on, Sure of Victory," *New York Times*, 15 April 1912 (first and second quotations); Joseph M. Dixon to Hiram Johnson, 22 April 1912, Hiram Johnson Papers.

41   Steven Biel, *Down with the Old Canoe: A Cultural History of the Titanic Disaster* (New York: W. W. Norton, 1996), 21–53.

42   "Roosevelt's Praise for Butt," and "Taft's Tribute to Butt," *New York Times*, 20 April 1912.

43 Hilles to Horace Taft, 19 April 1912, Charles D. Hilles Papers; Taft to Otto Bannard, 19 April 1912, series 7, case file 456, William Howard Taft Papers, LC. "Taft to Hit Back at Roosevelt Soon," *New York Times*, 23 April 1912.

44 "Taft Opens Fire on Roosevelt," *New York Times*, 26 April 1912; Pringle, *Taft*, 2:782.

45 "Colonel Says Taft Is the Disloyal One," *New York Times*, 27 April 1912.

46 "500,000 Turn out to Cheer Taft On," *New York Times*, 30 April 1912.

47 Dan Casement to James R. Garfield, 10 May 1912, Box 109, James R. Garfield Papers.

48 *New York Tribune*, 11 April 1912; Roosevelt, "The Right of the People to Rule," *Social Justice and Popular Rule*, 170.

49 "Roosevelt Unsafe, Taft Tells Ohioans," *New York Times*, 14 May 1912.

50 William B. McKinley to Herbert Parsons, 4 May 1912, Herbert Parsons Papers, Columbia University Library, New York; Taft to George Edwards, 10 May 1912, Charles D. Hilles Papers; Roosevelt to Arthur Hamilton Lee, 14 May 1912, in Morison, ed., *The Letters of Theodore Roosevelt*, 7:544; Pringle, *Taft*, 2:783.

51 "Roosevelt Unsafe, Taft Tells Ohioans," *New York Times*, 14 May 1912; "Battle Hard for Ohio Vote," *New York Times*, 15 May 1912; "20,000 Cheer Taft in Last Ohio Appeal," *New York Times*, 21 May 1912.

52 James Bryce to Edward Grey, 30 April 1912, Edward Grey Papers, FO 800/83, British National Archives, Kew.

53 Winthrop Murray Crane to Hilles, 15 May 1912, Harry S. New to Taft, 19 May 1912, Charles D. Hilles Papers; Root to Harry S. New, 22 May 1912, Elihu Root Papers.

54 James S. Sherman to Francis Hendricks, 24 May 1912, James S. Sherman Papers, New York Public Library; Taft to Otto Bannard, 25 May 1912, Charles D. Hilles Papers.

55 Gould, "Theodore Roosevelt, William Howard Taft, and the Disputed Delegates," 44–45.

56 Garfield Diary, 13 June 1912, James R. Garfield Papers; Gould, "Theodore Roosevelt, William Howard Taft, and the Disputed Delegates," 45–50.

57 The issue of the 1912 delegates and the correct result between Roosevelt and Taft is very complex. For the Taft side, *Statement Relating to Contests over Seats in the Republican National Convention* (Washington, DC, 1912) was reprinted in the *Congressional Record*, 62nd Cong., 2nd sess. (Washington, DC, 1912), 48, pt. 12: 523–577. The Roosevelt camp provided *A Stolen Nomination for the Presidency* (New York, 1912) and "Were the Delegates from Washington Stolen from Col. Roosevelt or Did They Belong to President Taft?" *Congressional Record*, U.S. House, 62nd Cong., 2nd sess. (16 August 1912), 11091–11115. Gilbert Roe, "The Truth about the Contests," *La Follette's Magazine*, 20 July 1912, 7–8, 27 July 1912, 8–9, 14, 3 August 1912, 7–9, 15, provides a perspective apart from the two sides. Roe was a former law partner of Robert La Follette.

58 John A. Sleicher to James S. Sherman, 16 May 1912, James S. Sherman

Papers; Root to George E. Dunham, 11 May 1912, Elihu Root Papers, discussed the chances of a compromise candidate.

59 Gifford Pinchot to W. P. Eno, 6 June 1912, Gifford Pinchot Papers, mentioned Roosevelt going to Chicago.

60 William Dudley Foulke to Roosevelt, 27 May 1912, Roosevelt to Foulke, 7 June 1912, William Dudley Foulke Papers, LC; Roosevelt to James Bronson Reynolds, 11 June 1912, in Morison, ed., *The Letters of Theodore Roosevelt*, 7:561.

61 Donald Richberg, "We Thought It Was Armageddon," *Survey* 61 (1929): 723; Ernest H. Abbott, "Purging the Ranks," *Outlook* 101 (1912): 472; Daisy Borden Harriman, *From Pinafores to Politics* (New York: Henry Holt, 1923), 99. Oscar King Davis, *Released for Publication: Some Inside Political History of Theodore Roosevelt and His Times* (Boston: Houghton Mifflin, 1925), 288–290.

62 Roosevelt, "The Case Against The Reactionaries," *Social Justice and Popular Rule*, 204, 211, 231

63 Hilles to Mrs. S. A. Willis, 17 June 1912, author's collection.

64 On the deliberations of the Wisconsin delegation, see "Reports of Meetings of the Wisconsin Delegation to the National Convention of the Republican Party to be held at Chicago, June 18, 1912," entry of 17 June 1912, James A. Stone Papers, Wisconsin Historical Society, Madison, which makes clear La Follette's unwillingness to assist Roosevelt or endorse McGovern. *The Chicago Convention: An Address by Gov. F. E. McGovern, delivered at Manawa, Wisc., August 16, 1914* (n.p., 1916), pamphlet in author's collection.

65 "Election of Senator Root as Chairman Gives First Advantage to President," *Washington Post*, 19 June 1912; Richard Harding Davis, "The Two Conventions at Chicago," *Scribner's Magazine* 52 (September 1912): 271. William Jennings Bryan, *A Tale of Two Conventions* (New York: Funk & Wagnalls, 1912), 34.

66 Rosewater, *Backstage in 1912*, 161–166; Robert M. La Follette, *La Follette's Autobiography: A Personal Narrative of Political Experiences* (Madison: Robert M. La Follette Co., 1913), 655; "Election of Senator Root," *Washington Post*, 19 June 1912; "Still Hope to Force the Unseating of 75 of the Taft Delegates," *New York Times*, 19 June 1912.

67 Richard Harding Davis, "The Two Conventions at Chicago," 270.

68 Rosewater, *Backstage in 1912*, 170–171; Philip C. Jessup, *Elihu Root*, 2 vols. (New York: Dodd, Mead, 1938), 2:195–201. Milton W. Blumenberg, comp., *Official Report of the Proceedings of the Fifteenth Republican National Convention* (The Tenny Press; New York, 1912), 122–123, 133–137, 282–304.

69 Oscar King Davis, *Released for Publication*, 308. For Hadley, see Henry J. Allen, "What Happened at Chicago," and Herbert S. Hadley to William Allen White, 25 September 1918, Herbert S. Hadley Papers.

70 Roosevelt to Sydney Brooks, 4 June 1912, in Morison, ed., *The Letters of Theodore Roosevelt*, 7:553.

71 Amos R. E. Pinchot, *History of the Progressive Party, 1912–1916*, ed. Helene Maxwell Hooker (New York: New York University Press, 1958), 165.

72 Roosevelt to the Republican National Convention, 22 June 1912, in Morison, ed., *The Letters of Theodore Roosevelt*, 7:562–563; Richard Harding Davis, "The Two Conventions," 273.

73 On the renomination of Sherman, see William S. Benet to Sherman, 26 June 1912, James S. Sherman Papers.

74 Republican National Committee, *Republican Campaign Text-Book, 1912* (Philadelphia: Press of Dunlap Printing Co., 1912), 271, 273, 276.

75 Hilles to Taft, 24 June 1912, Charles D. Hilles Papers. John Coit Spooner to Louis. T. Michener, 28 June 1912, Louis T. Michener Papers, LC.

CHAPTER 4 WOODROW WILSON AGAINST THE DEMOCRATIC FIELD

1 Geoffrey F. Morrison, "A Political Biography of Champ Clark" (Ph.D. diss., Saint Louis University, 1972), 299.

2 Genevieve Bennett Clark to John B. Brownlow, 16 January 1922, author's collection.

3 S. E. High to Claude Kitchin, 21 September 1916, Claude Kitchin Papers, University of North Carolina, Chapel Hill; William F. McCombs, *Making Woodrow Wilson President* (New York: Fairview Publishing, 1921), 208.

4 Edwin A. Weinstein, *Woodrow Wilson: A Medical and Psychological Biography* (Princeton, N.J.: Princeton University Press, 1981), sparked a long-running controversy about the impact of Wilson's health on his life and political career.

5 Wilson's relationship with Mrs. Peck is discussed in August Heckscher, *Woodrow Wilson* (New York: Scribner's 1991), 185–190; and in Phyllis Lee Levin, *Edith and Woodrow: The Wilson White House* (New York: Scribner's 2001), 124–132.

6 An excellent treatment of Wilson's press relations during this period is James D. Startt, *Woodrow Wilson and the Press: Prelude to the Presidency* (New York: Palgrave Macmillan, 2004).

7 "An Address in New York to the National League of Commission Merchants," 11 January 1912, in Arthur S. Link, ed., *The Papers of Woodrow Wilson*, vol. 24, *Jan.–Aug. 1912* (Princeton, N.J.: Princeton University Press, 1977), 32. Robert Alexander Kraig, *Woodrow Wilson and the Lost World of the Oratorical Statesman* (College Station: Texas A&M University Press, 2004), provides an interesting evaluation of Wilson's speaking style.

8 "A News Report of Another Busy Day in Illinois," 7 April 1912, in Link, ed., *The Papers of Woodrow Wilson*, 24:301.

9 For Texas, see Lewis L. Gould, *Progressives and Prohibitionists: Texas Democrats in the Wilson Era* (Austin: University of Texas Press, 1973), 58–66. Wilson to Joseph F. Guffey, 11 June 1912, in Joseph F. Guffey, *Seventy Years on the Red-Fire Wagon: From Tilden to Truman through New Freedom and the New Deal* (n.p.: privately printed, 1952), 38, provides background on Pennsylvania.

10 Edward Mandell House to Sidney E. Mezes, 25 November 1911, Edward Mandell House Papers, Sterling Memorial Library, Yale University, New Haven, Conn. Godfrey Hodgson, *Woodrow Wilson's Right Hand: The Life of*

Colonel Edward M. House (New Haven, Conn.: Yale University Press, 2006), is more sympathetic to House.

11 Cato Sells to Thomas S. Henderson, 18 March 1912, Thomas Stallworth Henderson Papers, Center for American History, University of Texas at Austin. Arthur S. Link, *Wilson: The Road to the White House* (Princeton, N.J.: Princeton University Press, 1947), 334.

12 William F. McCombs to Byron R. Newton, 6 October 1911, Byron R. Newton Papers, Sterling Memorial Library, Yale University, New Haven, Conn.; Ray Stannard Baker and William E. Dodd, eds., *The Public Papers of Woodrow Wilson: College and State*, 2 vols. (New York: Harper & Bros., 1925), 2:396.

13 Evans C. Johnson, *Oscar W. Underwood: A Political Biography* (Baton Rouge: Louisiana State University Press, 1980), 170–176, quoted on 174.

14 Morrison, "A Political Biography of Champ Clark," 1.

15 John E. Lathrop, "The Views of Champ Clark: An Authorized Interview," *Outlook* 101 (11 May 1912): 73.

16 Ray Stannard Baker, "Our Next President and Some Others," *American Magazine* 74 (1912): 132; Wilson to Mary Allen Hulbert Peck, 5 March 1911, Woodrow Wilson Papers, Manuscript Division, Library of Congress, Washington, D.C. (hereafter LC).

17 Arthur Willert to Geoffrey Robinson [Dawson], 10 March 1914, Archives of *The Times*, London.

18 Morrison, "A Political Biography of Champ Clark," 265.

19 Link, *Wilson: The Road to the White House*, 381.

20 Wilson to Nicholas L. Piotrowski, 13 March 1912, in Link, ed., *The Papers of Woodrow Wilson*, 24:242–243. Startt, *Woodrow Wilson and the Press*, 234–235, looks at Wilson and his relationship with the truth.

21 Link, *Wilson: The Road to the White House*, 353; John Morton Blum, *Joe Tumulty and the Wilson Era* (Boston: Houghton Mifflin, 1951), 43; Michael Kazin, *A Godly Hero: The Life of William Jennings Bryan* (New York: Alfred A. Knopf, 2006), 183–184.

22 Link, *Wilson: The Road to the White House*, 355; Link, ed., *The Papers of Woodrow Wilson*, 24:10.

23 For the Wilson-Harvey controversy, Link, *Wilson: The Road to the White House*, 359–378, remains the most detailed examination.

24 J. Franklin Jameson to George L. Burr, 6 June 1912, in Elizabeth Donnan and Leo F. Stock, eds., *An Historian's World: Selections from the Correspondence of John Franklin Jameson* (Philadelphia: American Philosophical Society, 1956), 150.

25 Link, ed., *The Papers of Woodrow Wilson*, 24:84, 111, 350, 395, 418.

26 "A News Report," 4 April 1912, in Link, ed., *The Papers of Woodrow Wilson*, 24:288.

27 "A News Report of an Address in Springfield, Illinois," 6 April 1912, in Link, ed., *The Papers of Woodrow Wilson*, 24:296.

28 "A News Item," 9 April 1912, in Link, ed., *The Papers of Woodrow Wilson*, 24:308; Link, *Wilson: The Road to the White House*, 412.

29 Wilson to James D. Phelan, 3 May 1912, in Link, ed., *The Papers of Woodrow Wilson*, 24:383.

30 Gould, *Progressives and Prohibitionists*, 76; Startt, *Woodrow Wilson and the Press*, 167–168.

31 Gould, *Progressives and Prohibitionists*, 81.

32 Morrison, "A Political Biography of Champ Clark," 295, 296.

33 Gould, *Progressives and Prohibitionists*, 80.

34 Wilson to Mary Allen Hulbert Peck, 17 June 1912, in Link, ed., *The Papers of Woodrow Wilson*, 24:82.

35 Francis Fisher Kane to Wilson, 23 June 1912, in Link, ed., *The Papers of Woodrow Wilson*, 24:496.

36 Honore Willsie, "Sound and Madness in Baltimore," *Colliers'* 49 (July 1912): 19; Francis E. Warren to George Pexton, 7 July 1912, Francis E. Warren Papers, American Heritage Center, University of Wyoming, Laramie.

37 On the organization of the Wilson forces in the Texas and Pennsylvania delegations, see Thomas B. Love to William G. McAdoo, 27 October 1930, Thomas B. Love Papers, Dallas Historical Society.

38 "Democratic Objections to Democratic Possibilities," *Literary Digest* 28 (1904): 398; Link, *Wilson: The Road to the White House*, 432.

39 Wilson to William Jennings Bryan, 22 June 1912, in Link, ed., *The Papers of Woodrow Wilson*, 24:493.

40 Link, *Wilson: The Road to the White House*, 443.

41 "A News Report," 1 July 1912, in Link, ed., *The Papers of Woodrow Wilson*, 24:517.

42 Democratic National Committee and the Democratic Congressional Committee, *The Democratic Text-Book, 1912* (New York: Isaac Goldman, 1912), 2.

43 Mark Sullivan, "Comment on Baltimore," *Collier's* 49 (13 July 1912): 10; Byron R. Newton, "The Wilson Campaign," 1921, Byron R. Newton Papers; Wilson to Mary Allen Hulbert Peck, 6 July 1912, in Link, ed., *The Papers of Woodrow Wilson*, 24:541.

44 Virginia Floy Haughton, "John Worth Kern and Wilson's New Freedom: A Study of a Senate Majority Leader" (Ph.D. diss., University of Kentucky, 1973), 33.

45 "Cheerful Democrats after Wilson Visit," *New York Times*, 22 July 1912.

46 See Kristie Miller, " 'Eager and Anxious to Work': Daisy Harriman and the Presidential Election of 1912," in *We Have Come to Stay: American Women and Political Parties, 1880–1960*, ed. Melanie Gustafson, Kristie Miller, and Elisabeth I. Perry (Albuquerque: University of New Mexico Press, 1999), 69–75, for the substance of this paragraph; quote on 73.

47 Link, *Wilson: The Road to the White House*, 487.

48 Taft to Helen Herron Taft, 23 July 1912, William Howard Taft Papers, LC.

49 "A Speech Accepting the Democratic Nomination in Sea Girt, New Jersey," 7 August 1912, in Arthur S. Link, ed., *The Papers of Woodrow Wilson*, vol. 25, *Aug.–Nov. 1912* (Princeton, N.J.: Princeton University Press, 1978), 5, 8.

50 Taft to Helen Taft, 8 August 1912, William Howard Taft Papers; "What Wilson Would Do," *Literary Digest* 45 (17 August 1912): 247.

CHAPTER 5 A SOCIALIST CELEBRITY RUNS FOR PRESIDENT
1 Nick Salvatore, *Eugene V. Debs: Citizen and Socialist* (Urbana: University of Illinois Press, 1987), 264.
2 "A News Report of a Campaign Address in Boston, April 27, 1912, and a News Report of a Campaign Address in Baltimore, April 30, 1912," in Arthur S. Link, ed., *The Papers of Woodrow Wilson*, vol. 24, *Jan.–Aug. 1912* (Princeton, N.J.: Princeton University Press, 1977), 366 (second quotation), 376 (first quotation).
3 Roosevelt, "A Confession of Faith," in *Social Justice and Popular Rule: The Works of Theodore Roosevelt*, ed. Hermann Hagedorn, national ed., 20 vols. (New York: Charles Scribner's Sons, 1926), 17:265.
4 Salvatore, *Eugene V. Debs: Citizen and Socialist*, 272, 392n24, touches on the issue of Debs and alcohol.
5 H. Wayne Morgan, *Eugene V. Debs: Socialist for President* (Syracuse, N.Y.: Syracuse University Press, 1962), 24.
6 Salvatore, *Eugene V. Debs: Citizen and Socialist*, is excellent on his early life. Also helpful is Ray Ginger, *The Bending Cross: A Biography of Eugene Victor Debs* (New Brunswick, N.J.: Rutgers University Press, 1949).
7 Morgan, *Eugene V. Debs: Socialist for President*, 50.
8 Salvatore, *Eugene V. Debs: Citizen and Socialist*, 246.
9 Hillquit is quoted in Ira Kipnis, *The American Socialist Movement, 1897–1912* (New York: Columbia University Press, 1952), 220.
10 Sally M. Miller, *Victor Berger and the Promise of Constructive Socialism, 1910–1920* (Westport, Conn.: Greenwood Press, 1973), 73 (both quotations).
11 Morgan, *Eugene V. Debs: Socialist for President*, 101.
12 Ibid., 114–115.
13 Eugene V. Debs to Fred Warren, 12 October 1910, in J. Robert Constantine, ed., *Letters of Eugene V. Debs*, vol. 1, *1874–1912* (Urbana: University of Illinois Press, 1990), 382.
14 Ibid., 385. For background on the McNamara–*Los Angeles Times* case, see Knox Mellon Jr., "Job Harriman: The Early and Middle Years, 1861–1912" (Ph.D. diss., Claremont College, 1972), 128–135.
15 Job Harriman to Morris Hillquit, 6 November 1911, Morris Hillquit Papers, Wisconsin Historical Society, Madison; Debs to Warren, 21 November 1910, in Constantine, ed., *Letters of Eugene V. Debs*, 1:389.
16 Harriman to Hillquitt, 19 December 1911, Morris Hillquit Papers.
17 Kenneth E. Hendrickson Jr., "Tribune of the People: George R. Lunn and the Rise and Fall of Christian Socialism in Schenectady," in *Socialism and the Cities*, ed. Bruce M. Stave (Port Washington, N.Y.: Kennikat Press, 1975), 83; Debs to Grace Brewer, 16 November 1911, in Constantine, ed., *Letters of Eugene V. Debs*, 1:432.

18 Salvatore, *Eugene V. Debs: Citizen and Socialist*, 248; Kipnis, *The American Socialist Movement*, 379–380.

19 Bruce Watson, *Bread and Roses: Mills, Migrants, and the Struggle for the American Dream* (New York: Viking, 2005), 184–185.

20 Debs to Theodore Debs, 21 April 1912, Debs to Thomas A. Hickey, 21 May 1912, in Constantine, ed., *Letters of Eugene V. Debs*, 1:473, 475.

21 *Proceedings: National Convention of the Socialist Party, 1912* (Chicago: M. A. Donahue, 1912), 4, 5.

22 David A. Shannon, *The Socialist Party of America: A History* (New York: Macmillan, 1955), 71.

23 Miller, *Victor Berger and the Promise*, 104.

24 *Proceedings: National Convention of the Socialist Party, 1912*, 137–143. Debs to Hickey, 21 May 1912, in Constantine, ed., *Letters of Eugene V. Debs*, 1:475.

25 *Proceedings: National Convention of the Socialist Party, 1912*, 199.

26 "Socialists Nominate Debs for President," *Dallas Morning News*, 18 May 1912. *Proceedings: National Convention of the Socialist Party, 1912*, 122, 128, 129–130.

27 *Proceedings: National Convention of the Socialist Party, 1912*, 133; Kipnis, *American Socialist Movement*, 407.

28 *Proceedings: National Convention of the Socialist Party, 1912*, 196, 197, 198.

29 Ibid., 164–165.

30 Debs to J. Mahlon Barnes, 31 May 1912, in Constantine, ed., *Letters of Eugene V. Debs*, 1:476–477.

31 Eugene V. Debs, "This Is Our Year: But Two Parties and But One Issue," 16 June 1912, Eugene V. Debs Internet Archive, http://www.marxists.org/archive/debs/works/1912/twoparties.htm.

32 Ibid.

33 Ibid.

34 Debs to John Spargo, 19 June 1912, Debs to Fred Warren, 19 June 1912, in Constantine, ed., *Letters of Eugene V. Debs*, 1:486, 487.

35 Debs to Fred Warren, 19 June 1912, Debs to Spargo, 19 June 1912 in Constantine, ed., *Letters of Eugene V. Debs*, 1:486, 488.

36 Theodore Debs to Edward Ellis Carr, 21 June 1912, Warren to Debs, 24 June 1912, in Constantine, ed., *Letters of Eugene V. Debs*, 1:489–490.

37 Debs to Members of the Socialist Party, ca. 20 July 1912, in Constantine, ed., *Letters of Eugene V. Debs*, 1:500–504, quoted on 504. The results of the referendum are given on 505n3.

38 George H. Goebel to Debs, 11 August 1912, in Constantine, ed., *Letters of Eugene V. Debs*, 1:538.

CHAPTER 6 THE BULL MOOSE CHALLENGE TO THE MAJOR PARTIES

1 Henry L. Stoddard, *As I Knew Them: Presidents and Politics from Grant to Coolidge* (New York: Harper & Bros., 1927), 410.

2 Bill Crawford, *All American: The Rise and Fall of Jim Thorpe* (New York: John Wiley & Sons, 2005), 161–169; "Sac and Fox Indian a Marvelous Man in Many Forms of Sport," *New York Times*, 21 July 1912.

3   "America First as Olympics End," *New York Times*, 16 July 1912.

4   Andy Logan, *Against the Evidence: The Becker-Rosenthal Affair* (New York: McCall, 1970).

5   *Austin Statesman*, 3 September 1912, ran a front-page picture of "Lieut Becker in Court." Logan, *Against the Evidence*, argues that Becker was innocent.

6   Walter Prescott Webb and Terrell Webb, eds., *Washington Wife: Journal of Ellen Maury Slayden from 1897–1919* (1962; reprint, New York: Harper & Row, 1963), 183.

7   For Roosevelt's earlier use of "bull moose," see Roosevelt to Marcus Alonzo Hanna, 27 June 1900, in Elting E. Morison, ed., *The Letters of Theodore Roosevelt*, 8 vols. (Cambridge, Mass.: Harvard University Press, 1951–1954), 2:1342. On the origin of the term in 1912, see John A. Gable, *The Bull Moose Years: Theodore Roosevelt and the Progressive Party* (Port Washington, N.Y.: Kennikat Press, 1978), 19; and "Bull Moose Suits Roosevelt," *Dallas Morning News*, 25 July 1912.

8   James S. Sherman to Frank S. Black, 5 July 1912, James S. Sherman Papers, New York Public Library; Theodore E. Burton to W. H. Phipps, 15 July 1912, Theodore E. Burton Papers, Western Reserve Historical Society, Cleveland; William Howard Taft to George H. Earle Jr., 9 July 1912, Charles D. Hilles Papers, Sterling Memorial Library, Yale University, New Haven, Conn.

9   George von Lengerke Meyer to Curtis Guild, 17 July 1912, George von Lengerke Meyer Papers, Massachusetts Historical Society, Boston.

10 Taft to James S. Sherman, 24 August 1912, Sherman Papers.

11 Hilles to Taft, 4 August 1912, Hilles Papers.

12 Republican National Committee, *Republican Campaign Text-Book, 1912* (Philadelphia: Press of the Dunlap Printing Co., 1912), 3.

13 Ibid., 7, 8.

14 Ibid., 15, 16.

15 Henry Cabot Lodge to James Ford Rhodes, 1 August 1912, James Ford Rhodes Papers, Massachusetts Historical Society, Boston.

16 George E. Mowry, *Theodore Roosevelt and the Progressive Movement* (Madison: University of Wisconsin Press, 1946), 157, noted the absence of Republican progressives behind the new party. For La Follette's alliance with Boies Penrose, see Taft to Helen Herron Taft, 26 August 1912, William Howard Taft Papers, Manuscript Division, Library of Congress, Washington, D.C. (hereafter LC). Jonathan Bourne to William S. U'Ren, 3 September 1912, Jonathan Bourne Papers, University of Oregon, Eugene.

17 Roosevelt to William Dudley Foulke, 1 July 1912, in Morison, ed., *The Letters of Theodore Roosevelt*, 7:568.

18 For the proposals about joint electoral tickets, see William Flinn to Theodore Roosevelt, 17 July 1912, E. A. Van Valkenburg to Roosevelt, 17 July 1912, and Joseph M. Dixon to Roosevelt, 19 July 1912, Theodore Roosevelt Papers, LC. For the events in Pennsylvania, see Richard James Donagher, "The Urban Bull Moose: A Case Study of Philadelphia and Pittsburgh," (Ph.D. diss., Fordham University, 1979), 135–139. Robert Sherman La Forte, *Leaders of*

Reform: Progressive Republicans in Kansas, 1900–1916 (Lawrence: University Press of Kansas, 1974), 189–197, considers the tangled situation in that state over the electors.

19 Roosevelt to E. A. Van Valkenburg, 16 July 1912, in Morison, ed., *The Letters of Theodore Roosevelt*, 7:577.

20 On Longworth's dilemma and the pressure applied to him, see "Named to Fight Longworth," *New York Times*, 22 August 1912, and Taft to Helen Taft, 29 July 1912, 11 August 1912, William Howard Taft Papers. Alice Roosevelt Longworth Diaries, 28 July 1912, Alice Longworth Papers, LC. I am indebted for this reference to Stacy Cordery.

21 The continuing controversy about the delegate contest can be followed in Republican National Committee, "The Truth about Those Delegates," in the *Republican Campaign Text Book, 1912*, 167–176 (pro-Taft); Roosevelt, "Thou Shalt Not Steal," in *Social Justice and Popular Rule: The Works of Theodore Roosevelt*, ed. Hermann Hagedorn, national ed., 20 vols. (New York: Charles Scribner's Sons, 1926), 17:232–242 (pro-Roosevelt).

22 "Third Party Called to Chicago Aug. 5," *New York Times*, 8 July 1912.

23 John A. Garraty, *Right-Hand Man: The Life of George W. Perkins* (New York: Harper & Row, 1960), 264–284, examines the role of Perkins in the Bull Moose struggle. Amos R. E. Pinchot, *History of the Progressive Party, 1912–1916*, ed. Helene Maxwell Hooker (New York: New York University Press, 1958), 164–181, presents an anti-Perkins perspective.

24 Sir Arthur Willert, *Washington and Other Memories* (Boston: Houghton Mifflin, 1972), 56. See also Lewis L. Gould, "The Price of Fame: Theodore Roosevelt as a Celebrity, 1909–1919," in *Lamar Journal of the Humanities* 10 (Fall 1984): 7–18.

25 Oscar King Davis, *Released for Publication: Some Inside Political History of Theodore Roosevelt and His Times, 1898–1918* (Boston: Houghton Mifflin, 1925), 342–351, explores Johnson's limits as a campaigner.

26 Roosevelt to Julian La Rose Harris, 1 August 1912, in Morison, ed., *The Letters of Theodore Roosevelt*, 7:589.

27 See Lewis L. Gould, *The Presidency of Theodore Roosevelt* (Lawrence: University Press of Kansas, 1991), 22–24, 118–122, 236–244, for Roosevelt's racial policies as president.

28 Davis, *Released for Publication*, 317.

29 "Roosevelt Men Bar Southern Negroes," *New York Times*, 2 August 1912.

30 Arthur S. Link, ed., "Correspondence Relating to the Progressive Party's 'Lily White' Policy in 1912," *Journal of Southern History* 10 (November 1944): 481.

31 Roosevelt to Julian La Rose Harris, 1 August 1912, in Morison, ed., *The Letters of Theodore Roosevelt*, 7:590.

32 "Roosevelt in Huff over Party Snarls," *New York Times*, 6 August 1912; "Won't Force Negro Party on South," *New York Times*, 7 August 1912.

33 Allen F. Davis, *Spearheads for Reform: The Social Settlements and the Progressive Movement, 1890–1914* (New York: Oxford University Press, 1967), 198;

Ethel Roosevelt to Kermit Roosevelt, [1912], Kermit Roosevelt Papers, LC.

34 William Menkel, "The Progressives at Chicago," *American Monthly Review of Reviews* 46 (September 1912): 314.

35 George Henry Payne, *The Birth of the New Party* (n.p.: H. E. Rennels, 1912), 306.

36 "How Women Won Roosevelt to Them," *New York Times*, 31 August 1912, a speech at Saint Johnsbury, Vermont, where Roosevelt discussed woman suffrage and how he thought about the role of women in policy issues. There is a typescript of the speech in the Theodore Roosevelt Papers.

37 Garraty, *Right-Hand Man*, 250.

38 Joseph L. Bristow to Roosevelt, 15 July 1912, Theodore Roosevelt Papers.

39 *The Autobiography of William Allen White* (New York: Macmillan, 1946), 484.

40 Richard Hofstadter, *The Age of Reform* (New York: Random House, 1955), 135; Alfred Chandler, "The Origins of Progressive Leadership," in Morison, ed., *The Letters of Theodore Roosevelt*, 8:1462–1465. This question is examined in detail in Donagher, "The Urban Bull Moose," 181–182.

41 Menkel, "The Progressives at Chicago," 311; "Hail New Party in Fervent Song," *New York Times*, 6 August 1912; Stoddard, *As I Knew Them*, 410.

42 "Songs to Be Sung at the First National Progressive Convention," August 1912 (Chicago: C. H. Congdon, 1912), author's collection.

43 "Roosevelt in Huff over Party Snarls," *New York Times*, 6 August 1912.

44 Ibid.

45 See Payne, *The Birth of the New Party*, 306, for the party platform.

46 Claude G. Bowers, *Beveridge and the Progressive Era* (Boston: Houghton Mifflin, 1932), 431.

47 There is an extensive literature on the corporation plank in the Progressive platform. See Edward A. Fitzpatrick, *McCarthy of Wisconsin* (New York: Columbia University Press, 1944), 160–163; Garraty, *Right-Hand Man*, 268–269; Gable, *The Bull Moose Years*, 98–102. Oddly enough, despite the efforts to suppress the wording, the offending language was printed in full in Payne, *The Birth of the New Party*, 311–312.

48 John Braeman, *Albert J. Beveridge: American Nationalist* (Chicago: University of Chicago Press, 1971), covers Beveridge's evolution into a progressive. On Beveridge's high opinion of himself, see Henry White to Henry Cabot Lodge, 1 May 1908, Henry Cabot Lodge Papers, Massachusetts Historical Society, Boston.

49 *"Pass Prosperity Around": Speech of Albert J. Beveridge, Temporary Chairman of Progressive National Convention* (New York: Mail and Express Job Print, 1912), copy in author's collection.

50 "Roosevelt Sole Convention Star," *New York Times*, 7 August 1912.

51 Roosevelt, "A Confession of Faith," in *Social Justice and Popular Rule*, 17:254, 257, 265.

52 Ibid., 17:279, 281.

53 Ibid., 17:284, 286–287.

54 "Roosevelt Sole Convention Star," *New York Times*, 7 August 1912.

55 "Negroes Quitting Colonel," *New York Times*, 8 August 1912. These remarks were published in *The Negro Question: Attitude of the Progressive Party toward the Colored Race*, pamphlet in the Theodore Roosevelt Collection, Houghton Library, Harvard University, Cambridge, Mass.

56 Roosevelt, "A Confession of Faith," in *Social Justice and Popular Rule*, 17:272, 279.

57 "Roosevelt Named, Shows Emotion," *New York Times*, 8 August 1912.

58 Ibid. See also, "Jane Addams Will Second Colonel," *Chicago Daily Tribune*, 6 August 1912. Rudyard Kipling's poem is "The Ballad of East and West" (1889).

59 "Roosevelt Named, Shows Emotion"; John Callan O'Laughlin, "Roosevelt Trip to Circle Nation; 2 Months on Road," *Chicago Daily Tribune*, 14 August 1912.

60 "How Women Won Roosevelt to Them," *New York Times*, 31 August 1912, "Speech Delivered by Colonel Roosevelt at a Banquet at Point of Pines, Mass. August 17, 1912," Theodore Roosevelt Papers.

61 "Speech of Hon. Theodore Roosevelt Delivered at Infantry Hall, Providence, R.I. Aug. 16, 1912," Theodore Roosevelt Papers.

62 "Mr. Roosevelt's Speech at St. Johnsbury, Vermont, Friday Evening August 30, 1912," Theodore Roosevelt Papers.

63 "Campaign Funds in 1904 and 1912," *Literary Digest* 45 (7 September 1912): 237–238. On the La Follette–Penrose alliance, see Taft to Helen Herron Taft, 26 August 1912, William Howard Taft Papers.

64 Belle Case La Follette and Fola La Follette, *Robert M. La Follette, June 14, 1855–June 18, 1925*, 2 vols. (New York: Macmillan, 1953), 1:447–448. For La Follette's resolution, see U.S. Senate, *Congressional Record*, 62nd Cong., 2nd sess. (24 August 1912), 11792–11793.

65 "Campaign Funds in 1904 and 1912," 237–238; J. Cal O'Laughlin to Roosevelt, 24 August 1912, Moses E. Clapp to Roosevelt, 27 August 1912, Theodore Roosevelt Papers.

66 "Campaign Funds in 1904 and 1912," 237–238; Roosevelt to Moses E. Clapp, 28 August 1912, in Morison, ed., *The Letters of Theodore Roosevelt*, 7:602–605.

CHAPTER 7 THE CLASH OF IDEAS

1 Ballard Macdonald and George Walter Brown, "Wilson, That's All," 1912 (Political Songs in America, Parlor Songs http//parlorsongs.com/issues/ 2002-11/this month/featureb.asp). The title of the song may have been in- spired by an editorial that James C. Hemphill wrote in the *Richmond Times- Dispatch* in November 1910 entitled "Wilson: That's All," which argued for Wilson's possible presidential candidacy.

2 "Campaign Methods," *Outlook* 96 (5 November 1910): 523. Michael E. McGerr, *The Decline of Popular Politics: The American North, 1865–1928* (New York: Oxford University Press, 1986), 148.

3 James D. Startt, *Woodrow Wilson and the Press: Prelude to the Presidency* (New York: Palgrave Macmillan, 2004), 201–205. For an example of how the Roosevelt campaign used cars, see "Circus Cars for Roosevelt," *New York Times*, 31 August 1912. Hilles discussed his campaign methods in Hilles to Taft, 4 October 1912, Charles D. Hilles Papers, Sterling Memorial Library, Yale University, New Haven, Conn.

4 "Women Taking Big Part in Politics," *Dallas Morning News*, 18 August 1912.

5 Ibid.; "Miss Boardman Won't Act," *New York Times*, 10 August 1912; "Woman's Help to Taft," *New York Times*, 22 August 1912; Eliot quoted in "Criticizes Jane Addams," *New York Times*, 21 August 1912. "Mr. Roosevelt's Speech at St. Johnsbury, Vermont, Friday Evening August 30, 1912," Theodore Roosevelt Papers, Manuscript Division, Library of Congress, Washington, D.C. (hereafter LC).

6 Harper quoted in "Asks If Roosevelt Set Suffrage Trap," *New York Times*, 10 August 1912. "Mrs. Atherton on Woman Moosers," *New York Times*, 28 August 1912. Jane Addams came to Roosevelt's defense; see Addams to Roosevelt, 26 August 1912; and her statement to the press, 26 August 1912, Theodore Roosevelt Papers.

7 "From the Diary of Oswald Garrison Villard, 14 August 1912, in Arthur S. Link, ed., *The Papers of Woodrow Wilson*, vol. 25, *Aug.–Nov. 1912* (Princeton, N.J.: Princeton University Press, 1978), 25–26.

8 On the extent of undecided voters, see "A Review of the World," *Current Literature* 53 (November 1912): 488.

9 Hilles to Taft, 31 July 1912, Charles D. Hilles Papers.

10 Walter Wilson to Hilles, 11 October 1912, Charles D. Hilles Papers.

11 "Taft Opens Attack on the Third Party," *New York Times*, 29 September 1912; Hilles to James S. Sherman, 29 August 1912, James S. Sherman Papers, New York Public Library; Sherman to Hilles, 4 September 1912, Charles D. Hilles Papers.

12 George Wickersham to Charles Nagel, 19 September 1912, Charles Nagel Papers, Sterling Memorial Library, Yale University, New Haven, Conn.

13 Wickersham to Nagel, 24 September 1912, Charles Nagel Papers; John T. Morse to Henry Cabot Lodge, 9 October 1912, Henry Cabot Lodge Papers, Massachusetts Historical Society, Boston.

14 Hilles to Taft, 4 August 1912, Hilles to Woodrow Wilson, 24 October 1912 (an open campaign letter released to the press), Charles D. Hilles Papers.

15 Taft to Helen Taft, 1 November 1912, William Howard Taft Papers, LC.

16 H. Wayne Morgan, *Eugene V. Debs: Socialist for President* (Syracuse, N.Y.: Syracuse University Press, 1962), 127–128.

17 For Debs in the Southwest, see James R. Green, *Grass-Roots Socialism: Radical Movements in the Southwest, 1895–1943* (Baton Rouge: Louisiana State University Press, 1978), 242–244.

18 Fred Warren to Eugene V. Debs, 8 August 1912, in J. Robert Constantine, ed., *Letters of Eugene V. Debs*, vol. 1, *1874–1912* (Urbana: University of Illinois Press, 1990), 535.

19 "Debs Classifies the New Hybrid," *New York Times*, 14 August 1912.

20 Eugene V. Debs, "This Is Our Year: But Two Parties and But One Issue," 16 June 1912, Eugene V. Debs Internet Archive, http://www.marxists.org/archive/debs/works/1912/twoparties.htm; "Debs Defines Bull Moosers," *New York Times*, 27 August 1912.

21 Green, *Grass-Roots Socialism*, 243–244.

22 "Socialists Cheer Debs 29 Minutes," *New York Times*, 30 September 1912.

23 "Red Flags Greet Debs," *Washington Post*, 19 October 1912.

24 Nick Salvatore, *Eugene V. Debs: Citizen and Socialist* (Urbana: University of Illinois Press, 1987), 264.

25 "An Address at a Farmer's Picnic at Washington Park, New Jersey," 15 August 1912, "A Speech to Workingmen in Peru, Indiana," 4 October 1912, in Link, ed., *The Papers of Woodrow Wilson*, 25:36, 334.

26 "Wilson Tosses Buttons from Train, Gets Warm Greeting in Massachusetts," *New Orleans Daily Picayune*, 27 September 1912; "A News Report," 26 September 1912, in Link, ed., *The Papers of Woodrow Wilson*, 25:270–271.

27 Bryan to Wilson, 18 August 1912, in Link, ed., *The Papers of Woodrow Wilson*, 25:46.

28 John Milton Cooper Jr., *The Warrior and the Priest: Woodrow Wilson and Theodore Roosevelt* (Cambridge, Mass.: Belknap Press of Harvard University Press, 1983), 60.

29 Ibid., 131. Roosevelt to Benjamin Ide Wheeler, 21 December 1911, in Elting E. Morison, ed., *The Letters of Theodore Roosevelt*, 8 vols. (Cambridge, Mass.: Harvard University Press, 1951–1954), 7:462.

30 Wilson to Mary Allen Hulbert, 29 September 1912, in Link, ed., *The Papers of Woodrow Wilson*, 25:285. The former Mrs. Peck was now divorced.

31 *The Autobiography of William Allen White* (New York: Macmillan, 1946), 493. See also Oscar King Davis, *Released for Publication: Some Inside Political History of Theodore Roosevelt and His Times* (Boston: Houghton Mifflin, 1925), 356–357.

32 "Two News Reports," 28 August 1912, in Link, ed., *The Papers of Woodrow Wilson*, 25:57.

33 Thomas K. McCraw, *Prophets of Regulation: Charles Francis Adams, Louis D. Brandeis, James M. Landis, Alfred E. Kahn* (Cambridge, Mass.: Belknap Press of the Harvard University Press, 1984), 108, 110.

34 "A Labor Day Address in Buffalo," 2 September 1912, in Link, ed., *The Papers of Woodrow Wilson*, 25:75.

35 "A Labor Day Address in Buffalo," 2 September 1912, and "An Address to the New York Press Club" 9 September 1912, **in** Link, ed., *The Papers of Woodrow Wilson*, 25:78, 123.

36 "An Afternoon Address at the Parade Grounds in Minneapolis," Link, ed., *The Papers of Woodrow Wilson*, 177.

37 "A Campaign Address in Indianapolis Proclaiming the New Freedom," Link, ed. *The Papers of Woodrow Wilson*, 327.

38 *Des Moines Register Leader*, 5 September 1912.

39 Davis, *Released for Publication*, 360; *Portland Oregonian*, 12 September 1912.

40 *Seattle Post Intelligencer*, 3 September 1912 (second quotation); "Crowds Brave Rain to Hear Roosevelt," *New York Times*, 3 September 1912.

41 John Wells Davidson, ed., *A Crossroads of Freedom: The 1912 Campaign Speeches of Woodrow Wilson* (New Haven, Conn.: Yale University Press, 1956), 119; "Roosevelt Bitter in Attack on Wilson," *New York Times*, 22 September 1912.

42 *New York Times*, 4 September 1912.

43 "Address to the New York Press Club," 9 September 1912, in Link, ed., *The Papers of Woodrow Wilson*, 25:124.

44 John Callan O'Laughlin, "Roosevelt Says Wilson Policies Oppose Progress," *Chicago Daily Tribune*, 15 September 1912. The complete text of Roosevelt's speech is printed in the *San Francisco Examiner*, 15 September 1912. A shorter version appears as "Limitation of Government Power," in *Social Justice and Popular Rule: The Works of Theodore Roosevelt*, ed. Hermann Hagedorn, national ed., 20 vols. (New York: Charles Scribner's Sons, 1926), 17:306–314.

45 "A Campaign Address in Scranton, Pennsylvania," 23 September 1912, in Link, ed., *The Papers of Woodrow Wilson*, 25:222, 224–225.

46 Ibid., 225. For Roosevelt's comments on the tariff, see "Roosevelt's Tariff Record," *New York Times*, 12 October 1912.

47 For Roosevelt's plan to develop the Mississippi Valley, see "Levee Convention, Memphis, Tennessee," September 16, 1912, Theodore Roosevelt Papers. Theodore Roosevelt, "The Progressive Party's Appeal," *Independent* 73 (24 October 1912): 944–949, assembled by his staff from Roosevelt's speeches, gives a convenient summary of the candidate's positions.

48 "Roosevelt Says Big Gifts Didn't Purchase Favor," *New York Times*, 5 October 1912.

49 "Wilson in His Steps, Declares Roosevelt," *New York Times*, 10 October 1912.

50 Roosevelt's speech in Chicago was printed in full, albeit with some typographical errors and transposed lines. See *Chicago Daily Tribune*, 13 October 1912.

51 Roosevelt, "The Leader and the Cause," 14 October 1912, in *Social Justice and Popular Rule*, 17:320.

52 "A Review of the World," 488.

53 "Sox Champions on Muffed Fly," *New York Times*, 17 October 1912,

54 Theodore H. White, *The Making of the President, 1960* (New York: Atheneum Books, 1961; reprint, Cutchogue, N.Y.: Buccaneer Books, [1999]), 294.

55 Stanley Cohen, *The Execution of Officer Becker: The Murder of a Gambler, the Trial of a Cop, and the Birth of Organized Crime* (New York: Carroll & Graf, 2006), 153.

56 Geoffrey C. Ward, *Unforgivable Blackness: The Rise and Fall of Jack Johnson* (New York: Vintage Books, 2006), 299–317.

57 Maude Howe Elliott, *Three Generations* (Boston: Little, Brown, 1923), 364. Roosevelt, "The Purpose of the Progressive Party," in *Social Justice and Popular Rule*, 17:335, 338, 339.

58 "Roosevelt Lets Cheers Go On," *New York Times*, 2 November 1912.

59 Roosevelt, "Governor Wilson and the Trusts," *Social Justice and Popular Rule*, 17:347. James Bryce to Edward Grey, 21 October 1912, Edward Grey Papers, FO 800/83, British National Archives, Kew.

60 "A Campaign Address in Madison Square Garden," 31 October 1912, in Link, ed., *The Papers of Woodrow Wilson*, 25:499, 500.

61 Taft to Horace Taft, 1 November 1912, Charles D. Hilles Papers.

62 "Kiss from Wife Tells Wilson He's President-Elect," in Link, ed., *The Papers of Woodrow Wilson*, 25:518.

63 The Prohibition Party's presidential candidate, Eugene Wilder Chafin, received 208,157 votes, and Arthur Elmer Reiner, the candidate of the Socialist Labor Party, received 29,324 votes as well in the balloting.

64 Taft to Charles Hopkins Clark, 8 November 1912, Charles D. Hilles Papers. Michael Haverkamp, "Roosevelt and Taft: how the Republican Vote Split in Ohio," *Ohio History*, 110 (2001-2002): 121-135 is a good treatment of the impact of the Roosevelt-Taft divide on the Republicans in a key state.

65 The presidential electors in California were elected directly by the voters. Two of the Wilson electors out-polled their Progressive counterparts in the very close contest in the state.

66 Joseph G. Cannon to Mabel Boardman, 18 November 1912, box 6, Mabel Boardman Papers, LC. I am indebted to Stacy Cordery for this reference.

67 For the contests that produced the Democratic pickups in the Senate, see James Wright, *The Progressive Yankees: Republican Reformers in New Hampshire, 1906–1916* (Hanover, N.H.: University Press of New England, 1987), 143–145; Robert Sherman La Forte, *Leaders of Reform: Progressive Republicans in Kansas, 1900–1916* (Lawrence: University Press of Kansas, 1974), 202–204; Jules Karlin, *Joseph M. Dixon of Montana*, pt. 1, *Senator and Bull Moose Manager, 1857–1917* (Missoula: University of Montana, 1974), 177–182.

68 Chester I. Long to Charles F. Scott, 16 November 1912, Chester I. Long Papers, Kansas State Historical Society, Topeka; Winthrop Murray Crane to Taft, 12 November 1912, conveying a letter from a "party worker," Charles D. Hilles Papers.

69 Henry F. Pringle, *The Life and Times of William Howard Taft*, 2 vols. (New York: Farrar & Rinehart, 1939), 2:845, 846; Taft to Charles F. Scott, 11 November 1912, Hilles to Crane, 12 November 1912, Hilles to Mrs. B. A. Wallingford, 20 November 1912, Charles D. Hilles Papers.

70 Roosevelt to Henry White, 12 November 1912, in Morison, ed., *The Letters of Theodore Roosevelt*, 7:639. For the postelection quarrels within the Progressive ranks, see John Allen Gable, *The Bull Moose Years: Theodore Roosevelt and the Progressive Party* (Port Washington, N.Y.: Kennikat Press, 1978), 152–153. Mark Bonham Carter and Mark Pottle, eds., *Lantern Slides: The Diaries and Letters of Violet Bonham Carter, 1904–1914* (London: Weidenfeld & Nicolson, 1996), 358.

71 Morgan, *Eugene V. Debs: Socialist for President*, 140.

72 Mark Lawrence Kornbluh, *Why America Stopped Voting: The Decline of Participatory Democracy and the Emergence of Modern American Politics* (New York: New York University Press, 2000), 90. Kornbluh's book is a stimulating look at these important issues. The figures cited are taken from his work.
73 Ibid., 111–115.
74 Ibid., 138–160.
75 John F. Reynolds, *The Demise of the American Convention System, 1880–1911* (New York: Cambridge University Press, 2006), is an interesting examination of one aspect of this process.

EPILOGUE
1   *New York Tribune,* 1 January 1913; *Washington Post,* 1 January 1913.
2   Mark Bonham Carter and Mark Pottle, eds., *Lantern Slides: The Diaries and Letters of Violet Bonham Carter, 1904–1914* (London: Weidenfeld & Nicolson, 1996), 356.

BIBLIOGRAPHIC ESSAY

There is an abundance of writing on the various participants and players in the 1912 election. What follows are the materials I have found most useful in writing the book. The list is selective and designed to direct those interested in further reading on the election to the most pertinent sources.

The personal papers of all four major presidential candidates are available on microfilm at major research libraries and through interlibrary loan. The papers of Theodore Roosevelt, William Howard Taft, and Woodrow Wilson are indexed and relatively easy to use. There are plans to digitize the Roosevelt papers. For Debs, abstracts of his correspondence have been placed online by Indiana State University at the "Debs Collection," http://odin.indstate.edu/about/units/rbsc/debs/debs-idx.html, and can be easily found by entering "abstracts in Debs correspondence" into a search engine.

The published documentary sources on the presidential election of 1912 are quite rich. Three of the four candidates have had their letters and documents from the contest published in one form or another. The most complete coverage has come for Woodrow Wilson. Arthur S. Link, ed., *The Papers of Woodrow Wilson*, vol. 24, *Jan.–Aug. 1912* (Princeton, N.J.: Princeton University Press, 1977), and *The Papers of Woodrow Wilson*, vol. 25, *Aug.–Nov. 1912* (Princeton, N.J.: Princeton University Press, 1978), are excellent for Wilson's private correspondence and public addresses. There is also still much of value in John Wells Davidson, ed., *The Crossroads of Freedom: The 1912 Campaign Speeches of Woodrow Wilson* (New Haven, Conn.: Yale University Press, 1956).

For Theodore Roosevelt, Elting E. Morison, ed., *The Letters of Theodore Roosevelt*, 8 vols. (Cambridge, Mass.: Harvard University Press, 1951–1954),offers in its seventh volume the cream of Roosevelt's outgoing mail in 1911–1912. Theodore Roosevelt, *Social Justice and Popular Rule*, vol. 17 of *The Works of Theodore Roosevelt*, ed. Hermann Hagedorn, national ed., 20 vols. (New York: Charles Scribner's Sons, 1926), has some of Roosevelt's important speeches in 1912 but by no means all of the pertinent public comments that he made.

For Eugene V. Debs, J. Robert Constantine, ed., *Letters of Eugene V. Debs*, vol. I, *1874–1812* (Urbana: University of Illinois Press, 1990), is an essential source for Debs as a political leader of the Socialists. Many of Debs's writings and speeches have been put online at the "Eugene V. Debs Internet Archive," http://marx.org/archive/debs/.

William Howard Taft has not interested historians as a letter writer, and the researcher must consult his personal papers in the microfilm edition from the Library of Congress (these can be accessed through "William H. Taft: A Register of an Addition to His Papers in the Library of Congress," http://www.loc.gov/rr/mss/text/taftwh.html). The president's speeches in 1912 must be gleaned from newspapers.

The election of 1912 did not produce the flood of campaign biographies that were so common just a decade and a half earlier. L. T. Myers, *Great Leaders and National Issues of 1912* (Philadelphia: J. C. Winston Co., 1912), has much relevant information and photographs of key personalities. George Henry Payne, *The Birth of the New Party or Progressive Democracy* (n.p., H. E. Rennels, 1912) has essays from many of the leaders of the Progressives.

The two major parties issued the customary "textbook" for the use of speakers and campaign workers. Republican National Committee, *Republican Campaign Text-Book, 1912* (Philadelphia: Press of Dunlap Printing Co., 1912), attacks both Roosevelt and Wilson. Democratic National Committee and the Democratic Congressional Committee, *The Democratic Text-Book 1912* (New York: Isaac Goldman, 1912), assails Taft and Roosevelt alike, largely over the tariff question.

Three parties published the proceedings of their national convention. Urey Woodson, ed., *Official Report of the Proceedings of the Democratic Convention of 1912* (Chicago: Peterson Linotyping, 1912), records what happened at Baltimore. Milton W. Blumenberg, comp., *Official Report of the Proceedings of the Fifteenth Republican National Convention* (New York, 1912), is essential for the Taft-Roosevelt encounter. As for the Socialists, *Proceedings: National Convention of the Socialist Party, 1912* (Chicago: M. A. Donahue, 1912), is very illuminating about the different political style of this radical party.

The most influential general accounts of the 1912 are contained in George E. Mowry, *Theodore Roosevelt and the Progressive Movement* (Madison: University of Wisconsin Press, 1946), and Arthur S. Link, *Wilson: The Road to the White House* (Princeton, N.J.: Princeton University Press, 1947). Books devoted to the election itself are Frank K. Kelly, *The Fight for the White House: The Story of 1912* (New York: Thomas Y. Crowell, 1961), Francis L. Broderick, *Progressivism at Risk: Electing a President in 1912* (New York: Greenwood Press, 1989), and James Chace, *1912: Wilson, Roosevelt, Taft and Debs—The Election That Changed the Country* (New York: Simon & Schuster, 2004). Broderick is by far the best of the group. Kelly and Chace both did no original research for their treatments of the election. Brett Flehinger, *The 1912 Election and the Power of Progressivism: A Brief History with Documents* (New York: Bedford/St. Martin's, 2003), is useful for the insights derived from the speeches and documents that it has assembled.

Several excellent books examine the role of the political parties in the election. David Sarasohn, *The Party of Reform: Democrats in the Progressive Era* (Jackson: University of Mississippi Press, 1989), makes a strong case that Wilson could have defeated either Roosevelt or Taft in a two-candidate race without a third major party in the field. For the Republicans, Norman Wilensky, *Conservatives in the Progressive Era: The Taft Republicans in 1912* (Gainesville: Florida State University Press, 1965), is good on the role of Charles D. Hilles in the Taft campaign. John Allen Gable, *The Bull Moose Years: Theodore Roosevelt and the Progressive Party* (Port Washington, N.Y.: Kennikat Press, 1978), is well documented and thorough on the Bull Moose campaign. H. Wayne Morgan, *Eugene V. Debs: Socialist for President* (Syracuse, N.Y.: Syracuse University Press, 1962), remains the best introduction to Debs as a Socialist electoral candidate.

To place the 1912 race in a larger context of the evolution of electoral politics, two books are thought provoking. Michael E. McGerr, *The Decline of Popular Politics: The American North, 1865–1928* (New York: Oxford University Press, 1986), examines changes in the way campaigns operated. Mark Lawrence Kornbluh, *Why America Stopped Voting: The Decline of Participatory Democracy and the Emergence of Modern American Politics* (New York: New York University Press, 2000), offers perceptive insights into why the 1912 election did not arouse great popular interest among the voters.

Of the major candidates in 1912, Woodrow Wilson has attracted the most attention from biographers and historians. *Wilson: The Road to the White House*, Arthur Link's first volume of his five-volume treatment of Wilson, mentioned above, is the place to start. James D. Startt, *Woodrow Wilson and the Press: Prelude to the Presidency* (New York: Palgrave Macmillan, 2004), is richer than its title indicates. It is a well-researched and very thorough account of Wilson's political rise. John Milton Cooper Jr., *The Warrior and the Priest: Woodrow Wilson and Theodore Roosevelt* (Cambridge, Mass.: Belknap Press of Harvard University Press, 1983), is the most probing account of the Wilson-Roosevelt interaction in 1912. Cooper's forthcoming biography of Wilson will be a major contribution to the historical literature on this important president.

Because of the presence of George Mowry's account of the postpresidential phase of Roosevelt's political career, the important biographies of the former president have stayed within that analytic framework. H. W. Brands, *T. R.: The Last Romantic* (New York: Basic Books, 1997), focuses more on Roosevelt's personality than on the campaign. Kathleen Dalton, *Theodore Roosevelt: A Strenuous Life* (New York: Alfred A. Knopf, 2002), is thoughtful and well documented with many leads for the researcher in her ample footnotes. Patricia O'Toole, *When Trumpets Call: Theodore Roosevelt after the White House* (New York: Simon & Schuster, 2005), is often critical of Roosevelt as a politician and a campaigner. Natalie Naylor, Douglas Brinkley, and John Allen Gable, eds., *Theodore Roosevelt: Many-Sided American* (Interlaken, N.Y.: Heart of the Lakes Publishing, 1992), contains several fascinating essays about the 1912 election and Roosevelt's postpresidential phase in general. Stacy Cordery, *Alice: Alice Roosevelt Longworth, from White House Princess to Washington Power Broker* (New York: Viking, 2007), has some excellent chapters about the effect of 1912 on members of the Roosevelt family.

William Howard Taft has been left out of the analysis of the 1912 election for the most part. Henry F. Pringle, *The Life and Times of William Howard Taft*, 2 vols. (New York: Farrar & Rinehart, 1939), has not been replaced as the best biography of the president. William Manners, *TR and Will: A Friendship That Split the Republican Party* (New York: Harcourt, Brace, 1969), made good use of the Taft papers but did not venture beyond the conventional interpretations of that time. Michael L. Bromley, *William Howard Taft and the First Motoring Presidency* (Jefferson, N.C.: McFarland & Co., 2003), has more about the workings of Taft's presidency and the political fortunes of the administration than its title might suggest.

Eugene V. Debs has been the subject of interesting biographies. Ray Ginger, *The Bending Cross: A Biography of Eugene Victor Debs* (New Brunswick, N.J.: Rutgers University Press, 1949), is older but still helpful. The standard modern treatment of Debs is Nick Salvatore, *Eugene V. Debs: Citizen and Socialist* (Urbana: University of Illinois Press, 1987).

Participants in the 1912 contest left memoirs of their roles in the various conventions and campaigns. Robert M. La Follette, *La Follette's Autobiography: A Personal Narrative of Political Experiences* (Madison, Wis.: Robert M. La Follette Co., 1913), outlines his grievances with Roosevelt. *Theodore Roosevelt: An Autobiography* (1913; reprint, New York: Charles Scribner's Sons, 1925) discusses his interpretation of the split with Taft while recounting the events of his life and times. William Jennings Bryan and Virgil McNutt, *A Tale of Two Conventions* (New York: Funk & Wagnalls, 1912), is most relevant for Bryan's view of the Republican convention. Victor Rosewater, *Backstage in 1912: The Inside Story of the Split Republican Convention* (Philadelphia: Dorrance & Co., 1932), gives the perspective of one of the Taft leaders. Oscar King Davis, *Released for Publication: Some Inside Political History of Theodore Roosevelt and His Times, 1898–1918* (Boston: Houghton Mifflin, 1925), spends much of its narrative on the events of 1912. Amos R. E. Pinchot, *History of the Progressive Party*, ed. Helene Maxwell Hooker (New York: New York University Press, 1958), offers the recollections of a very disillusioned Roosevelt supporter. Henry L. Stoddard, *As I Knew Them: Presidents and Politics from Grant to Coolidge* (New York: Harper & Bros., 1927), devotes several perceptive chapters to the events of 1912 on the Republican and Progressive side of the battle. *The Autobiography of William Allen White* (New York: Macmillan, 1946) looks back on the Roosevelt campaign and the Progressive convention with a blend of nostalgia and cynicism.

Biographies of the major players in the 1912 election provide further insights. John Braeman, *Albert J. Beveridge: American Nationalist* (Chicago: University of Chicago Press, 1971), is good on a leading Progressive. Michael Kazin, *A Godly Hero: The Life of William Jennings Bryan* (New York: Alfred A. Knopf, 2006), illuminates the transition from Bryan to Wilson. John A. Garraty, *Right-Hand Man: The Life of George W. Perkins* (New York: Harper & Bros., 1960), explores the influence of Roosevelt's closest adviser. John Morton Blum, *Joe Tumulty and the Wilson Era* (Boston: Houghton Mifflin, 1951), is very helpful on the Wilson campaign strategy. Nancy C. Unger, *Fighting Bob La Follette: The Righteous Reformer* (Chapel Hill: University of North Carolina Press, 2000), is good on the progressive alternative to Theodore Roosevelt. John Allen Gable, *Adventure in Reform: Gifford Pinchot, Amos Pinchot, Theodore Roosevelt and the Progressive Party* (Milford, Pa.: Grey Towers Press, 1986), is incisive on the role of the Pinchot brothers in 1912 and afterward.

A superb survey of women in the campaign is given by Jo Freeman, "The Rise of Political Woman in the Election of 1912," 2003, http://www.jofreeman.com/polhistory/1912.htm. Lewis L. Gould, "Theodore Roosevelt, William Howard Taft, and the Disputed Delegates in 1912: Texas as a Test Case," *Southwestern Historical Quarterly* 80 (July 1976): 33–56, looks at the main issue to come out of the Republican National Convention. Herbert F. Margulies, "La Follette, Roosevelt, and the Republican Presidential Nomination of 1912," *Mid-America* 58 (January 1976): 54–76, is a model study of the interplay between these two candidates through the Republican National Convention.

State and regional studies provide important information on the dimensions of the 1912 contest. Lewis L. Gould, *Progressives and Prohibitionists: Texas Democrats in the Wilson Era* (Austin: Texas State Historical Association, 1992), has a chapter on the Wilson campaign in that state. Robert Sherman La Forte, *Leaders of Reform: Progressive Republicans in Kansas, 1900–1916* (Lawrence: University Press of Kansas, 1974), is insightful about a Republican state where passions were intense. James Wright, *The Progressive Yankees: Republican Reformers in New Hampshire, 1906–1916* (Hanover, N.H.: University Press of New England, 1987), explores the fissures in a key northeastern state. James R. Green, *Grass-Roots Socialism: Radical Movements in the Southwest, 1895–1943* (Baton Rouge: Louisiana State University Press, 1978), traces the appeal of Debs and the Socialists to tenant farmers and others of the impoverished class in 1912. Michael Haverkamp, "Roosevelt and Taft: How the Republican Vote Split in Ohio in 1912," *Ohio History*, 110 (2001–2002): 121–135, is illuminating on the electoral impact of the Republican fissure.

For a key political issue, the protective tariff has attracted little scholarly attention. Richard Cleveland Baker, *The Tariff under Roosevelt and Taft* (Hastings, Neb.: Democratic Printing Co., 1941), is interesting on the Canadian reciprocity controversy. Paul Wolman, *Most Favored Nation: The Republican Revisionists and U.S. Tariff Policy, 1897–1912* (Chapel Hill: University of North Carolina Press, 1992), looks at the critics of protectionism within the Grand Old Party. Thomas K. McCraw, *Prophets of Regulation: Charles Francis Adams, Louis D. Brandeis, James M. Landis, and Alfred E. Kahn* (Cambridge, Mass.: Belknap Press of Harvard University Press, 1984), is very instructive on the trust issue and the views of Louis D. Brandeis.

Important documents, images, and recordings about 1912 have begun to appear on the Internet, and those materials should expand in the years ahead. "Teaching with Documents: Political Cartoons Illustrating Progressivism and the Election of 1912," www.archives.gov/education/lessons/election-cartoons, draws upon the resources of the U.S. National Archives. "Theodore Roosevelt on Film," at the Library of Congress's American Memory web site, http://memory.loc.gov/ammem/collections/troosevelt_film/index.html, gives a sense of Roosevelt in action in 1912. Woodrow Wilson campaign recordings can be found at "Woodrow Wilson Edison Campaign Recordings—1912," the Internet Archive, http://www.archive.org/details/woodwils1912. Taft's speech on "Popular Unrest" can be found at "History Matters: The U.S. Survey Course on the Web." historymatters.gmu.edu/5724.

INDEX